LIFTING THE VEIL ON ENROLLMENT MANAGEMENT

LIFTING THE VEIL ON ENROLLMENT MANAGEMENT

How a Powerful Industry Is Limiting Social Mobility in American Higher Education

Stephen J. Burd

Editor

HARVARD EDUCATION PRESS
CAMBRIDGE, MASSACHUSETTS

Paperback ISBN 9781682538920

Library of Congress Cataloging-in-Publication Data

Names: Burd, Stephen J., editor.
Title: Lifting the veil on enrollment management : how a powerful industry is limiting social mobility in American higher education / Stephen J. Burd, editor.
Description: Cambridge, Massachusetts : Harvard Education Press, [2024] | Includes bibliographical references and index.
Identifiers: LCCN 2023059377 | ISBN 9781682538920 (paperback)
Subjects: LCSH: Universities and colleges—United States—Admission. | Education, Higher—Economic aspects—United States. | Low-income students—United States. | Educational change—United States. | Educational equalization—United States.
Classification: LCC LB2351.2 .L54 2024 | DDC 378.1/610973—dc23/eng/20240122
LC record available at https://lccn.loc.gov/2023059377

Published by Harvard Education Press,
an imprint of the Harvard Education Publishing Group

Harvard Education Press
8 Story Street
Cambridge, MA 02138

Cover design: Ciano Design
Cover image credit: lvcandy/DigitalVision Vectors via Getty Images

The typefaces used in this book are Adobe Garamond Pro and Helvetica Neue.

CONTENTS

Introduction

In 2015, officials at the American Council on Education (ACE), the nation's leading higher-education lobbying group, made a startling discovery. They were shocked to learn from US Census data that the share of low-income students heading to college straight from high school had plunged during President Barack Obama's administration, despite the White House's successful efforts to substantially increase financial aid funding. While spending on Pell Grants, the government's primary source of aid for low-income students, had nearly doubled between the 2009 and 2014 academic years, the share of low-income high school graduates enrolling immediately into college had fallen by 10 percentage points, to 46 percent.

"Low-income students are much less likely to enroll in college immediately after high school than they were seven years ago, despite all of the efforts to increase their postsecondary participation," ACE's Terry Hartle and Chris Nellum wrote in a blog post.[1] While the ACE lobbyists said it was "unclear" why low-income student enrollment had dropped so precipitously, they offered five possible explanations:

- "Rapid price increases" at public colleges and universities, as a result of widespread state disinvestment, "may have led many students—particularly low-income students—to think that college is out of reach financially."
- Growing public skepticism about "the economic value" of attending college had discouraged low-income students from applying.

- The recovering economy, after years of financial crisis and recession, had enticed many to get jobs rather than go to college.
- The shrinking for-profit college sector, as a result of the Obama administration's increased oversight, had "disproportionally impacted low-income students."
- Potentially inaccurate census data was providing a misleading picture of what was happening.

There may have been some truth to these explanations, although the last one seems like wishful thinking. But while ACE found plenty of blame to go around for the troubling trend—stingy state legislators, a misinformed public, short-sighted students, overzealous regulators, and even faulty data crunchers—it let one major player off the hook: the colleges themselves.

And that omission is pretty remarkable, considering the dramatic transformation that has occurred in admissions and financial aid practices at both public and private four-year colleges and universities over the past four decades. Under the sway of the enrollment management industry's private consulting firms that develop strategies for student recruitment, many selective colleges are engaged in an arms race for the most desirable students: the best (and wealthiest) applicants they can attract. As a result, these institutions are leaving less-privileged students with fewer seats and larger funding gaps, which they can cover only by taking on substantial debt.

The multibillion-dollar enrollment management industry markets admissions and financial aid strategies and algorithms to colleges to improve their revenue and rankings. The firms that make up this industry have played a pivotal role in helping define the goals that colleges pursue and providing the strategies to achieve them. These companies' very existence depends on convincing campus enrollment managers, college presidents, and the institutions' boards that the schools' fortunes and even survival depend on using their products, which all too often disadvantage low-income students and students of color.[2]

Private colleges first adopted enrollment management policies and practices in the late 1970s and 1980s. In the previous three decades, these colleges had opened their doors wider to low-income students and students of color than ever before. Selective private college leaders had pledged to admit students regardless of financial need and to fully meet the need of students whose families could not afford to send them to college without this help.[3] Meanwhile, rapidly growing public universities kept their prices low enough that they were generally accessible for students, regardless of family income.

But those had been more prosperous times. With the economy in turmoil and the college-age population plummeting, many private colleges were struggling, and their commitment to meeting student need was wavering.[4] In the 1980s, the newly elected Reagan administration emphasized the private returns of higher education over public ones as it pushed Congress to slash federal student aid spending.[5] And *U.S. News & World Report* began ranking colleges, at first based solely on the reputational surveys that college presidents filled out, and, by the end of the decade, a simple set of metrics that could be easily gamed.

All these forces led to the emergence of an enrollment management industry that pushed colleges to operate more like businesses, focused on building their brands and bottom lines. Firms such as Maguire Associates, Noel-Levitz, Royall & Co., and RuffaloCODY entered the market, promising to help colleges become more competitive in recruiting the students that they wanted the most. These firms encouraged colleges to break down the firewalls that had been built between the institutions' admissions and financial aid offices and to use non-need-based aid, which they called "merit aid," to compete for high-quality and more-affluent students. And once some private colleges started using their financial aid competitively, it became difficult for others to resist for fear of being put at a competitive disadvantage.

Initially, private colleges tried to outbid their competitors by providing larger and larger merit-based scholarships. But over the years, they have adopted far more sophisticated strategies. Working with the consulting firms, many engage in "financial aid leveraging," an enrollment management practice in which they determine the precise price points they need to enroll different groups of students without spending a dollar more than is needed.[6] The biggest tuition discounts go to the highest-achieving students they have admitted and those who otherwise can afford to pay full freight and boost the institutions' revenue. Low-income students are often left with large funding gaps that could stymie their educational progress or force them and their families to take on substantial debt loads. Instead of removing barriers, these colleges are adding hurdles, making it more difficult for these students to go to college and earn a degree.

All of this would be bad enough if it were limited to private colleges. However, in the face of state disinvestment and the lure of rising up the rankings, many public universities have embraced the enrollment management strategies of their private college counterparts. At the urging of consultants, these once-low-cost schools, which for decades served as a gateway to the middle class, are increasingly employing their aid to lure affluent out-of-state students with good grades and standardized test scores to their campuses to increase both their revenue and rankings. Today, public universities spend billions of dollars annually on non-need-based aid, and many require low-income students and their families to take on heavy debt burdens to attend.[7]

Higher education is at a crisis point. But policy makers are not going to be able to head off this crisis unless they have a better idea of what the real problems are and who is responsible for them. However, despite how powerful and lucrative the enrollment management industry is, few people outside of academia (and even many within it) are aware of it or know what it does. As a result, the industry has received little attention in federal higher-education policy discussions. Higher-education hearings on Capitol Hill often focus on problems related to college access and affordability and student indebtedness. However, the words *enrollment management* are never uttered, nor are there mentions of *financial aid leveraging*, *tuition discounting*, or even the *merit aid arms race*. Not a single congressional hearing has focused on the extraordinary amount of influence that giant for-profit enrollment management firms, such as EAB and Ruffalo Noel Levitz (RNL), have over colleges' admissions and financial aid practices.

This edited volume aims to lift the veil on the industry and show how its efforts all too often disadvantage low-income students and students of color. Written by higher-education journalists and experts, researchers, a former college president, and former enrollment managers, the volume is the first book to focus on enrollment management as an industry. The book provides a history of how the industry came to be, identifies the major players, and shows how it has fundamentally changed the way that colleges recruit students and award financial aid, while operating mostly out of public view. The volume also offers a wide range of policy solutions that aim to rein in the industry and change the incentive structure in higher education so that colleges once again will serve as engines of opportunity rather than as perpetuators of inequality.

The book is divided into four parts. The first explores the history of enrollment management and of the consulting firms that dominate the industry. It also examines how the industry has evolved over time and in ways that enrollment management's original champions didn't foresee and some now regret.

The journalist and author *Neil Swidey* leads off the first part by writing in chapter 1 about the rise of both the enrollment management industry and *U.S. News & World Report*'s college rankings in the 1980s. While these data-focused forces started independently of each other, they became increasingly "symbiotic." According to Swidey, *U.S. News* ultimately provided the playbook for colleges to follow to rise up the rankings and gain greater prestige. The enrollment management firms promised to give colleges the strategies that they needed to play the game and beat their competitors. "Instead of passively accepting their fate, these colleges—with the right guidance from their consultants and their econometric modeling, data analysis, and behavioral science—could actively shape their futures. After all, there was no quicker way to increase a college's perceived prestige than to move up in the rankings." The result is that selective colleges, both public and private, have become ever more exclusive and expensive, values that *U.S. News* rewards, to the detriment of low- and lower-middle-income students alike.

In chapter 2, the higher-education journalist *Jon Marcus* provides a rich history of the enrollment management firms that dominate the business. Although they had modest origins, these consulting companies have evolved into a highly lucrative industry "dominated by a few big players that have diversified through acquisitions, often backed by private equity and investment funds that expect returns and constant growth." Marcus offers a balanced view of the business, showing how essential these firms have become in the "winner-take-all" landscape in which colleges find themselves—providing "expertise that most universities and colleges generally can't afford to build in house." But he also shows how they have pushed strategies that have made higher education less accessible and affordable, including encouraging public universities to jack up their tuition and provide generous discounts to affluent out-of-state students to increase their revenue and rankings. Despite growing alarm about these strategies, Marcus concludes that colleges are growing "more, not less, dependent" on these firms.

Don Hossler has spent more than forty years studying enrollment management, and he served as an enrollment manager for eight years. In chapter 3, he writes about the ethical dilemmas that he faced while serving as the vice chancellor for enrollment services at Indiana University Bloomington in the late 1990s and early 2000s. Overall, Hossler doesn't believe that there is anything "inherently wrong with enrollment management." Colleges need to be strategic and achieve their enrollment "goals in informed, intentional, and integrated ways." However, he agrees with critiques "about how enrollment management is too often being practiced—with colleges using enrollment management strategies that focus too much on increasing selectivity, optimizing net revenue, and pursuing prestige above all else." In the chapter, Hossler highlights the enrollment management practices that he finds most ethically problematic.

Part 2 of the book examines federal government policies and actions that helped fuel the growth of an enrollment management industry that often undermines the government's efforts to make higher education more accessible and affordable. In chapter 4, the former Education Department official and researcher *Jon H. Oberg* writes about how changes that Congress made to the federal student aid programs in the 1970s made it easier for colleges to use their own aid to pursue more-affluent students. The original Higher Education Act of 1965 envisioned having the government and colleges work together to increase low-income students' access to college. The statute created the Campus-Based Aid programs, each of which required colleges to partially match the federal funds that they received from these programs. By taking this cooperative approach, the federal government made an informal pact with colleges that each would complement the other in using financial aid to open the doors of college to those who could not afford to go to college without it.

But Congress, at the urging of the Richard Nixon administration, changed the equation in 1972 when it created the Pell Grant program and made it the primary source of aid for low-income students. As a voucher program, Pell Grants make no demands on colleges to use their aid to help financially needy students. Oberg argues that the Pell Grant program "set the table for the development of an enrollment management approach to student financial aid." Instead of complementing the government's efforts, many colleges use their aid to pursue wealthy students who can help them increase their revenue. Meanwhile, low-income students have become "a low priority" for colleges, "a population to exploit for other institutional purposes."

In chapter 5, the former Vassar College president *Catharine Bond Hill* writes that the federal government has been working at cross-purposes with itself when it comes to promoting college access for low-income students. While the Education Department annually spends tens of billions of dollars on federal student aid to make it easier for these students to obtain a postsecondary education, the Justice Department has aggressively enforced federal antitrust laws that prevent colleges from collaborating to ensure that they devote their aid to helping financially needy students. By doing so, the department has encouraged many selective colleges to embrace enrollment management and use their financial aid strategically to gain a competitive advantage.

Hill argues that the Justice Department's views on antitrust in higher education are misguided because of the important public mission that colleges play. However, she doesn't support giving colleges a blanket exemption because she doesn't believe that simply allowing colleges to collaborate will lead to meaningful changes in the way that they spend their student aid. Instead, she argues that Congress should give the exemption to colleges that enroll at least a minimum share of low-income students and meet their full financial need. Such a change, she argues, would justify access to both the antitrust exemption and the subsidies that colleges receive from the federal government, including access to federal financial aid funds and special tax treatment.

The book's third part takes a closer look at the enrollment management strategies that colleges employ in recruiting students and awarding aid and examines how they affect low-income students and students of color. In chapter 6, the researchers *Ozan Jaquette*, *Karina Salazar*, and *Patricia Martín* show how the student list business, which is a matchmaking intermediary connecting colleges to prospective students, caters to the institutions' enrollment management needs, helping them find the "right" students. For example, the

College Board and ACT, which dominate the business, make it easy for colleges to find students whose families can afford to pay full freight by including search filters in their list products that allow schools to target prospects in specific ZIP codes. In recent years, the College Board has introduced geodemographic search filters that allow colleges to target desirable prospects based on the past college-going behavior and socioeconomic characteristics of the schools that they attend and the neighborhoods in which they live.

The relationship between enrollment management firms, which often purchase names from the student lists on behalf of colleges, and the standardized admissions testing agencies generally has been mutually beneficial. But over time, there has been a blurring of the lines between them. The recent emergence of the giant enrollment firm EAB as a major player in the student list business especially troubles these researchers, as the company requires colleges to purchase expensive software or consulting services in exchange for access to its proprietary database of prospective students. "Should access to a substantial share of college-going high school students be restricted to the clients of a private firm?" they ask. "And should private firms be able to funnel prospective students toward their own clients and away from other colleges?"

Enrollment management is often talked about as having an iron triangle of three broad goals: increasing a college's revenue, raising the institution's profile, and making the student body more diverse. In chapter 7, the higher-education journalist *Peter Schmidt* writes that while colleges "generally give lip service to pursuing all three" of these goals, they haven't come close to giving them equal weight. In fact, the pressure on campus enrollment managers to raise revenue and rankings is so intense that they often "turn away members of disadvantaged populations" to achieve those goals. "Missing net revenue goals or overseeing a drop in the rankings is much more likely to get them fired than failing to meet diversity objectives."

In any case, Schmidt reminds us that prior to the 2023 Supreme Court decision *Students for Fair Admissions (SFFA) Inc v. Presidents and Fellows of Harvard College* and *SFFA v. University of North Carolina* that banned the use of racial preferences in college admissions, the court had limited colleges' pursuit of greater diversity to "an educational imperative realized by enrolling enough students from different backgrounds for all to benefit from access to new perspectives" rather than as a means to make up for past injustice or to provide equal opportunity to all students. As a result, achieving greater diversity was "an amorphous concept" that worked well with enrollment management because it maintained colleges' discretion to define diversity in ways that allowed them to "pursue their strategic objectives as they wish[ed]." Instead of making their campuses more socioeconomically and racially diverse, many colleges embraced enrollment management strategies that "kept their student bodies disproportionately white and wealthy."

In chapter 8, I warn that the financial aid leveraging strategies that the largest enrollment management firms have been aggressively marketing to colleges may lead to a subprime loan crisis. These strategies push colleges to use more and more of their institutional aid to offer the most generous tuition discounts to the best and wealthiest applicants to help them raise their prestige and improve their bottom line. To put it bluntly, leaving low-income students with large funding gaps is part of the game plan to get the students the colleges want most. As a result, many low-income families find they have little choice but to borrow hefty Parent PLUS Loans they likely cannot afford to cover these funding gaps.

Congress created the Parent PLUS Loan program in 1980 to help middle- and upper-middle-income students afford expensive colleges by allowing them to borrow up to the cost of attendance. For colleges leveraging their aid, these loans represent easy credit that they can offer the families of low-income students to cover funding gaps, as this debt is readily available so long as potential borrowers don't have bad credit. To make matters worse, low-income families are often unaware of the risks that they take on when they get PLUS Loans, which come with higher interest rates than federal student loans and offer less flexible repayment options. Incredibly, many colleges include PLUS debt in the financial aid packages that they offer students without explaining the terms and conditions of these loans. In other words, pushing low-income families to borrow PLUS Loans that they probably won't be able to repay has been a deliberate strategy that some enrollment management firms have been selling colleges.

In chapter 9, the author *Beth Zasloff* tells the story of a low-income student, Joanne, who experienced financial aid gapping firsthand when she was accepted into her first-choice school, Ithaca College. While Ithaca provides generous amounts of non-need-based "merit" aid to attract affluent students, it required Joanne's mother, a single woman who supports her family through a monthly disability check, to borrow a large Parent PLUS Loan to help pay for Joanne to attend. According to Zasloff, financial aid gapping is "merit aid's unfortunate corollary," leaving "fewer and worse options for low-income students, who often apply for aid with insufficient guidance and without parental support."

In telling Joanne's story, Zasloff shows that selective colleges that leave low-income students with substantial funding gaps not only put these students' families in an extremely precarious financial situation but also send a message to these students that they are not wanted as much as their more-affluent counterparts. "The enrollment management strategies that Ithaca and so many other selective public and private colleges have embraced have created campus cultures that favor the rich and white," she writes. "Wealthy students get the message that they are valued, while low-income students like Joanne are made to feel like second-class citizens who have to scrape and claw and put everything on the line for the chance of success."

Part 4, the book's final section, offers policy solutions that aim to curb the influence of the enrollment management industry, or at least reorient enrollment management policies and practices so they serve a far greater public purpose. In chapter 10, the higher-education writer and policy expert *Kevin Carey* argues that national price controls are needed in public higher education so that states will once again offer an affordable higher education to their citizens, regardless of family income. For much of their history, public universities' guarantee of "universal low pricing" not only opened the doors of colleges to low- and lower-middle-income students, but "also broadened the constituency and political support for higher learning," Carey writes. "It allowed public universities to bring people from different socioeconomic strata together, in a common place, for a common purpose." But over the last two decades, many public universities have embraced enrollment management and engaged in financial aid leveraging, raising their sticker prices and charging students vastly different prices depending on how much the institutions want them. This change has come at a great cost—undercutting "the role of higher education in building an inclusive, mutually supportive society."

While college lobbyists have long succeeded in keeping talk of higher-education price controls off-limits for policy makers, Carey sees hope in the popularity of the "Free College" movement. "People sense, correctly, that the United States used to offer a good deal to young people in the form of affordable public colleges, and that that benefit was revoked for cruel and stupid reasons. They want back what was lost." Requiring public universities to be free, however, is not the only choice that advocates for price controls have. "One could imagine a straightforward, graduated tuition schedule tied to household income. College could be free for many and affordable for all," he writes. "The key would be simplicity, affordability, and universality—a kind of federally mandated universal enrollment management disarmament for all public colleges and universities."

In the volume's final chapter, *Jerome A. Lucido*, a leading voice for reforming enrollment management, proposes a three-point plan that aims "to replace the current hypercompetitive enrollment environment that advantages those with advanced wealth and social capital to one that is based on cooperation for the greater good." Lucido, a former enrollment manager, argues that while "equity and fairness" cry out for change, his proposals are also in colleges' best interests because of "the dramatic demographic changes that this country is experiencing." While the number of high school graduates is expected to drop sharply, there are expected to be significant increases in the populations of low-income students and certain groups of students of color.

Lucido proposes substantially increasing the government's investment in higher education, including creating a new "Title I program for higher education," which would provide block grants to colleges to incentivize them "to enroll more low- and lower-middle-income students and increase their graduation rates." The proposal also calls on colleges to act together to "move away from destructive competition," and "publicly declare their commitment to advancing equity and inclusion," and establish "measurable progress goals" for achieving these goals. To put the plan in action, colleges would fight for an antitrust exemption from Congress. Finally, Lucido's proposal calls for "reforming enrollment management as a profession and a practice" so that campus enrollment managers would help "lead the charge toward equity."

Lucido concludes his chapter by asking whether the country "has the will" to take the steps needed to "lift up the coming generations who will hail primarily from populations who currently fare least well in the systems that we have built." Of course, before higher-education policy makers can do so, they will need to recognize the role that the enrollment management industry has played in transforming college admissions and financial aid in ways that have harmed low-income students and many students of color.

As I write in the book's conclusion, many higher education policy makers are in denial. They still believe that the federal government is in the driver's seat when it comes to setting the incentives by which public and private four-year colleges operate, much as it was at various pivotal points in the country's history. After all, the government spends tens of billions of dollars each year on student aid and provides colleges with enormous tax subsidies. But policy makers need to understand how much the government's influence has waned these past four decades, as four-year colleges have come increasingly under the thrall of private for-profit enrollment management firms. If they have any hope of solving the problems that have long bedeviled higher education, such as access, affordability, equity, and indebtedness, they'll have to acknowledge the industry behind the curtain.

My hope is that this volume will begin that process. Too much is at stake to continue to allow this extremely influential and profitable industry to continue operating in the shadows.

Part 1. An Introduction to the Enrollment Management Industry

CHAPTER 1

Reign and Ruin

The Rise of Enrollment Management and the U.S. News *College Rankings*[*]

Neil Swidey

In the mid-1980s, as the man lugged the twenty-nine-pound machine on the express bus out of St. Louis for his commute home each night, fellow passengers would often ask if he was a tailor. The question was understandable. The rectangular case he carried looked as if it housed a Singer sewing machine. In fact, it was an Osborne Executive 2 "portable" computer; inside the white plastic case was a detachable keyboard, two floppy disk drives, and a seven-inch screen.[1]

David Kalsbeek used that $2,500 computer to build the early data sets that would help give shape to the nascent world of enrollment management. Kalsbeek had been a philosophy major who liked to ponder deep questions. He was also an early-adopter computer nerd who found meaning in data. He schlepped his expensive personal computer back and forth to work so he could crunch numbers day and night, refining measures to assess student experiences. Kalsbeek worked in institutional research at Saint Louis University (SLU), a nearly two-century-old Jesuit school sitting just west of the Mississippi River. Like most universities in the 1980s, Saint Louis was made up of lots of siloed departments keeping their own records and doing business the way they always had: admissions over here, financial aid over there, the registrar over in that corner, the housing office over in the other.

For many years, SLU and nine other Midwestern Jesuit colleges had participated in an annual survey, sharing information about their admissions efforts and outcomes. Each school's dean of admissions would report a range of metrics. These included how much it had spent in marketing and recruitment, how much it had offered in total financial aid and scholarships, and how many applicants it had attracted—as well as where those applicants lived, what their races and standardized test scores were, and how many of them ended up enrolling. A few people hand-tabulated those results and then shared them with the group.

Kalsbeek brought those pen-and-pencil surveys into the computer age. He began by taking years of previous hand tabulations and feeding them into his Osborne Executive, allowing him to spit out spreadsheets showing trend lines for each of the ten colleges. The exercise produced some surprising results. For example, even if a school had a relatively small percentage of out-of-state students, his time-series spreadsheets could show that its out-of-state enrollment growth was outpacing the rest of the pack. He also revealed not just the percentage of student applicants that each college admitted and the percentage of students who accepted their admissions offers, but what would come to be known as its "draw rate"—the yield rate divided by the admit rate. This metric offered a better window into each college's relative market position, especially in the eyes of the all-important regional Jesuit high schools that functioned as feeders. Probably his most revealing—and, as it turned out, controversial—reports were the ratio-analysis spreadsheets on recruitment spending. He and his Osborne produced charts showing the relative bang for the buck over time that each college was getting, in the form of increased applicants, based on its spending on direct mail, travel, staffing, and other budget items.

He migrated his data onto transparencies for an overhead projector and then, during a workshop at Loyola University, presented his findings to the Jesuit group. One admissions dean immediately withdrew from the project. "I don't want to share my data," the man complained, "with anyone who can meaningfully make that much use of it."[2]

Kalsbeek did not invent enrollment management. That work in the 1980s to coordinate the functions of recruitment, enrollment, financial aid, and retention—and especially to use financial aid in ways that would goose the odds of students accepting admissions offers—had begun a decade earlier elsewhere. The most pioneering of this work had happened at another Jesuit school, Boston College (BC).[3]

Kalsbeek's innovation was how he sliced, diced, and presented all these metrics in a form that made it unmistakable how colleges were doing compared with their peers. Jon Boeckenstedt, a vice provost at Oregon State University and chronicler of the enrollment management field, calls Kalsbeek's work "to the best of my knowledge, the first-of-its-kind use of data benchmarking against a competitive set" in higher education.[4] When we first made contact, Kalsbeek recalled how a younger colleague who had attended presentations he gave on the use of analytics in enrollment management once compared him to Oakland A's general manager Billy Beane. Beane helped transform baseball, a national pastime, which like higher education, had long been governed by hunches, into stats-soaked, sabermetrics-obsessed *Moneyball*.[5] "Overstated, to be sure, but I did have the good fortune to be around at the dawn of this crazy thing called Enrollment Management and since I didn't have any professional experience in college admissions I HAD to approach and understand it analytically," Kalsbeek wrote in an email.[6]

Around the same time that Kalsbeek was injecting a metrics focus into how administrators ran their campuses, a man named Mel Elfin was doing the same in how the national media covered them. In the fall of 1986, the blunt-speaking, hard-charging, Brooklyn-born Elfin joined *U.S. News & World Report* as special projects editor. The son of a truck driver, Elfin had attended Syracuse University on full scholarship and later earned a master's degree from Harvard.[7] In 1964, while serving as *Newsweek*'s education editor, he had wowed the magazine's new boss, Katharine Graham, by hilariously roasting a departing colleague at an office send-off. The next year, when Graham tapped *Newsweek*'s Washington bureau chief, Ben Bradlee, to take the helm of her *Washington Post*, she chose as his *Newsweek* replacement that memorable editor with the Brooklyn accent and the cutting wit. Elfin remained *Newsweek*'s DC bureau chief for two decades. But by the mid-1980s, he was out and looking for a new home.

For many years, *U.S. News* had been viewed as the newsweekly version of the Ottoman Empire during its "sick man of Europe" decline. Media bold-types derided it as *U.S. Snooze*. By the time Elfin signed on, the real estate developer Mort Zuckerman was two years into his ownership of *U.S. News*. The combustible Zuckerman would cycle through four top editors in his first five years of ownership.[8]

As Elfin surveyed his special-projects portfolio at the sleepy weekly, he spotted an underappreciated gem: the "America's Best Colleges" rankings. *U.S. News* had begun its college rankings in 1983, on the heels of a similar college guide produced by *New York Times* education editor Edward Fiske (which featured a five-star rating system). The debut of the *U.S. News* rankings had been decidedly low profile, as they were sandwiched between an article on the economic recovery and another headlined "Bias Against Ugly People: How They Can Fight It." The magazine had mailed surveys to 1,308 college presidents, asking them to rank the highest-quality national universities and liberal arts colleges. About half the presidents responded.[9] Stanford and Amherst topped their respective lists. It was a simple reputational survey—a beauty contest (which may have given added significance to the placement of that feature on "ugly people").

The magazine didn't publish another college rankings issue until two years later. Why should it? It was preposterous to think that a sector as notoriously slow-moving as higher education could change appreciably in a single year. No matter. Elfin was a fiercely competitive editor who understood how to build buzz, especially among the prestige-seeking chattering classes. It didn't take him long to turn the "Best Colleges" rankings into an annual issue. On his watch, the magazine overhauled its formula while adding splashy feature stories and smart packaging to each year's special issue.[10]

Capturing the zeitgeist of the 1980s thirst for upward mobility, the *U.S. News* college rankings soon became a franchise. The rankings drove more than a few university presidents to distraction, even as they drove profits into the long-struggling newsweekly's coffers. "*U.S. Snooze* Wakes Up," crowed the headline to an *American Journalism Review* article on the magazine's rejuvenation.[11]

The field of enrollment management and the rankings at *U.S. News* both came into their own in the late 1980s. That these metrics-focused forces would go on to reshape the college landscape, whether for good or bad, is beyond debate. The most plausible interpretation is that each of these forces started out modestly, with defensible if hardly selfless intentions, only to turn into Frankensteins, bringing unintended consequences that Kalsbeek and Elfin never could have imagined. What's interesting, however, is how these forces are widely viewed as having done their transformational work independent of one another. In reality, they were symbiotic. It's a safe bet that neither enrollment management nor the *U.S. News* rankings would have taken on its dominant role had it not been for the other.

WHERE ENROLLMENT MANAGEMENT STARTED

In 1973, Jack Maguire was in his second year teaching theoretical physics at BC when his boss tapped him to take over the university's admissions office.[12] Founded during the Civil War to educate an emerging Irish Catholic immigrant community, BC by the early 1970s was on shaky ground. It was hemorrhaging so much money that it was nearing insolvency.[13] A big reason why Maguire left the physics department for the admissions office was that the university's bleak finances had seriously clouded his prospects for getting tenure. BC was facing other ominous numbers as well, in the form of declining applications and increasing early withdrawals.

Although admissions had long been the province of humanities types, Maguire deployed his mathematical, quantitative mindset to the job. Working with BC's new executive vice president, a dynamic former business professor named Frank Campanella, they cooked up a strategy that they called "enrollment management." The idea was to break down institutional silos and align the university functions of recruitment, admissions, financial aid, and retention—and do it all in a data-driven way. There were other people on other campuses testing similar approaches around the same time. "Were we the first and only ones to do it? You could make a case for lots of folks," Maguire says. "But the fact is, I had the great advantage of being a mathematician—a scientist—and knowing nothing about admissions. So I had all kinds of research to do. And that's why I relied on science."[14]

In 1976, with BC's turnaround underway, Maguire wrote an article for the university's alumni magazine laying out his ideas about enrollment management. Adopting the cautionary language that would dominate the college discussion decades later, Maguire warned about a looming demographic drop-off in the nation's supply of eighteen-year-olds. He also warned about the growing perception among young people that a college education offered too little payoff for its too-steep price tag (tuition and room and board at BC at the time was around $5,000 a year), and about the stark vulnerabilities facing institutions like BC that were highly dependent on tuition revenue.

Admissions offices tended to be passive places that let tradition, relationships, and instincts govern their decision-making. In contrast, Maguire advocated an active, quantitative approach. He ratcheted up both marketing efforts and surveys asking students why they enrolled—or left—and made changes to boost the former and reduce the latter. Because hundreds of BC students were dropping out or transferring each year, he adopted a laser focus on retention. And because BC was dealing with limited financial aid dollars and increasingly price-conscious families, he and his team began carving up aid money differently, with the aim of boosting both enrollment rates and tuition revenue. Instead of one-quarter of aid dollars going to each class, he directed one-third of the pie to the freshman class. And he began handing out modest tuition discounts in the form of ego-stroking "merit aid" scholarships to students who might not actually need aid but who might be persuaded to enroll at BC because of it.[15]

By 1980, BC's applicant pool had tripled from what it had been when Maguire took over, and other colleges were imitating his approach. Maguire figured that if he was going to be copied, he might as well be compensated for it. In 1983, he left BC to start his own consulting firm in enrollment management. (The year after Maguire left, BC stunned the football world with Doug Flutie's forty-eight-yard, buzzer-beating "Hail Mary" pass that sent the team to the Cotton Bowl for the first time in nearly half a century.[16] That attention produced a surge in applications from all around the country the following year, but Maguire rejects the conventional wisdom that credits the "Flutie bump" for the campus's reversal of fortune. "That is apocryphal," he says. "Our applications had tripled before Doug Flutie played a game."[17])

Maguire's timing in going out on his own was impeccable. A confluence of forces beginning in the 1980s put unprecedented strain on colleges—and the families trying to pay their kids' tuition bills. And those challenges dramatically increased the interest that colleges had in the efficiencies that Maguire and others in the emerging world of enrollment management offered. Those forces included:

- *Federal disinvestment in higher education under President Ronald Reagan*: In 1981, Reagan's budget director, David Stockman, wasted little time in setting the new administration's tone. "I don't accept the notion that the federal government has an obligation to fund generous grants to anybody who wants to go to college," he told Congress. "It seems to me that if people want to go to college bad enough then there is opportunity and responsibility on their part to finance their way through the best way they can." Within four years, the federal government had cut close to $1 billion from the federal student aid programs, including Pell Grants, the government's main source of aid for low-income students.[18]
- *Spikes in college prices and correspondingly large increases in federal student loan debt*: In 1986, students and their families borrowed nearly $10 billion in federal education loans—nearly a threefold increase from a decade earlier, after adjusting for inflation. At the time, the Reagan administration was doubling down on its efforts to shift the burden of paying for college from the government to the individual. "Who should pay the bill—the student or the cab driver who didn't even go to college?" asked Bruce Carnes, the top budget official in Reagan's Department of Education. "Nobody's holding a gun to these people's head and saying, 'You will take this loan, and you will go to this expensive school.'"[19]
- *Changing demographics*: Just as Maguire had warned, the potential applicant pool started to shrink, reversing an unusually long stretch of consistent growth. While just 6 percent of Americans had a bachelor's degree in 1940, that rate grew sharply each year from the end of World War II until the early 1980s. The federal GI Bill and Washington's massive investment in state university systems had helped fuel that growth, as had the draft deferments that were available to college students for much of the Vietnam era. But by 1983, the post-Vietnam growth rate in college completion fell by nearly half.[20] The fall-off came at the same time that the increasingly automated American economy began having much less use for blue-collar workers and a growing need for college-educated "knowledge workers."[21]

- *The rise of the Common Application*: The Common Application began modestly in 1975, when Vassar, Colgate, and a dozen other private colleges agreed on a standard form that applicants could photocopy and submit. By 1980, more than one hundred colleges had signed on.[22] (Those numbers would explode after the Common App went online in 1998. Today, more than nine hundred colleges use it.[23]) Making the application process easier helped boost the number of applicants those colleges received. However, because the Common App didn't require extra effort, a school could no longer be as confident in how genuinely interested applicants were in attending its particular institution.
- *The incredibly shrinking nation*: By the 1980s, two massive deregulation efforts—in the airline and telecom industries—combined to make far-away campuses feel a lot closer.[24] The rise of discount airlines meant that students could get back and forth from home to campus without having to add thousands of dollars in plane tickets to their budgets.[25] And the arrival of upstart long-distance carriers to compete with AT&T after the 1982 breakup of Ma Bell meant that those same students could call home each week without one parent saying, "We should let you go—this long-distance call is probably costing a fortune!"[26] These economic developments helped put far-flung students in play for colleges looking to expand their geographic reach, even if they couldn't yet match the Ivy League boast of having at least one student from every state in the country.
- *The 1980s arrival of yuppie status-seeking*: After acquiring the *House Beautiful* home and the shiny new Volvo, a natural outgrowth for young urban professionals (yuppies) was the corresponding desire to have stickers from name-brand colleges affixed to the rear window of that Volvo. The infatuation with prestige colleges helped widen the gulf between the haves and the have-nots in higher education, forcing nonelite schools to work that much harder to attract students.
- *The chill of government investigations*: For years, officials from elite private colleges had met each spring to compare and align the award packages that they were planning to offer students who had received acceptance letters from multiple selective schools.[27] The purpose of these meetings was to prevent accepted students from price-shopping for better deals as if

> they were just hunting for a set of radial tires. But an antitrust investigation that the US Department of Justice began in 1989 halted these meetings. The inquiry—and subsequent actions by the Justice Department—effectively ended any meaningful collaboration among colleges when it comes to how they spend their institutional financial aid.[28]

Collectively, these forces made it clear that a business-as-usual admissions approach would no longer cut it. Suddenly, the stakes became much higher for everyone, at the same time that the signals between colleges and prospective students became much weaker. Students had far more options and began submitting more applications, making competition for slots at the top schools all the more intense. And no matter where they looked, families faced price tags that were far steeper. Meanwhile, colleges—now unable to share information about aid packages with each other and less confident in their ability to detect genuine interest on the part of applicants—felt more at sea. Colleges were unsure of what they needed to do to nail down their incoming classes. This uncertainty was especially acute at nonselective colleges, which dominate the higher-education landscape. With the margin of error feeling vanishingly small, both colleges and students went looking for outside parties to help reduce their chances of making a costly mistake.

A MAGAZINE'S FAUSTIAN BARGAIN?

"There's a handful of people that run everything," the comedian Bill Hicks used to tell his audiences. No matter what presidential nominees promise on the campaign trail, "when you win, you go into this smoke-filled room with the twelve industrialist-capitalists who got you in there. This little film screen comes down, and a big guy with a cigar goes, 'Roll the film.' And it's a shot of the Kennedy assassination *from an angle you've never seen before*. . . . Then the screen goes up and the lights come up, and they say to the new president, 'Any questions?' "[29]

The joke had shades of truth for James Fallows. In the fall of 1996, he took over as the top editor of *U.S. News*. Even though the "Best Colleges" franchise had finally given *U.S. News* a way to stand out from the newsweekly pack, Fallows was not a fan of it. But any aspirations he may have harbored for deep-sixing the rankings soon collided with the harsh reality of how important they had become to the magazine's bottom line. Once he was inside the operation, it was as if he was looking at the Zapruder film from a completely unfamiliar angle.

Before joining *U.S. News*, Fallows had been the sober, thoughtful Washington editor for the *Atlantic Monthly*. The Harvard-educated journalist had previously been a speechwriter for President Jimmy Carter, a foreign correspondent, and an editor for the *Washington Monthly*. At the *Atlantic*, he trained his howitzer on higher education, criticizing the distorting effects of both the SATs and credentialism. American society is strongest, he argued, when access to opportunity is based on performance, not the stranglehold of credentialism. Instead of supporting the former, he complained, colleges were reinforcing the latter.

In his mind, the college rankings amplified the negatives of both the SATs and credentialism—and horse-race journalism in general. "They seemed to me to play on a wholly pernicious impulse—and pernicious in two ways," he would later say. "One was the idea that there was some kind of objective hierarchy of these institutions, just like saying 'best spouse' or 'best child.' There are differences among institutions of higher education, but the idea that one is best for a particular person is both preposterous on the merits, and also a disservice in negating what is best about American higher education, which is its range of institutions and options. Also, it was pernicious in its effects, because it made higher education an even more intense and internationalized arena of status competition."[30] Fallows's father had attended a tiny college that most people had never heard of, and yet, even without earning his bachelor's degree, he had managed to graduate from Harvard Medical School and become a pillar of his community. How many success stories like his father's would be precluded by the nation's growing obsession with status on the undergraduate level?

Earlier in his career, Fallows had worked at *Texas Monthly*, so he understood the reliance that city magazines long had on handing out crowns like "Best BBQ Joint." The college rankings sprang from that same place. "It's the eternal human fascination with this sort of numerology, matched with the modern-era status anxiety of colleges. In commercial terms, it was a brilliant insight," he says. "Unfortunately, it was damaging in all other ways."[31]

Of course, college rankings weren't the brainchild of *U.S. News*. The magazine had followed Edward Fiske's college guide onto the scene and arrived around the same time as other competitors, including one called *Lisa Birnbach's College Book*, by the author of the popular *Official Preppy Handbook*. In reality, college rankings have been around for more than a century. In 1910, a man named Kendric Charles Babcock traveled the country, and the following year, he published *A Classification of Universities and Colleges with Reference to Bachelor's Degrees*, rating each institution on a four-part scale.[32]

Still, there could be no denying that in terms of influence, the *U.S. News* rankings were in a class by themselves. Under the guidance of the projects editor Elfin, the rankings had shored up the long-shaky *U.S. News* business model. The annual college guide generated newsstand sales more than 50 percent above the magazine's usual numbers. Moreover, the rankings were no longer simply a magazine issue; they had also become a monster best-seller of a book, *America's Best Colleges*, racking up annual sales of about one million copies.[33]

Prospective students' parents obsessed over minor changes in the rankings each year, as did powerful alumni, trustees, and university marketing officials. Some college presidents celebrated the results—especially if their institutions climbed the list on their watch, knowing that record of improvement could make the leaders highly attractive to search committees at bigger schools looking for a new president. Other presidents complained that the list was bunk—incapable of measuring quality. During one national meeting, a college admissions official stood up and compared *U.S. News* to Satan.[34]

Regardless of the criticism, the rankings had become the measuring stick by which lots of people on and off campus viewed a college, so presidents had no choice but to deal with them. It was not uncommon for college presidents shut out from the top twenty-five or fifty to dismiss the rankings as "nothing but a beauty contest," only to turn around and trumpet the wisdom of *U.S. News* as soon as their own colleges managed to climb the charts.

In the years since the debut of the college list, Elfin and his deputies—the rankings managing editor, Alvin Sanoff, and data strategist Bob Morse—had worked to respond to criticism by rejiggering their algorithm and hoovering up more metrics. On top of academic reputation, they added measurements including selectivity, graduation rate, faculty resources, and alumni giving.

Selectivity, which boils down to the percentage of students that a college rejects, became an industrywide obsession thanks to *U.S. News*. How different was the world back then? In 1991, the acceptance rate at the University of Pennsylvania was 47 percent.[35] Think about that for a minute: nearly one out of every two applicants to that Ivy League school was admitted. In 1996, the acceptance rate at the University of Chicago was 71 percent, meaning nearly three out of every four applicants were admitted.[36] Lowering acceptance rates played a significant role in helping colleges climb the rankings. (In response to widespread criticism, the editors eventually reduced how much admit rates counted and, in 2018, eliminated them from the methodology altogether. By then, however, the damage had been done. Today, the admit rates for both Penn and the University of Chicago are under 6 percent.[37])

Given how high the stakes for rankings became in the 1990s, it should have surprised no one that any changes to the magazine's metrics would be met with corresponding efforts by some colleges to manipulate them.[38] A 1995 *Wall Street Journal* investigation by the reporter Steve Stecklow detailed a surfeit of gaming efforts by dozens of colleges.[39] For instance, the investigation compared the goosed statistics that many colleges reported to *U.S. News* against the real numbers that they reported to debt-rating agencies, where lying represented a violation of federal securities law. Some schools purged names from alumni lists to make their alumni giving percentage seem higher. Boston University reported the SAT math scores of its international students, which tended to be high, but not their verbal scores, which tended to be low. Rensselaer Polytechnic Institute boosted its selectivity rate by counting as "rejects" students who were admitted to a program other than the one to which they had specifically applied.[40]

After reading that damning *Wall Street Journal* article, the president of Reed College in Oregon pulled his institution out of the *U.S. News* rankings, refusing to report its data to the magazine. The rankings team punished Reed for its principled stand. While Reed had once occupied the number nine spot on the magazine's top liberal arts colleges, it now sank to the dreaded fourth tier on the list. In that low tier, *U.S. News* did not even dignify colleges with an actual numerical spot, instead giving only a range (122 to 161), and listing all the schools alphabetically. The backlash against *U.S. News* for this pettiness was intense, and the magazine retreated. The following year, Reed climbed to slot number 37. After the incident, Sanoff told *Rolling Stone* that when it came to Reed, "Let's just say we did not handle it the right way."[41]

Lost in all these controversies about the inherent value of the rankings was a little secret. There was a major beneficiary of the higher-ed landscape that *U.S. News* had reshaped, and it was the emerging enrollment management industry.

On the surface, enrollment management didn't focus on rankings, but rather on the quest to improve yield and maximize tuition revenue. Yet every time *U.S. News* fiddled with its algorithm in response to criticism, the editors went looking for new metrics to strengthen their argument that the rankings were a true measure of college quality.

Above all, what guru Jack Maguire—and his competitors in the increasingly crowded enrollment-management consultant space—offered their college clients was the ability to control their metrics. Or, at the very least, they could give them the appearance of control. Instead of passively accepting their fate, these colleges—with the right guidance from their consultants and their econometric modeling, data analysis, and behavioral science—could actively shape their futures. After all, there was no quicker way to increase a college's perceived prestige than to move up in the rankings.

In a rare nod to the cross-pollination between the rankings and enrollment-management sectors, the *U.S. News* "Best Colleges" guide in 1995 included a lengthy feature article headlined "The Consulting Game." The piece described a two-hour focus group involving seventy-five high school students in an auditorium in Concord, Massachusetts, comparing the process to the way that television networks tested sitcom pilots. The article, which introduced the *U.S. News* readership to the art and science of financial aid leveraging, focused on Maguire Associates, Jack Maguire's enrollment-management shop. It was written by Al Sanoff himself.[42]

Despite all the tinkering with the algorithm by the *U.S. News* team, the more popular the rankings became with the public, the more criticism the magazine received from college officials. By the time James Fallows took over the magazine, the student governments of close to two dozen colleges had passed resolutions calling on *U.S. News* to stop its numerical rankings. Some of the fiercest criticism came from Stanford, even though that university consistently enjoyed a perch at or near the top of the magazine's rankings. One Stanford senior, Nick Thompson, cofounded a group called Forget *U.S. News* Coalition, or FUNC. (Years later, Thompson would join the magazine world himself, writing critically for *Washington Monthly* about the *U.S. News* rankings and proposing a better mousetrap.[43]) And pretty much as soon as Fallows showed up at *U.S. News*, he received an indignant letter from Stanford's president, Gerhard Casper. "I hope I have the standing to persuade you that much about these rankings—particularly their specious formulas and spurious precision—is utterly misleading," Casper wrote, imploring the new editor "to walk away from these misleading rankings."[44]

Fallows had come to believe that the "Best Colleges" list was "a gimmick that was useful for *U.S. News* and, on the whole, socially detrimental."[45] In his bones, he knew that there was nothing meaningfully different between the number 1 school and the one in the number-10 slot. Yet he heard from parents who were crushed if their children didn't get an acceptance from a top-ten-ranked school. What's more, Fallows knew that the *U.S. News* rankings largely measured inputs—the resources of the institutions and the students whom they enrolled—rather than outputs. In other words, they were not based on how the schools actually educated students over four years, or how they improved their students' economic mobility once they left campus.[46] In that way, these rankings were not actually measurements of objective quality as much as they were mechanisms for privilege perpetuation.[47]

While *U.S. News* managers were coy about revealing their precise algorithm, they did disclose the types of measures they tracked. There was the college's reputation, which was an updated version of that original "beauty contest" based on surveys of other college leaders. There was student selectivity—a mix of standardized test scores, class rank, the percentage of students accepted, and, early in rankings' history, the percentage of those who enrolled—the "yield."[48] There were retention and graduation rates. And there were the college's endowment and other financial resources, its level of alumni giving, and the "quality" of its faculty, based on the crude measures of how many had obtained PhDs and how much they got paid.

Many college administrators worked to reverse-engineer the *U.S. News* algorithm to try to move up in the rankings. The desire for institutions to be seen as more selective produced some particularly odious behavior—incentivizing aggressive efforts by colleges to boost applications from students unlikely to be admitted, all so they could deny those applications and thereby appear more selective. The *Washington Monthly* summed it up this way: "In short, the perfect school is rich, hard to get into, harder to flunk out of, and has an impressive name."[49]

Fallows could not abide the status quo with the rankings. He had to do something. However, when he looked under the hood of the magazine's finances, he realized that many of his ambitious priorities for strengthening the journalism that his staff produced each week would be imperiled if he followed the Stanford president's exhortation to "walk away" from the lucrative annual rankings. A study at the University of California at Los Angeles around that time estimated that the "America's Best Colleges" issue of the magazine alone generated $5.2 million in sales each year, not including profits from advertising.[50]

Fallows tapped the respected National Research Council to do an independent, comprehensive review of its rankings.[51] Pulling the curtain back on the magazine's shrouded algorithm and methodology, the review was unsparing, suggesting an Oz-like absence of substance. "The principal weakness of the current approach is that the weights used to combine various measures into an overall rating lack any defensible empirical or theoretical basis," the report read. "Apart from the weights, however, we were disturbed by how little was known about the statistical properties of the measures or how knowledge of these properties might be used in creating the measures."

Given the business implications for the magazine, Fallows realized that killing the rankings was a nonstarter. Instead, he committed to making them better and more defensible. Among the reforms were creating separate lists for public and private institutions, as well as putting an end to the decimal points on each college's total score, which signaled a scientific precision behind the calculations that Fallows knew just wasn't there.

Before long, he installed a new team to run the rankings. Mel Elfin was out. Al Sanoff was also out. And where did Sanoff land? He became the vice president of Jack Maguire's enrollment management consulting firm, which he had profiled in *U.S. News* just a couple of years earlier. The force fields of rankings and enrollment management were moving even closer to one another. "I don't see my role primarily as telling people how to advance in the rankings," Sanoff told the *Chronicle of Higher Education* in 1998. "But certainly, it's possible that people will want to talk to me because I understand the rankings."[52]

The new special projects editor Lincoln Caplan, formerly of the *New Yorker*, whom Fallows hired to oversee the rankings brought in a statistical expert to improve the methodology. In his *Washington Monthly* piece, Nicholas Thompson reported that the new stats expert "found that *U.S. News* had essentially put its thumb on the scale to make sure that Harvard, Yale, and Princeton continued to come out on top, as they did every year until 1999."[53] Elfin had long argued that it made perfect sense for those three ultra-elite institutions to top the *U.S. News* rankings, but Thompson's article suggested that some questionable weighting measures had kept that Ivy troika's reign going. That all ended in 1999, when a new, purer statistical approach went into effect. Suddenly, sitting atop the *U.S. News* rankings was the small, heavily resourced, science, technology, engineering, and mathematics (STEM)–focused California Institute of Technology.

By the time the new methodology was in place, there was also someone new atop the *U.S. News* masthead. Three months shy of his second anniversary running *U.S. News*, Fallows had been shown the door.[54] The magazine's owner, Mort Zuckerman, continued his track record for impatience—souring on, and then replacing, yet another of his hand-picked newsroom leaders.

Fallows, Elfin, and Sanoff—three of the most influential players in either building or trying to reform the "America's Best Colleges" franchise—were gone from the newsweekly. Yet the *U.S. News* rankings marched on.

UNINTENDED CONSEQUENCES

Not long after Fallows took over at *U.S. News*, Don Hossler started his new job as vice chancellor of enrollment services at Indiana University. It marked a major change. Hossler had spent the bulk of his career studying enrollment management as a tenure-track faculty member. Now the academic had a chance to put his theories into practice.

His first exposure to the concept of enrollment management had been back in 1976, when he attended a small workshop about student retention at a hotel in Long Beach, California.[55] In 1984, Hossler published what is believed to be the first academic book on the subject. It was called, naturally, *Enrollment Management: An Integrated Approach*.

From the late 1970s through the mid-1980s, early adopters of the field of enrollment management had been finding each other. People like Hossler and

David Kalsbeek, with his twenty-nine-pound computer, would bump into each other at conferences, compare notes, and trade tips. The supportive community had grown slowly before exploding by the 1990s, when it moved from computer nerds tinkering with spreadsheets to big-money consulting firms competing aggressively while rapidly commercializing the enrollment space.

As the person now in charge of enrollment management for a flagship public research university, Hossler surveyed the changed late-1990s landscape. Some college leaders, like the president of Stanford, were still complaining about the *U.S. News* list, but most others had just accepted it as a reality that they had to deal with. At first, the list was primarily a concern for elite schools and those with aspirations to join their ranks. But as the categories expanded, and as lots of flagship public universities began functioning more like private ones, the *U.S. News* rankings became a reality for more and more schools. Meanwhile, the commercial success of the *U.S. News* list attracted more and more "best college" competitors, some of them aching to make their rankings stand out. This all reached peak absurdity when the *Princeton Review* introduced a new category by which it ranked colleges: best fire safety.[56]

As colleges invested ever more resources into boosting their rankings, those efforts often had a perverse effect of injecting more unfairness into higher education. After leaving *U.S. News*, Fallows returned to the *Atlantic*. In 2001, he wrote a withering exposé on how colleges were increasingly using binding early decision, which tended to favor privileged students, to boost their prestige. Fallows highlighted the example of the University of Pennsylvania. In its first rankings in 1983, *U.S. News* had not even included Penn in its list of national universities. By 2000, after years of heavily pushing early decision, Penn was clocking in at the number six spot, tied with Stanford.[57]

Hossler, with his deep understanding of college metrics from his decades of research into enrollment management, cast a gimlet-eye on the college rankings business. Still, he understood their appeal. They reminded him about a lesson that he learned once from a marketing book: when you're marketing a tangible product, you try to make it less tangible by creating an aura around it. With an intangible product, it works the other way. *U.S. News* had hit pay dirt by making higher education seem more tangible.

The orbits of enrollment management and the *U.S. News* rankings continued to track more closely. One year, when the top conference for enrollment management leaders—hosted by the American Association of Collegiate Registrars and Admissions Officers—met in Boston, Northeastern University capitalized. It bused all the attendees from their hotel to a swank space at the university featuring massive ice sculptures and an open bar, where they wined and dined them. "These were all higher-ed influencers," says Philomena Mantella, Northeastern's vice president overseeing enrollment management.[58] The elaborate reception was just one small part of a sophisticated strategy by Northeastern to reverse-engineer the *U.S. News* rankings.[59] Richard Freeland, Northeastern's president, set a goal of getting a university long dismissed as a "commuter school" to crack the *U.S. News* top hundred. (On Freeland's watch, Northeastern would do just that, climbing more than sixty spots.[60])

At Indiana University, Hossler employed the techniques of financial aid leveraging to improve the quality of the students that the university attracted, while also hitting the tuition revenue targets that his bosses had set. He knew that some people criticized those techniques as a way of taking money from poor students and giving it to their comfortable counterparts. But he felt that particular criticism missed the mark. For Ivy League institutions with enormous endowments, tuition revenue was an abstraction. For everyone else, it was a lifeline. Without enough revenue, a college wouldn't be able to keep the lights on, never mind fully fund lots of low-income students. Hossler knew that, when used strategically, modest tuition discounts in the form of merit scholarships could persuade more "full-pay" students to attend a college that they might otherwise forgo. And even with that discount factored in, the student would still be paying the college enough to help it subsidize needier students. It was simple math: even after an affluent student received, say, a 15 percent discount in the form of an ego-flattering "presidential scholarship," the remaining 85 percent of the tuition could potentially allow the college to underwrite more of the 100 percent discounts they needed to be able to enroll high-achieving poor students. (Of course, there's no guarantee that colleges seeking to keep their lights on will spend their money in this way.)

At its core, financial aid leveraging allows colleges to "buy" students for whom they wouldn't be able to compete otherwise. Critics liked to paint the beneficiaries of these practices as slacker rich kids with relatively high standardized test scores (which would help boost a college's *U.S. News* ranking) but unimpressive grade point averages. In other words, they were comfortable students who didn't feel the need to work very hard. But Hossler knew that these same aid techniques could be used in the service of nobler goals. Want to attract more smart young women to your STEM programs? Want more ethnic and racial diversity on your campus? Financial aid could be employed to help deliver those admirable results. So Hossler had no qualms about deploying these practices at Indiana University.

Three years into his job as vice chancellor for enrollment, Hossler asked two deputies to put together a report evaluating the impact of their aid-leveraging and other enrollment management techniques. As discounting became more common in higher education (by 2020, private colleges would be discounting their published tuition rates by, on average, a staggering 54 percent), overall tuition costs were driven up even faster.[61]

As he examined the report, Hossler first looked to see how the poorest students at Indiana University—those whose "expected family contributions" were zero—were faring. He was relieved to see that they were doing fine. But when he looked more closely at the numbers, his heart sank. Students who were lower middle class—those whose family incomes were quite modest, yet enough that they were expected to cover some chunk of the tuition—were clearly getting squeezed. Their Pell Grants and other sources of aid weren't keeping up with the rising costs of tuition and fees. "They were ending up having to borrow more money," Hossler says. "Every one of those percentages had gone up and looked worse for every one of those three years." He thought of the students whom he had been especially excited to attract to Indiana University, such as the promising Latina student from a working-class family in Gary, Indiana. He thought of the debt that she was having to take on as an unintended consequence of enrollment practices that he had long studied and more recently put into practice.

Oh my God, he thought, *what have I been doing?*[62]

"SCREWING POOR KIDS"

Within a few years, many others were asking the same question. A headline in a 2004 column that Hossler wrote in the *Chronicle of Higher Education* questioned whether enrollment management had "ruined" higher education. The following year, an *Atlantic* article headlined "The Best Class Money Can Buy" quoted the Williams College economist Gordon Winston making this assessment of enrollment management: "It's a brilliantly analytical process of screwing poor kids."[63] Written by Matthew Quirk, the story described how a growing number of colleges were abusing the system, with consequences far more nefarious than the unintended ones that Don Hossler had discovered in his own work. The article described how many enrollment managers were using more and more of their previously need-based financial aid dollars to fund "merit aid" discounts to attract wealthy students, while also egregiously "gapping" poor students. In many cases, they offered poor students financial aid packages that they knew to be hopelessly insufficient. "Called 'admit-deny,' this practice allows a college to keep poor students out while publicly claiming that it doesn't consider a student's finances when making admissions decisions," Quirk wrote.[64]

The *Atlantic* piece offered a stinging indictment, but it also pointed out that many college leaders were simply dealing with the reality of the arms race that *U.S. News* had helped spur. Since so many peer institutions were working to game the rankings and dangle merit-aid discounts to wealthy students in the hopes of "buying" students with higher test scores, most colleges could not afford to take the principled stand of unilateral disarmament. Trustees were putting intense pressure on college presidents to see their institution climb in the *U.S. News* rankings, and presidents were passing that pressure on to their vice presidents of enrollment management. The article described how the president of Virginia Commonwealth University walked around with a laminated card in his pocket to remind him of the school's goal to make it to the next tier in the *U.S. News* rankings. That president, incidentally, would earn a $25,000 bonus every year that Virginia Commonwealth managed to be ranked in the next tier.[65]

The *Atlantic* noted that there were some college officials who were managing to use the tools of enrollment management to achieve admirable goals. Case in point: David Kalsbeek, the early adopter who, in the 1980s, had used his Osborne Executive computer to put Saint Louis University in the vanguard of enrollment management. In 2005, Kalsbeek was serving as senior vice president of enrollment management and marketing at DePaul University in Chicago. DePaul had by then managed to become the nation's largest Catholic university, and the eighth-largest private college in the United States. Kalsbeek had used his sophisticated techniques to help DePaul expand its profitable professional programs and attract more full-pay students. Those moves had brought in enough money for the university to be able to enroll substantially more low-income and first-generation students and meet their financial needs.[66]

Back in 2005, it was unclear which forces in the enrollment-management world would ultimately win out—those determined to assist more disadvantaged students or those willing to disadvantage them even more. By 2013, when Kalsbeek teamed up with Hossler to write a journal article for *Strategic Enrollment Management Quarterly*, there was little question about which side was winning. In their article, the pair acknowledged the "hyper-competitive 'winner-takes-all'" landscape, which the forces of enrollment management had helped to shape. "Too often," they wrote, "enrollment management tools, techniques, and tactics have been used in ways that constrain equity outcomes for students from low-income and first-generation backgrounds."[67]

In a 2021 interview, Kalsbeek admitted that in recent years, the trend lines for the enrollment management field to which he had devoted his professional life have grown only more troubling. Early on, both enrollment management and the *U.S. News* rankings sought to bring order and a quantitative grounding to the world of higher education, which had previously been characterized by squishy notions like reputation. Kalsbeek had long argued that enrollment management, through its focus on data, trends, and intersecting dynamics, simply "crystallizes the trade-offs that exist," such as between boosting student diversity on the one hand and boosting net revenue on the other. In that way, it is value-neutral. It merely sets the table with clarity, allowing college leaders to make more informed choices about what their true priorities are. On some level, Kalsbeek continues to believe this.[68]

Yet on a deeper level, even an enrollment-management evangelist like Kalsbeek has begun to acknowledge the many ways in which these forces have worked to distort higher education. He accepts the criticism that "*U.S. News* just creates these incentives for us to spend more per student, and the only way to spend more per student is to make more per student, and therefore it's going to drive up our pricing," he says. And because of the addiction to merit-aid discounts and the corresponding tuition hikes that far too many colleges and their enrollment management officials have developed, the pricing structure in higher education is no longer sustainable. "We know that the sticker price is insane. We know it's indefensible," he says. "We know nobody can pay this. We know that the whole pricing financial aid industry has gotten all-confusing, particularly for more disadvantaged students."[69] (For his part, Maguire argues that college leaders erred by allowing *U.S. News* to provide the playbook for enrollment management. "Had institutions not abdicated their natural claim to define quality in higher education, they would have been the ones to determine what to measure and what to consider optimal outcomes," Maguire told the journalist Susan Paterno. "The rise of 'Best Colleges' rankings fueled a preoccupation with school status in the competitive battle for students."[70])

Meanwhile, the field of consulting firms working in this space—making enormous sums from colleges by promising to give them a competitive edge—has become improbably large and crowded. What began with small companies like Jack Maguire's now features not just longtime major players like Ruffalo Noel Levitz and Hardwick Day, but increasingly the world's biggest consulting firms, such as Deloitte and EAB. In 2022, the enrollment marketing company Carnegie acquired Maguire's firm, Maguire Associates.[71] Even Kalsbeek, who retired from his position at DePaul University, now works for a consulting firm, though his new employer, Human Capital Research, is a smaller one that has long specialized in higher education. The involvement of all these for-profit outside players "has elevated the expectation for a lot of institutions on how much can be done with data analytics, in guiding through a process, sometimes to supplant human judgment," Kalsbeek says. "That's the sad thing."[72]

It's also reality. The younger colleague who Kalsbeek recalled once comparing him to *Moneyball* star Billy Beane did that because, in the early days, both he and Beane were outliers. They were guys using crude—but, for the day, cutting-edge—computing to produce quantitative insights that their competitors couldn't see. At first, Beane's Oakland A's were the only team in baseball using these techniques to govern on-the-field decisions, while every other team continued to base all their moves on tradition and hunches. Then the Boston Red Sox followed his lead, and then a few other teams. Now, the outlier quants and their data analytics govern nearly every aspect of every game played by every ball club in Major League Baseball. Old-timers lament that these stats-obsessed nerds have ruined America's pastime, sapping it of its beauty and serendipity and inherent fairness. They can moan all they want, but just as in higher education, the quants have won.

CHAPTER 2

Going to a "Witch Doctor"

Colleges' Reliance on Enrollment Management Firms Grows Despite Alarm over Companies' Strategies

Jon Marcus

Unseasonably cool weather couldn't diminish the enthusiasm inside the low-rise office complex that was once the headquarters of the enrollment-management consulting firm Royall & Co.

Arranged around a grassy quadrangle beside a sprawling middle school on the northern outskirts of Richmond, Virginia, the three-building complex could be mistaken for a college campus. A retractable divider was pulled back to make room for about one hundred people in a conference room named for the admissions director, who was the company's first client. Cameras were set up for several hundred more to watch online.[1]

They were there midmorning on a Thursday in November 2019 to mark the thirtieth anniversary of when Royall, which initially specialized in sending direct mail for political campaigns, broke into the higher education game. Banners chronicled the company's thirty-year timeline, highlighting key events as the firm grew exponentially to become a behemoth in the lucrative enrollment management industry. One of the most critical of those events had been the company's $850 million sale in 2014 to the enrollment management consulting giant EAB, now housed in this complex and in three other offices, in Birmingham, Alabama, Washington, DC, and Minneapolis, Minnesota.[2] Another was EAB's $1.55 billion sale to an investment firm in 2017.[3]

At the Royall celebration, EAB executives and longtime clients offered greetings, and there were video tributes to the company's founder, Bill Royall, who attended but, ailing with the degenerative disease amyotrophic lateral sclerosis (ALS), did not speak.[4] He was accompanied by his wife, Pam Kiecker Royall, EAB's head of research for enrollment services. With their fortune, the pair had become art collectors and prominent philanthropists.[5] Then, after closing remarks, everyone broke for a lunch of flank steak, with meringue cookies—Royall's favorite dessert.[6]

That there are fortunes to be made in the for-profit enrollment management industry is hardly a surprise. This "academic-industrial complex" has been propelled by the increasingly complex science, and the high stakes for colleges and universities, of recruiting and retaining students and the revenue they bring. Where once institutions could sit back, wait for people to apply, and bestow on them the privilege of admission, now all but the most prestigious colleges and universities needed to aggressively recruit them. As the supply of students shrinks, competition for students continues to become only more intense.

Although most of the enrollment management companies are privately held and detailed information on revenue is visible only here and there, the industry now serves a market that one insider values at $15 billion a year in student recruitment, marketing, enrollment, retention, financial aid, and other services.[7]

Pioneered by characters with unlikely origins in fields such as telecommunications and shaped by technology masterminds with Silicon Valley–caliber celebrity, the enrollment management business has come to be dominated by a few big players that have diversified through acquisitions, often backed by private equity and investment funds that expect returns and constant growth.

EAB is one of the giants in the industry. Another is Ruffalo Noel Levitz (RNL), the product of an expensive merger in 2014, when RuffaloCODY acquired Noel-Levitz for an undisclosed sum to create a single enrollment-management and fundraising consulting company with 1,800 clients.[8] At the time of their merger, EAB and Royall reported a combined net income of more than $25 million.[9] The same year, Noel-Levitz revenues were estimated to be more than $35 million.[10]

Several midsized firms also play a big role in the field. Smaller ones keep cropping up too, some created by top managers who jumped ship from the behemoths and others by institutional enrollment vice presidents who hung up a shingle. A few nonprofits, including the College Board, ACT, and the American Association of Collegiate Registrars and Admissions Officers (AACRAO), have also gotten in on the act of providing enrollment consulting services.

These consultants can provide expertise that most universities and colleges generally can't afford to build in house. They have data at their fingertips collected from among not just one but hundreds of client institutions, helping them spot trends that are hard to see at ground level. They can put together solutions much more quickly than is possible in the infamously slow-moving culture of higher education. And they bring long-term outsiders' perspectives to campuses that can't see beyond the next year's class.

Colleges depend heavily on these companies to help them shape their classes. According to a 2019 survey that EAB conducted, 90 percent of private colleges and 36 percent of public universities have hired consultants to help them use their financial aid to recruit students.[11] These firms offer a wide range of services to colleges, with some providing products or strategic advice to colleges and universities that have large and sophisticated enrollment management offices of their own. But some less well endowed colleges, with smaller administrative staffs, rely on these private companies to largely develop and carry out their recruiting and financial aid strategies.

Enrollment consulting services are expensive. Private colleges and universities sometimes list enrollment management consultants as among their five highest-paid independent contractors in their financial statements, which they're required to report to the Internal Revenue Service (IRS). Bryant University in Rhode Island paid Royall $419,744 in 2017, for example; in 2019, Linfield University in Oregon paid RNL $330,992.[12] Public flagship and research universities are also increasingly dropping big sums on these firms. Between 2010 and 2018, the University of Alabama paid $1.9 million to the College Board and $349,000 to ACT for student data and $4.4 million to Hobsons for consulting services, the advocacy group Third Way found by filing public-records requests.[13]

Despite how lucrative and influential the enrollment management industry is, few people in the wider public, or even in academe, know of it or understand what it does. "If people were to learn about how some of this is done, it would create intense cynicism about the college process," says Jim Jump, the academic dean and director of college counseling at St. Christopher's School in Richmond, Virginia, and former president of the National Association for College Admission Counseling (NACAC). "Enrollment management serves colleges really well. I'm not sure it serves the public really well."[14]

The enrollment management industry has pushed a strategy of high tuition and high financial aid, even at public universities, on the principle that offering generous discounts will attract the students that consultants exhort their client institutions to relentlessly pursue—increasingly higher-income ones, who bring revenue and rankings-boosting SAT scores and grade point averages (GPAs). It's simple, as one top enrollment-management consulting company executive explains: "I've got to have enough room under the top-line sticker price" to provide inducements of the size that will attract desired students.[15]

Pursuing this strategy has caused colleges to shift a significant proportion of institutional financial aid from need-based to so-called merit-based, meaning more money flowing to students who need it less. Non-need-based financial aid is now growing faster than the need-based kind. Students from families with incomes of $120,000 or higher at public universities, for example, get an average of $5,950 more than federal guidelines show they need; those from families with incomes of $200,000 or higher get $7,860 more. At private universities and colleges, people in those earnings categories receive about twice these amounts more than they need.[16]

"Aid used to be a charitable act, and now it's become a competitive weapon," says Lloyd Thacker, the founder and executive director of the Education Conservancy, who has pushed for reform of college admissions. A former private school college counselor, he says that he "saw the amount of aid offered to those kids quadrupled. These kids didn't need aid. They were being bought."[17]

Colleges' generosity to students from relatively affluent families comes at a cost. Public and private colleges and universities alike over the past two decades have significantly reduced the share of financial need they meet, leaving lower-income students and their families with hefty funding gaps. To attend these institutions, they and their parents have to take on heavy debt loads each year that can amount to nearly as much as their annual earnings, or more.

The practice is taking a huge toll on the colleges themselves. Private, non-profit colleges have gotten so locked into this cycle that they now give back more than half the tuition revenue that they receive from first-year students in the form of discounts to meet ever-challenging enrollment targets, according to the National Association of College and University Business Officers.[18] Even as colleges appear to be raising their prices faster than inflation, this has slowed growth in net revenue at the average institution to less than the inflation rate.[19]

"There's both the economic and ethical aspects of this issue," says S. Georgia Nugent, the president of Illinois Wesleyan University, who has long criticized the escalating use of merit aid and tuition discounts. "From students' and society's points of view, the limited resources you have are not being directed as much as they should or could be to the population that most needs those resources." As for colleges, she says, "it's obviously not sustainable. Any business where you're giving away more than you're taking in, that's not a sustainable model."[20]

When it comes to recruiting students, enrollment management companies often provide products and strategies that aim to help colleges rise up the *U.S. News & World Report* rankings and make them appear more exclusive. Consultants have pushed such tactics as early decision, for example, which benefits wealthier applicants from better-resourced high schools and fills seats at the expense of lower-income, first-generation, and racial-minority students.[21]

Early decision "is a great deal for colleges. It's a great deal for students who know where they want to go," says Jump. But "there's always been a question about how equitable it is." In the enrollment-management era, he says, "what's changed about early decision is that colleges very strategically are taking a huge portion of their class early and they're doing that to lower their admit rates, which is factored into the rankings."[22] He's speaking about selectivity, or the proportion of applicants accepted; the more students are admitted early, the fewer seats are available in the regular admissions cycle, making it harder for other applicants to get in. Colleges have also been accused of encouraging students to apply, with personalized letters and emails, for the purpose of rejecting them. The more students who are recruited and then denied admission, the more selective a college or university can claim to be.

Enrollment management industry officials generally chafe at the criticism that they've made higher education more inequitable. They're convenient scapegoats, they say, when the forces responsible for this are far beyond their control. They argue that a shift in public officials' view of higher education as a private rather than a public good, as well as the subsequent state and federal government disinvestment, are the roots of a problem for which they're often blamed.

Still, even a few of the industry's own biggest names say they worry about the direction it's taken. Jack Maguire, who left Boston College to start his own consulting company in 1983 from his dining room table, with his wife and daughter as employees, describes some of the tactics of enrollment outfits with "the nastiest word I can think of: Trumpian, with all kinds of intrigue."[23] Tom Williams, head of a firm, Ingersoll Williams and Associates, that would merge with Noel-Levitz and become one of that company's early principals, who has since spun off his own enrollment management business, says that outside consultants have led higher education down a dangerous course—including by pushing such strategies as tuition discounting, a major reason why some small colleges are going out of business.[24]

Colleges have outsourced a lot of things that they used to do themselves—dining and custodial services, bookstores, fundraising—that have given rise to lucrative for-profit industries that now provide those services under contract. Entrepreneurs have also found profitable footholds in such things as tutoring, test prep, rankings, and college admissions counseling, among others.

But the enrollment management business has become as big as it is almost invisible to the people it affects the most: students and their families. "It's hard for me to think of an academic or programmatic change—maybe online learning—which has had a comparable growth over as short or maybe an even longer period as enrollment management," says Richard Freeland, the former president of Northeastern University and the Massachusetts commission of higher education and a historian of higher education, who went on to become a senior consultant at Maguire.[25]

FROM HUMBLE BEGINNINGS TO MULTIBILLIONS

Iowa may seem an unlikely place for some of the major players to be clustered in an industry that serves higher education. But it's where the University of Iowa education professor Everett Franklin Lindquist developed the ACT, which was first administered on November 7, 1959, setting in motion a chain of events that would make his state the birthplace of a disproportionate number of enrollment management providers.[26]

First, in Iowa City, there was the ACT itself, whose Interest Inventory is one of the principal lists of prospective college students, collected from test-takers and sold to colleges to use in their recruiting efforts. The nonprofit would grow to have annual revenues of $349.4 million and later launch an acquisitions spree to add still more recruitment services for sale to higher education clients.[27] In 1984, two top ACT executives, Lee Noel and Randi Levitz, would leave to found Noel-Levitz, a recruitment and retention company that produced training videos and developed an early alert and intervention system that universities could use to improve student retention.[28] Thirty miles away in Cedar Rapids, Al Ruffalo was working for the telecommunications company Teleconnect, which sold telephone systems and eventually long-distance service; Ruffalo made a name for himself and the company by hiring celebrity athletes and paying them nominal fees and stock options for endorsements. Telecommunications deregulation and the breakup of AT&T led to Teleconnect being acquired by MCI in 1991, and Ruffalo decided to leave and start his own business—RuffaloCODY, his name and the initials of his partners—helping colleges and universities use telemarketing for fundraising.[29] Across town, Stamats (pronounced "Stay-mates"), which had been founded decades earlier as a publisher of custom magazines, steered into the business of providing marketing and market research services to higher-education institutions.[30]

Sorting through the ensuing evolution of the enrollment management consulting business is an exercise rooted as much in genealogy as in history, with family and professional connections and few degrees of separation. It also reveals how modest the origins of what would quickly become a multi-billion-dollar business were.

Stuart Weiner, the admissions director at Blackburn College in Carlinville, Illinois, set himself up as an admissions marketing consultant in 1973, naming his company Stuart Weiner Associates. He hired Ron Ingersoll, a biology professor turned enrollment management dean, and Ingersoll's wife, Dori, and offered recruiting and telemarketing services to mostly small, Midwestern colleges. "We just called it using the telephone," says Tom Williams, who was brought on board part-time in 1980 from Adrian College, where he worked at that time and which was a client of what was by then called Weiner Ingersoll.[31]

By 1982, Ingersoll bought out Weiner, renamed the company the Ingersoll Group, and moved it to Denver. Williams joined full time, and it became Ingersoll Williams. Then he bought out Ingersoll and hired an ACT vice president, David Crockett (yes, a direct descendant of the folk hero and frontiersman, says his son, Kevin Crockett, who would go on to work for Noel-Levitz and then became president of RNL).[32] The company became Williams Crockett until, while at a conference speaking about the then-new idea of financial aid leveraging—using financial aid to enroll the right students and studying precisely how much it would cost to recruit them—Williams was handed a message from Lee Noel.

"Back then there was a concept of enrollment management but there was no comprehensive provider of those services," remembers Williams.[33] Noel thought that their two companies, together, could become one. So, in 1992, they merged, keeping the name Noel-Levitz but with Williams as a principal, and pushing the idea of financial aid leveraging.[34] (It wasn't the end of the roller-coaster ride; the student loan guarantor USA Group bought Noel-Levitz in 1995 in an early example of emerging outside interest in the investment potential of enrollment management that would intensify in the 2010s.[35])

Back east, Jack Maguire, who is credited with being the first to use the term *enrollment management*, started his own consulting company in 1983 in his house in the historic town of Concord, Massachusetts, with his wife—a former college admissions director—as chief executive officer (CEO) and their daughter as their sole employee. They called it Revolutionary Ideas before renaming it Maguire Associates, and had one client: Boston College, which Maguire had gotten to hire him in exchange for staying in his job for one more admissions cycle before he left.[36]

That was the same year that Bill Royall started in the political marketing business; he would become famous for an email audaciously sent to thousands of potential donors soliciting money for Bill Clinton at almost the exact moment Clinton got the Democratic presidential nomination in 1992.[37] By then, however, Royall was already pivoting into higher education, helping colleges more precisely target the names on the lists that they licensed from ACT and an even bigger source of leads: the College Board, the parent of the SAT. Using a rudimentary form of predictive analytics, Royall narrowed down the prospects to the ones most likely to be interested, and response rates jumped from about 9 percent to as high as 19 percent.[38] He also came up with the idea of sending applications to students with their information already entered, and waiving application fees the way that credit card companies had started waiving membership charges. This "rapid app" helped clients including Rensselaer Polytechnic Institute, the University of Minnesota, and Marquette University sharply raise their application numbers—and, as a consequence, their selectivity, a major factor in those all-important rankings—although critics complained that many of these applicants were far less likely to enroll, depressing yield rates.[39]

In 2007, the Advisory Board, which did strategic research for financial and healthcare clients, started to expand into student and academic affairs consulting. A few years after that, it launched its Student Success Collaborative, which used technology to warn universities when students were at risk of dropping out.

Providers organized national conferences to drum up business. In 1987, for example, the Noel-Levitz partners printed a brochure, loaded up some vans in Iowa City, and drove to Washington, DC, to put on the first National Conference on Student Retention. No one was more surprised than they were when 1,200 people showed up, in roles that ranged from academic advising to residential life. It was a receptive audience, Kevin Crockett says. Before then, "there wasn't a home for people who were being charged with that activity on campus."[40] The next opportunity the private sector saw was in marketing and advertising institutions to prospective students. Marketing was at the time a concept so foreign to universities and colleges that a story in an education journal in 2006 about the idea was titled "The M Word."[41] But some higher-education marketing consulting firms had already quietly been at it for a while. Carnegie Communications—named for the building at their alma mater, Penn State, where the two principals met and came up with the idea in 1985—began by publishing a magazine for prospects called *Private Colleges & Universities* in which it sold space to institutions. "It was very taboo to advertise back then," says Meghan Dalessandro, the chief operating officer at what is now called Carnegie Dartlet. The partners, one of whom ran a national daily newspaper advertising business, "had to get across to [higher-education] folks that it was okay to advertise. You weren't allowed to even say that word at the beginning." After a while, in an early version of lead generation, they added inquiry cards to the magazine, which students could fill out and mail back to the publisher to send along to admissions offices. Carnegie Dartlet does the same thing now online for private and public universities alike, through a product that it calls CollegeXPress.[42]

Marketing "was rejected for so long because it felt so corporate," says Elizabeth Scarborough Johnson, the chair of the research, strategy, and communications firm Simpson Scarborough. "I have all those stories of being kicked out of presidents' offices for using the M word. I walked out with my hand raised saying, 'You'll need me someday. You'll be calling me later.' "[43] Marketing alone proved not enough to offset their enrollment challenges, so public and nonprofit colleges turned to a recruiting tactic that was filling up all those huge for-profit universities: lead generation, the same process that in other sectors is used to drum up sales leads.[44] Now, when consumers searched for information or responded to unsolicited emails or late-night TV ads about colleges, careers, or scholarships, their information would be collected and sold to institutions—in many cases, without the users' knowledge or consent. "As the technology became more pervasive and available, the entrepreneurs that were helping businesses generate leads and develop customers saw a really great opportunity in colleges," says Robert Massa, a longtime enrollment and marketing officer who worked at Dickinson, Drew, and Lafayette colleges and Johns Hopkins University and now teaches at the Rossier School of Education at the University of Southern California.[45]

Yet another private-sector tool started to be sold to colleges and universities as data science became more fine-tuned and technology evolved—customer relationship management systems (CRMs), which can automate much of the basic communication and scheduling functions of admissions offices. It does such things as use keywords to raise a college to the top of a search, target advertising to specific audiences, track inquiries, and automate follow-up emails.

Some admissions offices got their CRMs from mainstream providers such as Salesforce, which dove into the education market in 2015; by 2020, it had 8,000 customers show up at its higher education users' summit, which was held virtually because of COVID-19.[46] The Ingersoll Group and Tom Williams built a rudimentary early recruitment–focused CRM called the Enrollment Management Action System, later combined with the Telecounseling software developed by Noel-Levitz, renamed EMASPro, and sold to Education Systems.[47] Soon companies popped up to focus solely on enrollment CRM. One was Technolutions, whose Slate information management system would become the one most associated with the field—and whose Slate Innovation Summit annually draws 2,500 users who come to watch its founder and chief executive, Alexander Clark, announce the latest advances through a face mic, Steve Jobs–style and sometimes flanked by performers from the Blue Man Group. (In a nod to all this pageantry, the event has been renamed the Slate Innovation Festival.)

Developed by Clark to allow his alma mater, Yale, to release admissions decisions online, Slate would soon be able to track every contact between an institution and a student. It transmits 1.6 billion emails and seven million text messages per year for its 1,200 university and college clients, and what look like handwritten note cards (spoiler—they're not) to applicants and admitted students.[48] Enrollment managers collect so much information about prospective students that these officials are able to track applicants' activities online, including what pages of a college's or university's websites they've visited and for how long, and to score the odds that they would accept an offer of admission.[49]

As companies jockeyed to position themselves in this increasingly crowded market, some executives jumped ship to start their own firms and there was a spree of acquisitions and mergers. The biggest were that $850 million purchase of Royall by EAB, followed by the $1.55 billion sale of EAB three years later. "We all fell off our chairs," says Tom Green, the associate executive director for consulting and strategic enrollment management at AACRAO and editor-in-chief of the journal *Enrollment Management Quarterly*. "We had no idea that anything anyone was doing was of that kind of value."[50]

But those were only the most noticeable of a biblical succession in which companies begat other companies in a race for market share. In 2018, ACT bought the National Research Center for College Admissions (NRCCUA),[51] which two years earlier had taken over the research firm Eduventures.[52] In order to straddle the higher-ed and K–12 markets, Hobsons U.S. acquired Naviance, which provides planning and advising systems for high schools;[53] RepVisits, which schedules high school visits by college recruiters;[54] College Confidential, an online forum for students and parents;[55] the CRM platform Intelliworks;[56] and Starfish Retention Solutions,[57] among others. ("Hobsons is buying everything," one enrollment management vice president quips.) Civitas Learning bought College Scheduler.[58] The higher-education digital-marketing agency mStoner acquired the software development firm Global Image.[59] The media company Alloy Partners bought Carnegie Communications before one of its principals bought it back.[60] Then Carnegie combined with Dartlet.[61]

Royall & Co. merged with the direct marketing and enrollment management company Hardwick Day.[62] After it picked up Royall, EAB added the retention company GradesFirst[63] and YouVisit, which produces virtual campus tours;[64] when colleges started jettisoning their requirements that applicants submit SAT and ACT scores during the COVID-19 pandemic—accelerating the test-optional movement and jeopardizing an important source of leads for enrollment-management offices—EAB also acquired Cappex, a website that 1.5 million high school students use annually to search for colleges and scholarships, whose information it said would allow it to "connect our partners with Cappex's growing student audience... amid continued market turbulence."[65] It later acquired Concourse Global, which lets students who otherwise might not consider college submit their academic and extracurricular records anonymously before applying and hear back from admissions offices about whether they might be accepted and how much financial aid they'd get.[66]

RuffaloCODY scooped up the research firm the Austen Group[67] and, after it had acquired Noel-Levitz and become RNL, added the campus visit and recruitment app Render Experiences and the digital marketing agency Converge.[68] RuffaloCODY also acquired Scannell & Kurz—cofounded by Jim Scannell, who had been best man at Jack Maguire's wedding and worked for him before starting his own firm.[69]

Private equity firms, investment funds, and even student lenders were showing interest. "When we first started back in 1991, private equity firms didn't pay attention to companies like RuffaloCODY," Al Ruffalo remembers.[70] But then the companies started bringing in real money and posting steady and impressive growth that seemed to flow in inverse proportion to the fortunes of their clients—the number of students attending university and college took its biggest dip ever in the 2010s, falling about 12 percent, even as some of the biggest enrollment management firms were seeing huge paydays from acquisitions.[71]

It was Vista Equity Partners, a $57 billion firm that invests in technology companies, that paid $1.55 billion for EAB in 2017, for instance—even more than the health-care side of parent the Advisory Board went for.[72] RNL is backed by the $21 billion equity investor Summit Partners.[73] Civitas Learning got a $60 million growth investment in 2015 led by the private equity company Warburg Pincus.[74]

Entrepreneurs from outside education also saw an opportunity. Huron, founded by former partners of the Arthur Andersen accounting firm, for instance, served other sectors including business and health care but expanded its higher-education practice from forty consultants when it began in 2002 to nearly nine hundred.[75] The creative agency 160over90, part of the sports, entertainment, and media conglomerate Endeavor, went from serving customers including sports franchises, beer companies, and hotel chains to producing marketing campaigns for the University of California at Los Angeles and the University of Virginia.[76] "There are companies in other verticals saying, 'We can play in higher education,'" says mStoner cofounder and co-owner Michael Stoner.[77]

The enrollment management industry has come to encompass so many services and products that no one tracks how big it has become. There are a few clues, however. The LeadsCouncil, which represents lead generators that serve higher education and other industries, has grown to 450 members.[78] The number of companies that provide marketing technology services to higher-education and other clients has mushroomed 5,233 percent, from 150 in 2011 to 8,000, according to an annual survey.[79] But the simplest illustration of the transformation of enrollment management is the exhibit hall at the annual conference of NACAC, the admission counseling association. Once a handful of vendors glad-handing prospective customers in a small conference room had by 2019 grown to 205, filling an 87,000-square-foot swath of Louisville's Kentucky International Convention Center.[80]

Principal sponsors of the NACAC conference typically include the likes of EAB, Slate, Salesforce, ACT/NRCCUA, the Common App, the College Board, CollegeNet, and Carnegie Dartlet. There are also newer entrants ranging from the college-ranking service Niche to the online video production company AlliedPixel. Out on the floor of the exhibit hall are rows of vendors offering branded paperweights and stress balls and services described in the impenetrable language of technology: operational efficiencies, web-based software solutions, enterprise-class functionality, modular-based architecture. Beyond the big booths reserved for EAB, the College Board, Slate, Hobsons, ACT, and RNL, these include CRM and admissions management software providers ZAP Solutions and EnrollmentRx and marketers Collegis Education, Waybetter Marketing, BlueFuego, and Fire Engine RED. On one side of the cavernous room is the texting platform Cadence; on the other is leads-chaser LeadSquared.

The industry had helped transform students into high- or low-quality "starts" and "leads." Distributing financial aid has been transformed into "leveraging" (some inside higher-ed prefer "financial aid optimization"), and successfully enrolling an admitted student is now an "admit-to-deposit conversion." Back on campus, and even in the corner offices of a few enrollment management companies themselves, people were starting to wonder if it had all gone too far.

SHORT-TERM BENEFITS, LONG-TERM FOLLY

It was at one of the first editions of another product of the College Board—its annual winter Higher Ed Colloquium—that the keynote speaker sounded an early alarm about some worrying effects of the enrollment management industry. Andrew Delbanco, the Alexander Hamilton Professor of American Studies at Columbia University, told his audience of campus leaders gathered in Laguna Beach, California, that competition for students seemed to be reducing universities' commitments to them. Leveraging financial aid often meant shifting it from lower- to higher-income applicants, Delbanco warned. Vying for a better ranking in *U.S. News* was encouraging colleges to prioritize prestige over access. So was hurrying to lock in students by expanding early acceptance.[81]

That was in 2002. Delbanco's warning would be echoed by others in the ensuing years, but the industry's momentum didn't slow down—it speeded up. The hypercompetition for full-pay students and high-achievers who would help colleges rise up the rankings only intensified as enrollment continued to decline before plummeting by nearly 1.5 million students during the COVID-19 pandemic.

How much the enrollment management industry is to blame for the direction that higher education has taken is up for debate. Industry officials say that there are larger forces at play, and even some critics of the arms race agree.

"I don't know how much to fault the enrollment-management industry," says S. Georgia Nugent. In addition to the punishing enrollment trends, she says, "part of the cause is a change in our culture." Before financial aid became a recruiting weapon, Nugent says, people thought that it was reasonable for tuition from students who could afford to pay for college to subsidize their classmates who couldn't. She adds, "Over time, we have become a coarser culture. We have become a much more me-focused culture. And then of course our economic situation has changed, so that all socioeconomic levels are more anxious now about their economic future."[82]

Still, even college presidents admit that they are uneasy about the ways that the enrollment management industry has pushed a combination of high tuition and escalating amounts of financial aid to reel in students and fill slots. In a survey of presidents whose colleges used financial aid to shape their classes, most said they believe in principle that non-need-based financial aid conflicts with higher education's goals and values, and they wish that they could slow the growth of merit aid. But that could put them at a competitive disadvantage. They said that outside consultants increasingly control their financial aid policies. They have found themselves "using aid to buy students from competitors," one president in the anonymous survey said. "It hurts the public interest," added another. The effect is "to reward the rich for being rich, to perpetuate class divisions, to make distributions of wealth worse," said a third.[83]

"What's fascinating is that nobody likes this," says Thacker of the Education Conservancy, who wrote up a report based on these interviews with private college presidents. "Not students, not presidents, not parents, not deans. None of these presidents thought they were doing the right thing. They all disliked this game."[84]

They keep hiring the consultants who make the rules, however. "We have gotten to a point where we have become an integral effort to game the social compact system and we go to a witch doctor to tell us how to do it," a college president said in the survey.

Beyond the effects on students of these tactics, there have been counter-productive consequences for colleges. Feeding expectations for financial aid, for instance, pushed some private, nonprofit schools' discount rates—the proportion of revenue from tuition that they hand back to entering students in the form of institutional grants or discounts—to nearly 55 percent.[85] Rapid apps may have increased the number of prospects in the pool, but they also made it easier for students to apply who weren't particularly interested in an institution. That lowered yield, which meant that recruiters had to scramble for more applicants in a dog-chasing-its-tail scenario that sent them back for help again to the consultants.

Those companies have "basically contributed to the destruction of the integrity of the enrollment funnel," says the enrollment management industry executive Tom Williams, referring to the cone-shaped progression that begins with lots of prospects and turns them into a slightly smaller quantity of applicants, which becomes an even smaller number of admitted students and then a still-narrower jackpot of deposit-paying freshmen. Williams means that new approaches such as targeted digital advertising don't give prospective students the chance to decide on their own whether they actually want to go to the college that recruited them, making them less likely to enroll if they're accepted. "There's no difference between that and a low-quality inquiry," he says. "So that leads to the vendor-driven strategy where it's in the vendor's interest to sell you more names."[86]

Other strategies have proved to be of short-term benefit but equally long-term folly. Luring students with generous financial aid, only to reduce the offers the next year—a practice called *front-loading*—contributes to high dropout rates; 26 percent of students, on average, don't come back for their sophomore year, a figure that has remained fairly unmoving for decades.[87]

That means that colleges are constantly trying to improve retention rates, another service that the consulting firms stand ready to sell them.

There is little oversight or regulation of enrollment management practices like all of these, and little indication that it's high on the priorities of regulators and politicians more focused on issues such as student loan debt. As enrollment continues to plunge, colleges and universities appear more, not less, dependent on these strategies to stay in business. They foresee only more bad news on the enrollment front, including another long-anticipated downturn thanks to a decline in the number of births during the Great Recession of 2008 that will further reduce the number of eighteen-year-old prospective college students in the mid-2020s by 11 to 20 percent.[88] Any hope of a rebound after that was dashed by birth-rate data showing an even sharper drop in the number of children born during the pandemic.[89] So while there remain voices of alarm about the way that enrollment management drives decision-making, colleges and universities are becoming only more dependent on it.

"Arguably the best solution would be to not spend any of these dollars externally on vendor services but funnel all of that money directly to students," says Kristin Tichenor, a senior advisor to the president and the former senior vice president for enrollment and institutional strategy at Worcester Polytechnic Institute, who moonlights as a consultant. "The challenge is if you do that, student financial need is infinite, so you would spend the money very quickly on deserving students but not provide the institution with the broad range of students that it needs."[90]

CHAPTER 3

A View from the Inside

Reflections of a Former Enrollment Manager

Don Hossler

In evaluating enrollment management, it is important to make a distinction between the concept and how it is too often practiced. There is nothing inherently wrong with enrollment management, which enables institutions to pursue their strategic goals in informed, intentional, and integrated ways. College leaders who desire to make their campuses more socioeconomically and racially diverse can and do use the tools and strategies that enrollment management offers to achieve these goals.

At the same time, the critiques that many thoughtful higher-education observers have made about how enrollment management is too often being practiced—with colleges using enrollment management strategies that focus too much on increasing selectivity, optimizing net revenue, and pursuing prestige above all else—are fair criticisms.[1] Too often, enrollment management tools, techniques, and tactics have been used in ways that constrain equity outcomes for students from low-income and first-generation backgrounds.

In making this critique, we must not view the past with rose-colored glasses. Throughout the history of higher education in this country, private and public colleges and universities have used the strategies and tools *of their day* for both admissions and financial aid strategies as they competed for students. Indeed, one only need read John Thelin's book *Higher Education and Its Useful Past* (1982) and Frederick Rudolph's *The American College and University: A History* (1980), with their historical analyses of the admissions activities undertaken in the past, to know that we would be naive to think that questionable activities have not occurred before. Rupert Wilkinson's *Aiding Students, Buying Students: Financial Aid in America* (2005), a comprehensive history of the goals and purposes of campus-based financial aid, shows that colleges have long used their own financial aid dollars in ways that were beneficial to the institutions, including by awarding merit aid to get the students that they wanted. In other words, there never was a golden age when colleges existed solely to serve society's needs and didn't care about their bottom line.

The economist and longtime college president Howard Bowen made this clear in his 1980 book *Revenue Theory of Higher Education*, in which he laid out the following four principles explaining colleges' behavior:

- The dominant goals of institutions are educational excellence, prestige, and influence.
- In their quest for greater excellence, prestige, and influence, there is virtually no limit to the amount of money that an institution will spend.
- Each institution will raise all the money it can.
- Each institution will spend all it raises.

What has changed since Bowen wrote his book is the scale at which colleges and universities are pursuing these goals, aided by an industry that has provided them with increasingly sophisticated tools and strategies to help them manage the enormous challenges that they face in trying to gain competitive advantage over their peer institutions. Over the last four decades, offices of enrollment management have gone from a new management idea found at a handful of private colleges to a major organizational structure found at most nonprofit postsecondary education institutions, including public universities. As a result of the rapid expansion of campus enrollment management organizations, an array of corporate consulting firms have emerged to create an industry that supports this important organizational function. Some of these companies provide distinct services, such as social media specialists, graphic design staff, and research analysts to help sophisticated campus enrollment management organizations carry out their efforts more effectively. But many small and some midsize colleges rely on these corporate consultants even more heavily because they lack sufficient resources to have full-time professionals in all areas of enrollment management. They depend on consulting firms to develop and help carry out the strategies needed to fulfill the expectations of boards of trustees, presidents, and other senior campus administrators.

At this juncture, a logical question to ask is: Why do institutions need all these specialized services and professional expertise? As enrollment management organizations have evolved, the competitive forces among four-year public and private institutions have only increased. Demographic patterns always influence the intensity of the competition among colleges. Even when there are fewer students graduating from high school, college presidents still expect enrollment management organizations to maintain or increase enrollment. Meanwhile, many financially strapped private colleges need help coming up with strategies to fill their slots and raise revenue. At the same time, state disinvestment from their higher-education systems has pushed public universities to pursue full-pay students from other states more aggressively, ratcheting up a financial aid arms race. And many states have put in place performance-based budgeting plans that reward colleges for graduating students in a timely manner.

And then there are the college rankings. *U.S. News & World Report's Best Colleges* was the first comprehensive college ranking scheme that focused upon undergraduate education that gained wide attention. Rankings have become big business, which is in part responsible for the rise of enrollment management. While families have always had a general level of awareness that a small group of private and public colleges and universities were the most prestigious in the country, there was no consensus as to the relative prestige, or ranking, of all four-year institutions across the country. Ranking schemes have changed this. These ranking products have created the illusion that quality is easily measured and one can quantify one college's quality compared to another's.

The pursuit of ever-higher rankings has become a pernicious fact for many colleges. Recent ranking scandals at the business schools of Temple and Rutgers universities, and a 2022 book challenging the foundations of ranking schemes written by Colin Diver, the former president of Reed College, provide ample evidence of the problems with college rankings.[2] They show how easily colleges can manipulate the metrics to move up in the rankings.

There are many thoughtful approaches to building a college's prestige—such as increasing the quality of an institution's academic programs—but it can take more than a decade for these strategies to pay off. The average tenure of a college president is just five to seven years. This short time frame inevitably leads presidents to pursue short-term, expensive strategies that promise an immediate rankings boost. This desire for a quick payoff often leads to one of the most troubling practices: *the use of financial aid to acquire students who have higher admissions test scores, who are more likely to graduate, and who are likely to bring more tuition revenue to their institutions.* In an era when the majority of colleges cannot come close to meeting student demand for need-based financial aid, every dollar used to enroll students who do not require aid can diminish access for those who have moderate and high levels of financial need.[3]

Again, there is nothing inherently wrong with efforts of enrollment management organizations to carry out their responsibilities in efficient and effective ways. At the same time, senior administrators need to hold in tension the purpose—the mission—of their institutions. It is my personal bias that when there is tension between the mission and purpose of a university and enrollment management decisions, serious consideration must be paid to the mission statement before enacting enrollment strategies that are inconsistent with it. And while it is sometimes difficult to separate the strategies that colleges implement on their own from those that they pursue as the result of their work with an external vendor or consultant, there clearly have been excesses, which I will explore later in this chapter.

Too often, critiques of enrollment management take place in a vacuum. As influential as some campus enrollment managers are, it is ultimately college presidents, provosts, deans, and even the board of trustees that set the schools' enrollment priorities. It is the enrollment manager's job to inform these discussions and to use enrollment tools and strategies to achieve the results that the institution's leadership desires. This point is not intended to be a defensive one from someone who has served as an enrollment manager. I believe that it is an important consideration to keep these complexities in mind when considering proposals to curb problematic practices.

Regardless of the criticisms leveled, enrollment management is here to stay. Colleges can't just hope that *enrollments happen*. In the rest of the chapter, I am going to reflect on my experiences in enrollment management, identify some of the most problematic practices, and offer my thoughts on the best paths forward for changing the incentive structure around enrollment management and finding ways to regulate its excesses.

NAVIGATING TENSIONS BETWEEN VALUES AND ENROLLMENT GOALS

At this point in the chapter, I think it's important to provide some background on my own experiences with enrollment management. I've spent forty years studying the factors that influence college enrollments. As Neil Swidey's chapter in this volume (chapter 1) indicates, I first became aware of the concept of enrollment management at a small conference on student retention that was held in Long Beach, California, in 1976. Eight years later, I published what I believe to have been the first academic book on the subject of enrollment management, *Enrollment Management: An Integrated Approach*. And for more than twenty years, I served as the editor of the College Board's *Enrollment Management Review*, which highlighted and discussed research in the field.

In 1997, the chancellor of Indiana University's flagship campus made me an offer that I couldn't refuse: to become an enrollment manager myself. In my new role, I was able to see firsthand how the competing institutional goals of enhancing access, enrolling a more diverse student body, increasing net tuition revenue, and enrolling more high-ability students creates inevitable tensions between the values espoused in mission statements and the enrollment goals of enrollment management organizations.

When I started as the vice chancellor for enrollment services, the primary charge that the chancellor assigned me was to boost tuition revenue by increasing the number of out-of-state students, who pay higher tuitions than in-state students. The state of Indiana funds its public universities less generously than some contiguous states. As a result, Indiana University Bloomington has historically had to enroll large numbers of higher-paying out-of-state students to make up the difference. Unfortunately bringing in a substantial number of students from other states generally means enrolling fewer in-state students. The pressure on campus enrollment managers to achieve the twin goals of raising more revenue and increasing prestige can be intense and far removed from universities' mission of teaching, research, and service.

My marching orders were to increase tuition revenue, not to increase the quality of the entering students. I quickly focused on how financial aid could influence the enrollment decisions of *pretty good* nonresident students. These students would add far more to the *margin* than in-state students. Recruiting the best out-of-state students would have been too expensive because top students attract substantial merit-aid offers from other universities. To achieve our assignment, we worked with an outside economist who helped our internal research staff learn how to best determine the effects of financial aid on nonresident students. With this assistance, we developed statistical models that helped us figure the modest amounts of merit aid that we would need to provide to increase the enrollment of these *fairly good* out-of-state students. The strategy worked. Within a year of putting these models into effect, we saw an increase of four hundred students and a substantial growth in net tuition revenue.

But I made one unfortunate miscalculation. When I began as an enrollment manager, I assumed that state and federal financial aid would be sufficient to meet the full financial needs of low- and moderate-income in-state students. But in my third year as the senior enrollment officer, I discovered that my assumptions had been wrong, and that federal and state aid was not meeting the full need of moderate-income Hoosier students—those who were eligible for some federal financial aid, but not the maximum Pell Grant. A review of our data convincingly showed that unmet need—financial aid gapping—was becoming a substantial problem for lower-middle-income, in-state students, forcing them to accrue large amounts of debt. To my dismay, I realized that my strategies had become part of the *equitable access problem*.

After some sleepless nights, I worked with my team to create a set of analytical tables for senior campus policy makers that demonstrated the case for more need-based financial aid. It took three years for us to convince the university's leadership that we needed to allocate additional institutional financial aid to close the unmet need gap. While we weren't able to award enough money to completely eliminate the gap, we were able in the fourth year to produce a large reduction in unmet need. It is worth noting that senior leaders rejected our recommendation to reallocate some merit aid to need-based aid to completely close the gap. Instead, several years later, the university made raising money for need-based aid a top priority of a major fundraising campaign that it was conducting and attributed my advocacy for it as one reason for this campaign. Can I count this as a success, or should I have resigned earlier over this important ethical issue? Like many enrollment management priorities, my response is, *I don't know.*

Similar scenes play out at colleges frequently. For example, at one large public research university, a colleague was let go when he resisted the president's suggestion to provide less information to prospective students about the requirements to be admitted at this selective public flagship. The president's intent was to get more students to apply so the institution could reject more students and thus appear more selective. Another professional friend withdrew his name from consideration for an enrollment manager position after the college's president revealed his plan to increase the number of applicants while holding the number of admitted students constant to make the institution look more selective. Similarly, I was recruited for a position at a highly selective public research university where the only goal that the president articulated was to increase the average SAT scores of the entering class so the institution would rise in the rankings. Unfortunately, none of these enrollment goals is unusual.

There's at least one other decision I made as an enrollment manager that still troubles me. At the time, I commissioned a first-rate external research firm to help us better understand why some admitted students decided to enroll and others did not. One of the firm's findings revealed that high-ability students were more likely to enroll if they knew that they were admitted to their intended major program. The Bloomington campus had a long tradition of having first-year students enroll as undecided students. Except for a very small honors program, all students were treated the same during their first academic year, and they were not allowed to select a major until they had explored a range of disciplines as part of their general education. This policy harkened back to an era when the liberal arts dominated the intellectual climate of the Bloomington campus.

As a result, most of the university's professional schools started admitting high-performing first-year students directly into the majors of their choice, and the number of direct admit students increased rapidly across most majors. Many of these students had academic credentials that made them eligible to become part of the honors program, forcing it to expand significantly. Today, the university has a large, separate honors college, with its own building and residence hall exclusively serving these students. In honors programs at most colleges and universities, students, who are more likely than not to come from affluent families, have greater access to full-time faculty members, benefit from smaller class sizes, often receive larger financial aid awards, and frequently live in their own special residence halls, separate from the rest of the student body.

At the time, I found myself in a position where I was advocating for direct admission into majors and for the expansion of honors programs, even though I had qualms about doing so. During discussions of the study, I would often say the following: "Personally, I do not believe students should be asked to declare their major until their sophomore year and I am not a fan of honors programs. Students should have time to explore, and honors programs are inconsistent with the historical mission of public institutions. But my job at the moment is not to reflect upon my own preferences but rather to offer you the best information I have on what would help you to enroll more high ability students."

In retrospect, I still ask myself whether I should have opposed these moves, arguing that moving in this direction would be harmful to the university's mission and public purpose.

ETHICAL LAND MINES IN ENROLLMENT MANAGEMENT

I recently conducted both a Google Scholar search and a general search on the terms *ethics* and *enrollment management* (there are hundreds of these reports generated by consulting groups and colleges). It is remarkable how little attention has been given to ethical considerations of undergraduate enrollment management efforts. An electronic search of these terms combined yields at best only two or three entries. Given the rapid development of institutional policies and practices, a critical look is long overdue. In this section, I am going to highlight some of the policies and practices that I find most potentially problematic.

Predictive Analytics and Demonstrated Interest

Colleges can use student background characteristics, geographical proximity, initial student contact, and application dates to establish early predictions for new student enrollment. Similar analyses can be undertaken to forecast the number of students who will return and persist each year. These predictions help institutions to be good stewards of their financial resources. The sooner that college leaders have the information needed to determine whether the enrollment of undergraduate students is likely to increase or decline, the more effectively they can spend or save dollars on the margins—which is a good thing.

Admissions offices often purchase the names and addresses of high school juniors or seniors who have taken either the ACT or SAT exam. These names can provide insights in different ways. For students who have already applied, test scores, as well as information that the students provided ACT or the College Board about their academic interests and extracurricular activities, can help admissions staff refine their recruitment efforts. Colleges can also purchase the names and information of students who have not applied and attempt to recruit these individuals as well.

However, there are also questionable uses for predictive analytics. Researchers from the University of California at Los Angeles and the University of Arizona have documented public universities' use of geodemographic analyses to identify high schools to visit, particularly those out of state, where they are likely to find large numbers of wealthy students.[4] The researchers found, for example, that the University of Alabama visited only 33 percent of high schools in Alabama in 2017, while concentrating its recruiting efforts at more-affluent high schools in other states. At the same time, the University of Alabama has invested heavily in scholarships to attract National Merit Scholars from around the country.

In their quest for nonresident students and/or institutional prestige, recruiters at some public institutions, including the University of Alabama, spend less time traveling to parts of their home states where there are large numbers of low-income Black and Latino students, as well as low-income rural white students. Recruiting practices like these raise questions about the mission of public universities, which were founded to serve students from their home states. (To be fair, not all public universities in the study fit this pattern. For example, the University of Nebraska concentrated on in-state recruiting, visiting 88 percent of the state's high schools.)

In addition, enrollment management offices increasingly use econometric techniques in ways that enable colleges to treat similar students differently.

The goal is to determine which students are most likely to enroll if admitted. Generally, colleges consider students who contact the admissions office multiple times and visit the campus to have demonstrated interest in the institution. Universities can use these behavioral indicators in their admissions and financial aid decisions in ways that are both beneficial and harmful to these students.

These efforts have become very sophisticated. Customer relations management (CRM) tools enable enrollment organizations to use Internet Protocol (IP) address–matching technology to track web browsing at individual households. These tools give schools the ability to see how long an IP address remains on a college website. This software also makes it possible for admissions officers to track the pages that a prospective student views on the college's website and see how long that student spends on them. If the student fills out a request for information or event registration form on the website, this tool provides data to help shape *customer journeys* tailored to each individual student's interests. The combination of the browsing history of individual prospective students and information collected from registering for a campus visit can be used to develop *prospect personas*, which inform future communications and campus visits for prospective students. And they give the colleges the ability to gauge a student's demonstrated interest in their institutions.

For example, the University of Wisconsin at Stout uses software provided by Capture Higher Ed to place cookies on the computers of prospective students who visit campus admissions websites, according to the *Washington Post*. Subsequently, the campus receives a report with a link to a student's private profile, which includes twenty-seven pages that the student viewed on the school's website and the length of time spent on each page. The report also includes an algorithm that predicts the probability of whether that student would enroll if admitted.[5] The *Post* identified colleges and two vendors of these tracking services, Capture and Ruffalo Noel Levitz (RNL). The newspaper interviewed admissions staffers at twenty-three colleges, examined contracts and emails obtained from twenty-six public universities through open-records laws, and used a web privacy tool to confirm the presence of Capture's tracking software on thirty-three universities' websites.[6]

Many prospective students and parents believe that showing more interest in a college will benefit them in admissions. This is true, but there can also be a cost to demonstrating interest, of which they are generally unaware. Some colleges provide less generous institutional aid awards to students with higher scores of demonstrated interest because enrollment managers presume that it will take less aid to induce these applicants to matriculate. The money saved can go to desirable applicants, who may need more convincing to enroll, or for other institutional priorities—and this will leave more dollars to fund *the institutional margins.*

Cost of Attendance and Financial Aid Award Letters

How financial aid is marketed and awarded is another enrollment management function that is especially ripe for a critical review. In 2019, University of Pennsylvania researchers examined the websites of colleges and universities to determine how the institutions described how much they cost and how students and their families pay for college. The authors found that many institutions fail to provide easily accessible, complete, and factual information about their costs. Unfortunately, this strategy of obfuscation is all too common, as colleges attempt to make the total cost of attendance appear lower than it actually is. As a result, prospective students and their families are often left in the dark about the true cost of attendance and the likely financial aid packages that students might anticipate, so they are unable to make informed decisions about which college to attend.[7] Colleges not only need to provide this information but must do so no later than early in the second semester of prospective students' senior year.

In addition, students and their parents often find financial aid award letters to be confusing. This is especially true for students from low-income families or who are the first in their families to go to college. In 2018, the progressive think tank New America and the Boston-based nonprofit group uAspire documented an array of problems with award letters, including the use of confusing jargon, the failure of colleges to identify the full cost of attendance, and the inclusion of Parent PLUS Loans, which allow families to borrow up to the college's full cost regardless of their income or whether or not they will be able to repay the debt, in the financial aid award.[8] Financial aid is a complicated subject. It is easy for campus enrollment managers or vendors to create award letters that make it sound as though student loans and PLUS Loans are another form of scholarship.[9] Colleges appear to engage in these deceptive practices so that students who have been accepted won't be scared off by the college's price tag. The practices have garnered a great deal of attention in recent years. As a result, both the US Education Department and the National Association of Student Financial Aid Administrators have released guidelines for aid award letters that aim to discourage or prevent colleges from engaging in such chicanery.[10]

Merit Aid, Tuition Discounting, and Financial Aid Gapping

The use of financial aid to acquire students has become commonplace among both public and private four-year colleges and universities. Using sophisticated analytical techniques, colleges can target financial aid dollars to induce prospective students to apply and subsequently enroll. Because the practice has become so widespread, it's extremely difficult for any institution to resist for fear of being put at a competitive disadvantage. However, participating in this arms race has become a major problem for many colleges, as these scholarships are generally not funded by endowment funds but rather are awarded as discounts off of tuition. Providing tuition discounts leaves colleges with less money to fund the renovation of buildings, hire more faculty, and provide more student support services.

The widespread use of tuition discounting also harms financially needy students who don't receive sufficient aid. These students are left with large funding gaps, meaning that their colleges are not giving them as much financial aid as the government estimates they need to afford to attend the institutions based on their family's income. The troubling practice of *financial aid gapping* has become common at both public and private institutions, with the average gap being $16,000 at private colleges and $11,000 at public universities. The reasons for these gaps vary. Regional public institutions often have relatively little in the way of aid to offer financially needy students. Public flagship universities typically have large institutional aid budgets, but they often use a substantial amount of these dollars for non-need-based aid to attract out-of-state students. Some private colleges are relatively wealthy but may still elect to spend more of their financial aid dollars on merit. Far too often, private colleges don't have a lot of resources and leave large unmet need gaps in their aid offers.

The effects of gapping are harmful in many ways.[11] Students and their parents accrue large loan debts through the federal student loan program;

Parent PLUS Loans, which can cover up to the full cost of attendance; and even private loans, which are often more expensive than federal student loans and have fewer consumer protections. Unmet financial need can also directly affect the probability of a student persisting and graduating from college. Little is known about the extent to which college administrators take the responsible step of discouraging students from matriculating if the students and their families must take on excessive debt to attend.

In the 2018–2019 academic year, the average discount rate at private colleges was 52 percent. Many public universities are reluctant to disclose their discount rates to avoid media headlines reporting on the large amount of financial aid they are awarding to out-of-state students, which wouldn't play well with state legislators or the public. Even after subtracting the costs of financial aid, nonresident students enrolled at public universities typically still pay substantially higher tuition rates than in-state students.

While most public and private four-year colleges are heavily involved in tuition discounting and gapping, it is also true that some of the wealthiest and most prestigious colleges are still committed to meeting students' full financial need. However, these institutions can achieve this only by limiting the number of low-income students they enroll. In other words, it is not uncommon for elite private institutions to determine in advance how many low-income students they want to fund. They will then control the number of low-income students they admit, even if more low-income applicants are eligible for admission. They employ this strategy to control how much institutional aid is allocated to these students. In essence, very few schools are need-blind throughout the entire process.

In these ways, enrollment management policies and tuition discounting all too often accentuate problems in college access and success for low-income students and others who have significant amounts of financial need.[12]

WHERE THE BUCK STOPS

In looking for solutions to the troubling practices that I have outlined, it's important to recognize a significant factor that has resulted in the outsized role of enrollment management organizations: the career mobility of presidents, provosts, and other ambitious senior campus administrators.

Historically, colleges named presidents and provosts from their own faculty, and it was not uncommon for these individuals to remain at one institution for their entire careers. In 1986, only 17 percent of college presidents had previously served in that position elsewhere. In comparison, well over half of all sitting presidents in 2017 had either been a president, interim president, or provost at another campus prior to their current presidency. If former academic deans are included, almost 75 percent of all presidents came from one of these senior administrative positions.

As I wrote earlier, the tenure of most college presidents is now just five to seven years. Provosts and presidents who want to move on to their next job have a relatively short time to prove that they are effective college leaders. It is hard for them to improve the faculty or to raise sufficient dollars to build several new buildings when their tenure is so limited. However, with a clear set of goals and sufficient amounts of financial aid, it is possible in a short amount of time to enroll a more diverse student body, increase net-tuition revenue to enhance the margin, move up in college rankings, improve persistence and graduation rates, and/or improve other enrollment-related outcomes. Not surprisingly then, deans, provosts, and presidents who have career aspirations to move to more prestigious administrative roles look to both internal and external enrollment management organizations for quick ways to make an impact.

To amplify this point, I worked for several years with two professional organizations to develop a data tool that would provide senior college leaders, including board members, with a better understanding of how their peer institutions were spending their financial aid. It was my hope that in the light of day, these officials might be concerned about how much money they were spending on non-need-based aid, potentially disadvantaging low-income students and students of color. Unfortunately, I found that most college officials and board members were not interested in using these data and, at times, seemed more concerned about the public relations optics rather than the inequities reflected in the comparative data.

In addition to college presidents, faculty members and alumni have a stake in making their institutions more selective. It has been my experience that while professors will voice concerns about equity enrollment outcomes, such as lack of diversity on campus, many have an underlying desire for their colleges to move up in ranking schemes. It is hard to find a faculty member who would not be happy to have more academically talented students in the classroom. The problem is that many faculty members are unaware of the costs of attracting those students. They are unaware that providing more generous merit scholarships or tuition discounts may mean that there are fewer dollars available for the institution to become more diverse or for other purposes, such as renovating laboratories, hiring more faculty, or increasing the amount of information technology (IT) support staff.

For their part, many alumni pay attention to college rankings and express concern if a college's ranking drops. I once had a meeting with the Indiana University alumni board at which questions were raised about why Indiana was not higher-ranked and why we were not making a greater effort to enroll more high-ability students. I responded in a scholarly way about all the factors related to rankings, and then, in a tongue-in-cheek manner, I pointed out that many of *them* might not have been admitted if Indiana University had been more selective at the time they attended.

CHANGING THE INCENTIVES

Market pressures will only continue to intensify at public and private four-year colleges unless federal, state, and institutional policy makers find ways to change the incentive structures in higher education and regulate the excesses of enrollment management. To be clear, enrollment management isn't going away. Colleges have far too many reasons not to let enrollments just happen. Nevertheless, the federal government and states can take significant steps to reduce market pressures and produce more equitable outcomes.

Colleges cannot solve these problems on their own. But even if they wanted to, the US Justice Department has forbidden them from collaborating on financial aid and tuition-discounting policies by threatening lawsuits under the Sherman Antitrust Act, as will be discussed in chapter 5. The inability of colleges and universities to meet and discuss the problems associated with high tuition and high financial aid pricing models has only accentuated the competition, which has led to ever-increasing expenditures to attract the most sought-after students. As my colleague Jerry Lucido has provocatively observed, the government has regulated the markets for professional sports in a manner that allows teams to communicate and set boundaries around the competition for professional athletes. Shouldn't higher education be allowed to do the same?

Joseph Stiglitz, a Nobel laureate economist, has argued that it is the role of the federal government to regulate markets to ensure equality. The government made a huge investment in this effort in higher education when it created federal financial aid programs in the late 1960s and early 1970s. The Pell Grant and Stafford Loan programs were designed to provide all students access to public and private colleges regardless of tuition costs. Colleges have greatly benefited from these programs, which have enabled them to enroll more students and maintain or increase the academic programs that they could offer. But policy makers made a big mistake when they designed these programs: they didn't require colleges to meet any accountability metrics to continue participating in them. Congress could have required colleges, for instance, to guarantee that they would meet the full financial need of Pell Grant recipients and provide them with the academic support that they would need to persist and graduate.

Federal policy levers are needed to create incentives for colleges to admit and graduate more low-income students and better support them. Because states exert more influence over colleges within their geographical boundaries, there's a role for states to play as well, working with the federal government to coordinate efforts to regulate higher-education markets and reduce the level of inequality. Using state performance funding models, many states have attempted to create incentives for public institutions to enroll and graduate more low- and moderate-income students. These efforts have not produced the hoped-for results. Research suggests that the funding goals that states establish change too often, and the dollars that they provide are insufficient to bring about enrollment changes. To achieve their goals, states need to provide sufficient funding and stability so the goalposts that colleges are trying to meet don't keep shifting.

In addition to performance-based funding, states should expand high school dual-credit programs, which enable students to earn both high school and college credits. These programs increase the odds that students will make the transition from high school to postsecondary education successfully.

Colleges also have an important role to play. Senior campus policy makers, including enrollment officers, provosts, presidents, faculty leaders, and board members, need to review their enrollment management strategies periodically to ensure that they are promoting equitable access and success to all potential students. Among other things, these college officials should carefully examine whether their policies build upon federal and state financial aid programs for low- and moderate-income students to increase access and success, or else undermine those efforts by redirecting their aid to wealthier students.

Overall, there needs to be greater collaboration between institutional, state, and federal policy makers. Among other things, the federal and state governments should support the creation and existence of ethical codes for admissions, financial aid professionals, and senior enrollment officers. These codes can serve as guidelines for enrollment management organizations, as well as other senior campus policy makers. The Department of Justice made a grave error in 2019 when it threatened a lawsuit against the National Association for College Admission Counseling (NACAC) accusing the organization of placing illegal restraints on the ways that colleges compete in the recruiting of students. This misguided action spurred only greater destructive competition among less-selective schools.[13]

Organizations like NACAC need the ability to establish professional ethics that can result in the right valuing of enrollment management organizations. By *right valuing*, I am suggesting that the enrollment management efforts of colleges and universities should be more consistent with their mission statements and senior campus leaders and trustees should reduce the use of enrollment management techniques to acquire more prestige based on the academic ability of the students whom they seek to enroll. I am also suggesting that enrollment management organizations spend less on their marketing efforts so colleges can provide more need-based financial aid and academic support for low- and moderate-income students, as well as a first-rate education for the student body overall. If colleges spend less money competing for students, the size and scope of the enrollment management industry will shrink and be put to better use.

Part 2. How the Federal Government Helped Fuel the Growth of Enrollment Management

CHAPTER 4

The Design of Federal Student Aid Made Enrollment Management's Worst Practices Possible

Jon H. Oberg

The term *enrollment management* alludes to the systematic use of research data from many sources to shape the composition of a student body in order to achieve a college's strategic goals. Enrollment management can be used for good ends, compatible with federal grant programs to assist low-income students, such as increasing student access, retention, and achievement. It started that way. But for the past several decades, colleges have predominantly used enrollment management to achieve other institutional goals, such as raising prestige rankings at the expense of financially needy students or to displace federal student grants for the benefit of unrelated campus projects. The unprecedented reliance of low-income students and their families on unwanted loans that they often cannot repay is in no small part attributable to deliberate enrollment management strategies that have exploited vulnerable students and families.

This chapter traces the development of enrollment management in the context of the Higher Education Act of 1965 (HEA). While the 1965 Act itself envisioned the coordination of federal, state, and institutional efforts to increase low-income access to college, changes that Congress made to the law in 1972, at the urging of the Nixon administration, created student aid programs without effective coordinating mechanisms to ensure that colleges and states retained sufficient "skin in the game" to keep the parties from working at cross-purposes. Funding choices made by the Reagan administration a decade later set the stage for the preeminence of loans rather than grants for the next four decades, with even less coordination of effort among the levels of government.

The viewpoint of this narrative, in which I express increasing alarm as the nation drifts away from the original purposes of the HEA, comes from my personal experience as a state official, a staff member of the US Senate, the chief executive of the Association of Independent Colleges and Universities of Nebraska, US Department of Education congressional liaison for higher education, and researcher at the Education Department. I also propose a set of remedies to problems created by the widespread misuse of enrollment management.

THE EDUCATION OF A BUDGET ANALYST

My introduction to a concept that would be fundamental to enrollment management, in the broadest sense of the term, began in the early 1970s, when I was a budget analyst for the state of Nebraska. Among my duties was to review the annual budget of the University of Nebraska, a public flagship institution: all funds, all revenues, and all expenditures.

Congress had just reauthorized the HEA, with much input from the Nixon administration. The Education Amendments of 1972 established several new student aid programs, including the Basic Education Opportunity Grant (BEOG) program. The 100 percent federally funded grants—which later would be renamed Pell Grants after Claiborne Pell, the senator who originally sponsored the BEOG legislation—were to be phased in over four years, with a new class added each year. (For simplicity's sake, I will refer to BEOGs from here on as Pell Grants, even though the name change wasn't made until 1980.)

When the Pell Grant program started, I asked University of Nebraska budget officials how the grants would be handled, especially for eligible students who were already receiving state grants or tuition remissions. The answer: Pell Grants would replace state grants. And what would happen to the newly freed up state funds? University officials declined to say, other than that they were not returning the money to the state treasury. We struck a compromise: the institution could use the funds to build a new pharmacy college building.

This was a lesson in understanding the fungible nature of money and the principle of displacement, or substitution. Congress was spending money for one thing but, in effect, some of the money would actually be going for something else. There has never been any visible federal effort to evaluate how Pell Grants work; that is, how much grant aid financially needy students receive overall, and whether this support makes college more affordable for these students.

In the original HEA, Congress had established the Campus-Based federal grant, loan, and work-study programs, each of which required matching funds and maintenance of effort on the part of institutions.[1] Without those safeguards, Pell Grants ushered in greater fungibility in student financial aid packaging, making it more difficult to know to what ends the congressional appropriations were being put. Pell Grant displacement, in time, would become one of the dubious practices of enrollment management.

As part of the same HEA reauthorization in 1972 that created Pell Grants, Congress also established the State Student Incentive Grant (SSIG) program, which offered a 50-50 match with states to encourage them to provide more grants to financially needy students. Like the Campus-Based Aid programs of 1965, SSIG was a cooperative federalism effort. But SSIG never caught on. Colleges lobbied hard for the more fungible Pell Grants rather than increasing the SSIG budget.

Another creation of 1972 was Sallie Mae, a government-sponsored enterprise established to handle the growing need for a national secondary market for the bank-based Guaranteed Student Loan program, which had its genesis in the HEA. Guaranteed federal student loans also required no institutional match or maintenance of effort and, like Pell Grants, were fungible with state and institutional student aid efforts. Student loans could be offered to students as financial aid, displacing many types of grants.

The Pell Grant and Guaranteed Student Loan programs soon grew, leaving the Campus-Based Aid programs and SSIG in the dust. The predominance of these voucher-type programs set the table for the development of an enrollment management approach to student financial aid. Rather than ensuring that federal grants and loans were used in a cooperative federalism tradition, colleges could move resources around to target or untarget individual students or groups of students based on data gathered about them, depending on institutional objectives. They could even reduce their institutional aid efforts in favor of other priorities, which might have nothing to do with student aid of any kind.

None of these practices were apparent during my first encounter with enrollment management, which was positive. I attended a conference at which an admissions officer at a small private college in Illinois described how his institution was focusing on retention. The college staff was gathering as much data as they could about their students, including the dropout risks that the students faced. The college would then tailor financial aid packages, along with academic support services, to students who needed the most help to persist. This effort impressed me, as the college was using federal student-aid funds as part of an inclusive effort to target those who needed the help the most. Colleges, I thought, might actually deploy financial aid better than federal and state governments and charitable groups that raised private funds for scholarships. If this was the direction that enrollment management was taking, then more power to it.

REAGAN CUTS GRANTS—AND COLLEGES REACT

In 1979, I started work at the US Senate. Among my duties was staffing the Senate Budget Committee, where I witnessed the Reagan administration's push in 1981 to cut federal grants and force college students to rely more on loans. The administration's embrace of loans over grants sparked two reactions from colleges: increased adoption of the "higher-tuition, higher-grant-aid" model of institutional budgeting; and, to complement it, more reliance on an "equity packaging" rationale for developing students' financial aid packages. Tuition went up, but many colleges promised to return the extra revenue to needier students in the form of grants to achieve so-called vertical equity based on students' ability to pay. With more institutional grant aid at their disposal from higher tuition, some institutions also adopted policies of looking across sources of aid to achieve horizontal equity among individuals with the same level of financial need, as determined by federal need-analysis standards.[2]

Under equity packaging, institutional aid could be adjusted up or down in individuals' student aid packages, solely at the discretion of the college. If, for example, a private scholarship organization sent a check to a college to help a needy student, the college would make sure that the student got that particular award, but then it would reduce the amount of institutional aid that it provided that student accordingly, so that student wouldn't be better off than other financially needy students. In effect, the college shared the private scholarship award equitably with students demonstrating the same level of financial need. This type of financial aid displacement, however, left the student who received the scholarship no better off than before receiving it.

Colleges could engage in this type of aid packaging only with the cooperation of the US Department of Education. Colleges lobbied hard to require students to identify in their applications for federal student aid all forms of financial support they were receiving, using the argument that this was for equity purposes and in the best interest of financially needy students overall. The federal student-aid application also asked students to indicate if they were agreeable to taking out loans. In these ways, the Education Department complied with the wishes of colleges that were relying increasingly on revenues from student debt.

In the mid-1980s, I served as the executive director of a state-level association of thirteen private nonprofit colleges and universities in Nebraska. As part of my duties, I often traveled to Washington to work on federal legislation and appropriations, trying to obtain more funding for Pell Grants. Based on my experience with the University of Nebraska a decade earlier, I was concerned that when Congress increased Pell Grant funding, institutions could displace their own institutional aid to spend on their own priorities instead of on financially needy students. I was therefore prepared, as a representative of colleges, to accept more congressional guardrails crafted to prevent displacement, for the purpose of getting more Pell funding for these students.

But most college lobbyists were not. Midway through the Reagan presidency, under the aegis of the American Council on Education (ACE), college leaders and lobbyists gathered to visit our respective congressional delegations to make the case for more federal student aid. We met first in the Rayburn

House of Representatives office building to receive our charge from the ACE president, Robert Atwood. A college president in the audience spoke up to emphasize how important it was to impress on Congress that colleges like his were in financial trouble because they had to increase spending for institutional aid, and Congress needed to increase Pell funding so he could direct his own college's resources elsewhere. Atwood reacted viscerally. "No! Don't say that!" he exclaimed. The message, he said, must be "Pell is for students," regardless of the reality of internal college budgeting. "Don't get into your institution's own budgeting procedures," he admonished.

As illustrated by this exchange, many institutions were using enrollment management not to achieve higher retention or greater equity but rather to prop up institutional finances. Student loans were put into financial aid packages as never before, sometimes not distinguished from grants but lumped together simply as "federal student aid" in financial-aid award letters. No federal standards existed to ensure that colleges used these letters to help students make enrollment decisions and make sure that they understood the various types of aid being offered. Colleges were increasingly using institutional grants as so-called merit aid to pursue financially desirable students—those who had no financial need but could be persuaded to enroll when offered scholarships that appealed to student or parental vanity. Low-income students often became a low priority, a population to exploit for other institutional purposes.

Colleges sought to employ admissions officials with the kinds of data collection and student financial aid skills to make enrollment management an integral part of overall strategic planning. Some colleges created "dean of enrollment management" positions. Colleges without their own internal capabilities turned to outside consultants, who offered to develop custom-made enrollment management plans to fit institutional objectives, no questions asked. Some of the consulting organizations were affiliated with lenders in the student loan industry, which saw profit potential in moving grants out of students' aid packages in favor of loans.

Colleges exhibited considerable secrecy about enrollment management plans, whether internally or externally prepared. They considered the plans proprietary information and kept them confidential. Colleges complained among themselves as to which of them might be gaining advantage by using questionable practices. The National Association of Student Financial Aid

Administrators had no code of ethics worthy of the name. One aid officer complained to me that a competing institution was putting the maximum amount of federal student loans into packages as a starting-point assumption, around which student need and federal regulations were tailored creatively to fit. Many aid officials were becoming alarmed at the "merit-aid arms race" for affluent students that was developing. Some aid administrators were disgusted that the very survival of their colleges increasingly depended on how they played the merit aid game. But the enrollment management industry was telling institutions that it had the answers, and they would be taking undue risks not to go along.

The US Department of Education raised no concerns about any of this. These were the Reagan years, in which oversight and evaluation were considered overregulation. And there was a loud contingent within the higher-education community who liked the status quo.

LESSONS ABROAD

During much of the George H.W. Bush administration, I was in Berlin studying, writing, and teaching. Among the subjects that caught my interest was the German student-aid program, known by its abbreviation *Bafög* rather than the ponderous *Bundesausbildungsförderungsgesetz.*

Bafög was a cooperative federalism effort with a fixed ratio of federal-to-state funding, with no displacement between levels of government. It also was half-grant, half-loan, so there was no displacement of grants by loans. For a few years in the 1980s, grants were totally replaced by loans. The reliance on loans hurt low-income student access badly, and, as a result, the German government soon went back to including grants in the *Bafög* program. This experience made a lasting impression on me.

When I came back to the States, I started working again in Washington, this time as a civil servant for the Department of Education's Office of Legislation and Congressional Affairs under the Clinton administration. I found little interest either in the Education Department or in Congress in issues of enrollment management, cooperative federalism programs, or program evaluation efforts. The overriding grant issue at the time was how to deal with a budget shortfall in the Pell Grant program, not whether (or how) the program was making higher education more affordable for low-income students.

By President Bill Clinton's second term, the HEA was due for reauthorization and the Department of Education's leaders were more receptive to new ideas. During the government shutdown of 1996, I wrote an academic paper from my home entitled "Testing Federal Student-Aid Fungibility in Two Competing Versions of Federalism."[3] Based on its findings, I advocated within the Education Department for greater support of the Campus-Based Aid and SSIG programs, which were less susceptible to enrollment management manipulation. Education Secretary Richard Riley and Deputy Secretary Mike Smith were convinced and pushed for more funding and a higher profile for these programs. But the White House's Office of Management and Budget thought otherwise, cutting the proposed increases and, as usual, proposing to eliminate SSIG. In the end, congressional supporters of SSIG succeeded in getting its name changed to Leveraging Educational Assistance Partnerships (LEAP), although they were unable to fund the program properly. The Campus-Based Aid programs, however, got a hard-fought increase in funding, a small concession to the cooperative federalism programs established in 1965.

A dust-up with the higher-education community came about over the Clinton administration's Hope Scholarships, which were not scholarships but tuition tax credits that were meant to make higher education more affordable for middle-income students. After Congress approved the program, Bowdoin College's financial aid director said that he would take the tax credit into account when packaging student aid by reducing institutional aid for those who received the Hope Scholarships, based on the college's enrollment management approach. Bowdoin's stance prompted Secretary Riley to write a letter to the higher-education community, urging colleges not to undo a benefit that was supposed to help families pay for college. The credits had not been created for colleges to pocket the money themselves.

After the Bowdoin incident, and the realization that institutions' enrollment management plans could be undermining federal grant as well as tax credit programs, Secretary Riley wrote once again to institutions, this time to dissuade them from undermining Pell Grants. Riley was the only education secretary ever, in my experience, to show high-level interest in how financially needy students fared in the aid-packaging process.

A RESEARCH AGENDA

In 2001, to strengthen a weak postsecondary finance research effort, I moved to the Education Department's Office of Educational Research and Improvement (OERI), which was soon to be renamed the Institute of Education Sciences (IES). I worked in the little-known National Center for Education Research (NCER), a component of IES. NCER was not known for its research because it did very little. It was well matched with another component, the National Center for Education Evaluation, which did little evaluation of federal education programs, especially postsecondary ones.

In creating a research agenda at IES, I recalled that during the 1998 reauthorization of the HEA, when I was working in the Office of Legislation, I received a call from George Conant, a leading Republican staff member with the House of Representatives committee in charge of rewriting the law. He wanted to put into the legislation a requirement for a study of how institutional practices (i.e., enrollment management) might be counterproductive to the goals of the HEA. We discussed the language, and it was incorporated into the law.

So on arrival at IES, I proposed a study based on that 1998 provision to determine whether financial aid packaging was being used to enhance or thwart federal financial aid programs. The reaction at IES was lack of interest. Nevertheless, I proceeded with IES tolerance, but no support.

My study was the first research to show that many colleges were putting private student loans into packages before federal loans, with their better terms.[4] It also demonstrated racial disparities by income, in that colleges were disproportionately steering low-income minority students to loans while providing institutional grants to middle- and upper-income minority students.

There were other troubling findings. Presumably, if federal student aid were working as advertised, when Congress increased spending on Pell Grants for low-income students, financially needy students' borrowing would go down. But that was not the case. I found that loans to financially needy students went up, regardless of Pell Grant funding. The research suggested that colleges were displacing Pell Grants by redirecting their institutional aid for recruiting more-affluent students. As a result, low-income students were no better off, and in many cases they actually were worse off, having to take on substantial loan debt, with the largest debt loads going to low-income

Black students. My research foretold a student-loan repayment crisis in future years, marked by troubling racial disparity, which has now come about.[5] The current student-loan crisis is rife with racial imbalance.

While writing the paper, I asked colleagues at the National Center for Education Statistics (NCES) to disaggregate borrower race from income in their public reports so it would be easier to determine if, as I suspected, low-income minorities were being left with disproportionate student-loan burdens. NCES declined, indicating that the sample sizes might be too small to do so and that granularity at that level could inadvertently violate NCES survey confidentiality agreements. I was also told that colleges had advised NCES to keep race and income reports separate. As a quantitative analyst myself, I did not buy the first two excuses, but as a person with decades of experience in the politics of higher education, I totally understood the third.

Based on my findings, I talked to Education Department colleagues at the Office of Federal Student Aid (FSA) about how their own software was likely being misused. FSA offered colleges, at no cost, a financial aid packaging program known as EdExpress. Many of its subscribers were colleges that could not afford to hire enrollment management firms with their customized proprietary packaging software. EdExpress allowed colleges to move financial aid around to meet institutional objectives, regardless of whether that meant loading up low-income students with loans and using Pell Grant increases to displace institutional aid to increase merit scholarships, or for whatever purposes the institution wanted.

"But that's how financial aid works," my FSA colleagues replied. They told me that so long as the Pell Grant was put into the package first, colleges could package aid as they saw fit. When I expressed concern about colleges manipulating institutional aid, they replied, "It's their money," repeating the view of the higher-education associations to the detriment of the interests of the financially needy. With FSA officials parroting the arguments of college lobbyists, I concluded, the federal student-aid programs were running off the rails.

I was not the only researcher who found that enrollment management techniques were often incompatible with improving higher-education access for low-income students. A few months after I published the 1997 paper on grant fungibility, Sarah Turner, an economist at the University of Virginia, independently wrote of a process that colleges engaged in to "undo the targeting" of Pell Grants.[6] After my 2003 paper, several economists looked at the Pell displacement issue and concluded that some institutions were capturing large shares of the funds for their own uses instead of using them to reduce the amount of student debt that they were requiring low-income students and their families to borrow. The economist Leslie Turner put the annual amount of Pell Grant funding that colleges were capturing at six billion dollars.[7] But it was not just academics who were concerned. In 2005, the journalist Matthew Quirk wrote an exposé in the *Atlantic* headlined "The Best Class Money Can Buy." He displayed to readers an unflattering portrait of enrollment management and explained that some college officials were concerned that many of the practices that the institutions were engaged in were tarnished by being the tool of misplaced priorities.[8] The higher-education trade press followed with articles about the bad image that enrollment management was creating for itself.[9]

Despite these journalistic efforts, there's little evidence to suggest that policy makers pay attention to enrollment management or know much about it. Major changes are needed but will be difficult to achieve unless higher-education policy makers gain a better understanding of enrollment management and are willing to acknowledge that the federal student aid programs are not achieving the purposes that the HEA set out for them.

REMEDIES

Enrollment management can be used to enhance rather than undermine the federal student aid programs. The Education Department can ensure that colleges are doing so in a variety of ways, such as better administering existing law by adding or reconfiguring appropriations and by making legislative changes. But they must first familiarize themselves with enrollment management instead of continuing to turn a blind eye toward it.

The Secretary of Education can take actions *under current law* for the immediate benefit of students, families, and taxpayers in the context of improving enrollment management, such as the following:

- Require Department of Education offices that deal with postsecondary education finance to familiarize themselves with the theory and practice of enrollment management. The starting point should be to look at the current profound problems of inequitable postsecondary access, completion, and debt, and to examine the role that enrollment management has played in creating or exacerbating these problems. The unfortunate reality is that there is no consensus as to whether the federal student aid programs have worked effectively. Compared to a half-century ago, access gaps by socioeconomic and racial and ethnic status have worsened and student-loan debt has reached levels beyond anything previously imaginable. Perhaps all would be even worse without the federal student aid programs, but an examination of enrollment management's impact on these trends is long overdue.

- Assess current law provisions to determine their applicability to enrollment management practices. Student aid program authorizations contain language as to what uses funds may and may not be put. For example, the Pell Grant authorization statute does not suggest that it would be proper for colleges to manipulate the grants using enrollment management techniques so that they serve other ends, such as funding merit aid or constructing pharmacy buildings.
- Instruct program reviewers in the office of FSA to examine enrollment management practices at selected colleges and universities. These reviews could include institutions that volunteer to show how their practices, informed by data collection, enhance the goals of the HEA. The reviews must also include institutions that may be reluctant to disclose their procedures or their contracts with enrollment management companies. The HEA and its regulations specifically demand transparency in the awarding and packaging of financial aid, including criteria for determining the amount of student financial aid awards, whether federal, state, local, private, or institutional.
- Implement, as necessary, statutory "limitation, suspension, and termination (LS&T)" provisions in cases where program reviews show that an institution's enrollment management practices are functioning contrary to the purposes of the federal student aid programs. In reality, the education secretary would likely give warnings to allow institutions to bring themselves into compliance. However, actual use of the LS&T authority in circumstances where it is warranted would send

a strong signal to colleges not to undermine the federal student aid programs.

- Direct the Office of Postsecondary Education to explore enrollment management accreditation, to use recognition of private enrollment management consulting companies directly or through established institutional accreditors to endorse approved practices at colleges. This process would be a way to reward colleges that enhance rather than undermine HEA programs and to discourage bad practices.
- Use the College Scorecard to help students and their families better understand how student aid is awarded and packaged. Make certain that these individuals are informed that they have a right to know all sources of student financial aid and how the information that they provide on their Free Application for Federal Student Aid (FAFSA) and other financial aid applications is going to be used in the aid-packaging process. Colleges engaging in any form of aid displacement, including for students receiving private scholarships, should be required to disclose that information to students and to all outside sources of aid, as it may influence those sources' giving. The Education Department must be clear that colleges are prohibited from engaging in any aid-packaging practices that undermine the federal student aid programs.
- Involve the Department of Justice in discussions of the benefits of good enrollment management practices, and how they should be used to further the purposes of HEA programs. These positive practices would include cooperative efforts among colleges that agree to follow a code of admissions and financial aid ethics. Historically, the Justice Department has discouraged institutions from such efforts, much to the dismay of many institutions that have had the best interests of students at heart. Although Justice Department officials may believe that these codes violate antitrust laws, they should be reminded that antitrust laws are to protect consumers, and one of the best ways to protect college students as consumers is by not losing sight of the purposes of HEA and the federal student aid programs.

The proposals given here, whether carrots or sticks, may unfortunately collide with the financial realities facing certain colleges. Even in the best of times,

I have heard frank acknowledgments from college aid officials that if they are *not* able to manipulate federal aid for their institution's benefit, they will go under financially. They explain that they need to go after well-to-do students with merit aid, even if it means loading up low-income students with debt. They argue that they need to work over every federal grant and tax credit dollar to take pressure off their aid budgets, even if it means obfuscating and denying that they do it.

It's clear that many colleges are struggling and pushing low-income students and their families into taking on heavy debt loads that they may not be able to repay. A much greater federal investment is needed. Many higher-education advocates will argue that all that is needed is a substantial funding boost for Pell Grants. But that is not the answer, as there is a lack of empirical evidence across institutional sectors that increases in Pell Grant funding result in lower student debt or a lower net price paid by Pell Grant recipients. Instead, the education secretary should do the following:

- Include in any annual appropriations request a sum to assist colleges with their enrollment management programs, to aid both institutions that are already doing a good job and those that need help abandoning bad practices. Such spending could truly be described as helping both students and institutions simultaneously. This is not a small sum; it would surely be several billion dollars annually, based on enrollment management research undertaken in the academic community. The Education Department should also conduct its own research to fulfill its statutory mandates. Not to prejudge any such research, but community colleges and nonselective public universities would likely be rewarded for doing the best they can with their limited resources, while private nonprofits, public flagship and research universities, and minority-serving institutions would be the most in need for funds to turn their enrollment management efforts around in order to complement rather than diminish the purposes of federal student aid. Under this new program, funds could be distributed on a formula basis, but institutions would have to commit to before-and-after audits from the Education Department to show how the funds were used, with the possibility of repayment and penalties for misuse.

- Reprioritize student-aid appropriations requests to benefit cooperative federalism programs. The Campus-Based Aid programs—the SEOG and College Work-Study—are still on the books and could be funded at much higher levels to take advantage of their matching and maintenance-of-effort qualities, which help to limit financial aid shell games by enrollment managers. Lawmakers could either provide new funding or redistribute funds from the Pell Grant program or, even better, from higher-education tax credits and deductions, which disproportionately benefit the non-needy. SEOG is particularly well suited for a substantial funding boost, as it is popular with institutions for its flexibility and the ease of its matching requirements at schools with their own institutional aid.

In terms of rewriting the HEA, the education secretary should consider putting the following legislative options before Congress:

- Change the current Campus-Based Aid distribution formulas, which are based too much on former, badly outdated enrollment patterns. This change should be made with a hold-harmless provision so no college receives less under a new formula, but authorize a much higher level of appropriations so all institutions benefit.
- Add cooperative federalism mechanisms to the federal grant and loan programs that do not have them so that colleges have skin in the game. Adding these mechanisms would be true to the original HEA vision that was intended by Congress in 1965. These requirements need not be onerous, but they have to be sufficient to engage cooperative commitment so that all levels—federal, state, and institutional—pull together in the same direction rather than compete to exploit each other.
- Another possibility that policy makers should consider is starting over legislatively, essentially scrapping the HEA, after reviewing the experience of other countries that have successfully increased low-income access, kept tuition affordable, and operated student loan programs that do not rely on a for-profit industry that exploits students. My own experience suggests that Germany could be a model in the way that it has, as a federal republic, balanced the contributions of national and state governments and the division between grants and loans.

Adopting some of or all these recommendations would have salutary effects. Current federal student-aid efforts would go further because they would not have to sail against the countervailing winds of bad enrollment management practices. Many institutions would be relieved to be freed from an enrollment management arms race in which they are unsuited to compete. And student financial aid and admissions officers would no longer have to worry so much about how, legally and ethically, to juggle their often-competing obligations to students, families, institutions, and oversight agencies.

Five decades of federal student-aid programs working at cross-purposes with enrollment management is too long.

CHAPTER 5

The Justice Department's Views on Antitrust in Higher Ed Have Bolstered the Enrollment Management Industry

Catharine Bond Hill

For more than thirty years, the US government has been working at cross-purposes with itself when it comes to promoting college access and affordability for low-income and working-class students. The US Department of Education annually spends tens of billions of dollars, through both federal grant and loan programs, to make it easier for lower-income students to obtain a postsecondary education. But the Education Department can't do the job alone; it needs colleges to supplement its efforts by devoting their institutional financial aid dollars to the same students. However, since the early 1990s, the Justice Department has been aggressively enforcing federal antitrust laws that have prevented colleges from collaborating to ensure that they spend institutional aid on financially needy students.

The Justice Department's actions have helped fuel the growth of an enrollment management industry that has encouraged colleges to use their own financial aid dollars to compete for students from upper-middle-income and wealthy families, in search of net revenue and prestige. As a result, many low- and lower-middle-income students are not admitted to selective colleges, even though they are just as qualified as their more-privileged peers, and sometimes even more so. Others who are admitted simply can't afford to attend. And those who do matriculate are being left with larger and larger funding gaps, forcing them and their families to take on a substantial amount of debt to afford to pay the tuition. The lack of institutional support has also made it much more difficult for low-income students at these colleges to succeed, as many feel that they have no choice but to work long hours at jobs off campus, attend part time, or even "stop out," leaving school with the hope that they will return at some future point.

It doesn't have to be this way. The federal government should have a coherent set of policies in place that encourage colleges to complement federal student aid programs by working together to design admissions and financial aid policies that help, instead of hinder, the educational progress of students who are most in need of financial aid.

This chapter will provide a brief history of how we got here, analyze the question of whether federal antitrust laws should apply to nonprofit colleges, and offer a proposal that would provide selective colleges with a limited exemption from these laws in exchange for a commitment to better serve the public good. Under this proposal, these schools would be required to agree to educate a more socioeconomically diverse student body and provide adequate need-based financial support to ensure low-income students' success. Any failure to live up to this commitment would put the exemption's future at risk.

At a time of growing inequality in this country, it is not unreasonable to expect selective colleges, which receive substantial public subsidies, to open their doors as wide as they can to students who can't afford to attend school without help.

AVOIDING BIDDING WARS

To understand how we got to the point where the government is working at cross-purposes, it's important to review the history. Since 1965, when Congress first approved the Higher Education Act (HEA), federal student aid programs have enjoyed strong bipartisan support, in recognition of the public benefits of increasing educational attainment for those who could not afford it otherwise. Today, the federal government annually provides nearly thirty billion dollars of federal grants to more than seven million students, many of whom come from families with yearly incomes of less than thirty thousand dollars.[1] The original legislative champions of the HEA believed that low-income students would primarily pay for college with the help of grant aid rather than federal loans, which were created primarily to help middle-income students pay for college.

In embracing need-based aid, the federal government was actually following the lead of selective private colleges. More than a decade before the HEA, private college leaders recognized that they needed to become more systematic in their use of student aid rather than continuing to take a scattershot approach. To try to prevent schools from getting into bidding wars for the students whom they most desired, selective private college leaders embraced the notion of providing need-based financial assistance to students whose families could not afford to send them to college without that help.

As part of that effort, about 150 private colleges and universities formed Overlap Groups around the country in the 1950s, made up of institutions that tended to receive applications from the same students. The groups generally developed common standards to use in assessing students' financial need, and many of them banned the use of non-need-based aid at participating institutions.[2] The most prominent group, known as the Ivy Overlap Group, consisted of the eight Ivy League colleges and the Massachusetts Institute of Technology (MIT). The Ivy Overlap Group coordinated the financial aid offers that the member-schools would make to individual promising prospective students who had been admitted to more than one of the institutions to ensure that they would not use their financial aid dollars to compete for those students.

The universities wanted to avoid an arms race that would force them to waste precious funds on high-achieving, higher-income students whose families could afford to pay full freight. The Ivy League institutions' leaders believed that by preventing costly bidding wars, they were standing up for the principle that financial aid should be used exclusively to meet financial needs and, therefore, they were bolstering the government's mission of ensuring college access for all students regardless of their financial circumstances.

The Ivy Overlap Group's meetings were held in secret. Little was known about them until 1989, when the *Washington Post* ran an exposé of the Ivy

Overlap Group that accused it of carrying on "a price-fixing system that OPEC [the Organization of Petroleum-Exporting Countries] might envy." That article caught the attention of the Justice Department, which began its own inquiry into these practices.[3]

After investigating the schools for more than two years, the Department of Justice in May 1991 charged the Ivy League universities and MIT with violating the Sherman Antitrust Law. The Justice Department argued that the Ivy Overlap Group's activities were a clear case of price-fixing that was forcing some students and their families (including wealthier ones with high-achieving students) to pay more than they would have if the schools were not colluding.

The Ivies quickly reached a settlement with the Department of Justice through a consent decree barring such cooperation for ten years absent changes in legislation, while admitting no culpability.[4] Many of the institutions that signed the consent decree believed that their behavior had been legal, but they wanted to avoid an expensive legal fight with the government.

MIT, however, refused to settle, and the case went to trial in the US District Court in Philadelphia. The lead attorney for MIT accused the Justice Department of mistakenly assuming that higher-education institutions were "indistinguishable from a manufacturer of toaster ovens or porcelain fixtures."[5] He argued that the court should take into consideration "the legitimate non-economic values" that nonprofit educational institutions promote, suggesting that any efficiency losses could be traded off against other charitable objectives that benefit the public.[6] MIT also argued that forbidding collaboration among colleges over how they spend financial aid would lead to an arms race for the best students that "would undermine efforts to maintain educational access and opportunity and impede socioeconomic diversity, which would lessen the overall quality of education."[7]

The federal district court sided with the Justice Department. MIT appealed, and the Third Circuit Court of Appeals in Philadelphia ruled in 1993 that the district court had not taken MIT's position that the Ivy Overlap's activities bolstered the government's mission of promoting college access for low-income students adequately into account. The appellate court remanded the case to the district court for further deliberation on a "rule of reason" basis, rather than the "quick look" basis of the earlier decision. "Overlap may in fact merely regulate competition in order to enhance it, while also deriving certain social benefits," the Appeals Court stated, adding that if that was the case, the Overlap Group's actions would not violate the Sherman Act.[8]

A new trial would have given MIT the possibility of prevailing over the Justice Department and showing that the department's views on antitrust in higher education were misguided. However, MIT negotiated a settlement with the department instead, which allowed colleges to come together and discuss financial aid policies broadly, if they agreed to admit students regardless of financial need (except for foreign students and students off the wait list) and to meet students' full financial need with federal, state, and institutional grants and loans. The agreement also prohibited colleges from discussing individual students' aid offers or future tuition or faculty salary levels.[9] Both MIT and the Justice Department claimed victory.[10]

Following up on the consent decree and settlement, Congress in 1994 enacted Section 568 of the Improving America's Schools Act (IASA), which allowed some of the conditions of the MIT settlement to apply to a broader group of colleges and universities under a limited antitrust exemption. Section 568 applies to institutions that admit all students on a need-blind basis and allows them to establish common approaches to awarding institutional financial aid. It does not allow any discussion of aid awards for individual students, as took place during meetings of the Ivy Overlap Group.

In 1998, a group of presidents from eligible institutions formed the 568 Presidents Group to work on common principles for awarding need-based aid. Establishing this group has not proved an effective means of controlling the competition for students through the use of financial aid. Importantly, membership in the group is limited to the relatively small number of institutions that remain need-blind in the admissions process. Many institutions that use non-need-based aid to compete for students are not need-blind and therefore do not qualify to participate. In addition, some schools that qualify have not joined the group, maintaining their independence to award aid as they see fit. As of 2020, only twenty-one colleges and universities are members, showing how guarded many institutions are about how they spend their institutional aid dollars.[11]

THE JUSTICE DEPARTMENT FLEXES ITS MUSCLE

In the years since MIT's settlement, the competition for affluent students with good grades and test scores has become ever more intense at both public and private colleges and universities, leading to the arms race that MIT predicted. Many college leaders who are caught up in the competition are unhappy with the direction that higher education has taken. They have found it difficult, however, to disengage unilaterally for fear of putting their institutions at a competitive disadvantage. These leaders have argued that collective action is needed to limit the use of non-need-based aid.[12] But the Justice Department has remained a roadblock, threatening more antitrust lawsuits.

In January 2013, a group of private college presidents held a session at a Council of Independent Colleges (CIC) Presidential Institute entitled "Collaborative Efforts of Student Aid and Admissions Policies," where they unveiled a draft statement of principles for discussion. Among the topics discussed were colleges' use of non-need-based aid to attract students and how colleges must work together to curtail the practice and recommit to using their aid to meet students' needs. Collaboration, the leaders said, would eliminate the risk of acting alone.

The Justice Department's antitrust division got wind of the discussions and apparently decided that they needed to be shut down. In May 2013, the department sent letters to several college officials who had participated in the session, expressing concern about efforts by colleges to work together to curtail the use of merit aid and instructing these officials to preserve documents related to the discussions. The CIC responded that the session involved a "free exchange of ideas" and there was no agreement for collective action. However, the department's letters had the intended chilling effect: they effectively ended the discussions.[13]

The Department of Justice's next target was the code of ethics and professional practices of the National Association for College Admission Counseling (NACAC). The Justice Department launched an investigation into NACAC's code of ethics several years ago, alleging that certain provisions in the code restrained competition among colleges for students in violation of antitrust laws. In September 2019, NACAC members voted to eliminate several portions of the ethics code, worried that litigation and further investigation threatened the organization's survival. The provisions in the code that were deleted would have barred colleges from doing the following:

- Offering financial or other incentives solely to applicants who apply under early decision programs;
- Recruiting students after they have submitted a deposit at another institution;
- Recruiting transfer applications from previous applicants or prospects unless those students inquired about transferring.

The Department of Justice argued that these practices, including the ban on poaching students from a school after they have enrolled, reduced competition that could lead to better deals for these students. NACAC officials and many of the association's members defended the provisions, saying that they help keep colleges from using scarce resources to compete for students who have already chosen the college they want to attend, and which otherwise might be used to meet financial need. However, under pressure from the Justice Department, NACAC voted to amend the code of ethics voluntarily, with the hope that these changes would be considered adequate to allay the Department of Justice's antitrust concerns and put an end to any further action. The organization also voted to give its board the temporary authority to make further changes in the event of "extraordinary legal circumstances."[14] Ultimately, NACAC and the Justice Department settled in December 2019, with the organization confirming that it had withdrawn the provisions that the Justice Department had claimed restricted competition for students.[15]

The Department of Justice, however, appears to have additional targets. Lately, department officials have set their sights on colleges' early-decision programs, which require students who are admitted to both accept the admissions offer and withdraw all applications from other institutions. Students, their parents, and school counselors are required to sign a statement that the students will take these steps, if admitted, in exchange for being considered early. At issue in the Justice Department's inquiry is whether colleges should be allowed to share the names of students admitted early with other schools that are close competitors. The exchanging of names is an attempt to enforce this agreement, with schools reserving the right to revoke the acceptances of any students who have violated their commitment. The Department of

Justice has contacted several schools, asking them to preserve documents relating to this practice.[16]

With the Justice Department becoming even more aggressive of late, it is important to determine whether its interpretation of antitrust in higher education stands up to scrutiny. Do college leaders and lobbyists have a case to make that the department's views are misguided? The next section takes a closer look at that question by examining whether federal antitrust laws should apply to nonprofit colleges.

"PART-CHURCH AND PART–CAR DEALER"

Gordon C. Winston, one of the first economists to think systematically about the economics of higher education toward the end of the twentieth century, liked to refer to colleges and universities as "part-church and part–car dealer."[17] Winston, who spent almost half a century at Williams College, referred to colleges in this way because they serve an important public mission while at the same time providing a private good to paying individuals. Higher education contributes to a nation's human capital with many positive externalities for the economy and society, such as productivity growth and equal opportunity and social mobility, while at the same time, it is a service purchased by students and their families to improve their future earnings potential, a very private good. These competing purposes or roles of higher education have contributed to an intriguing history of interaction between our nation's antitrust laws and colleges and universities.

Winston's characterization of colleges as "car dealers" certainly suggests that they participate in the market for educational services, competing with each other for students (customers) and faculty (inputs) just as other industries do. Even though they are nonprofit, colleges, like corporations, face budget constraints and have to worry about sources of revenue to sustain their operations. They, therefore, face incentives to charge prices that generate revenue to help balance their budgets. As a result, it could be in the financial interests of colleges and universities to attempt to fix prices with competitors to increase tuition and revenue, allowing them to either spend more on their current operations or capital projects or save for spending in the future. Similarly, they could fix the prices (i.e., salaries) they are willing to pay faculty, which would also free up resources for other purposes. What they cannot do with the added revenue is distribute any excess of revenue over expenditures to shareholders or owners, since nonprofits do not have these due to their nonprofit form. Nonprofits can in fact make profits: they just cannot distribute them to shareholders or owners. Of course, employees of nonprofits, from managers to staff, can benefit from increased revenue in the form of added compensation or more advantageous working conditions, at the expense of their students (i.e., the customers). The constraints on compensation come through the nonprofits' boards of trustees and, in part, through the Internal Revenue Service (IRS) code and requirements to report and demonstrate that the compensation of the highest-paid employees of the nonprofit is not excessive.

Given their nonprofit form, does it make economic sense to subject colleges to antitrust laws, even if they have some attributes of car dealers? Will antitrust laws encourage them to compete in a way that increases efficiency and benefits consumers?

The concept of efficiency on which the antitrust laws are based is fairly straightforward: in a competitive market, given a certain set of assumptions, economists demonstrate that consumer welfare is maximized. And if competition is impeded for some reason, such as collusion or monopoly, then consumer welfare is reduced. Under those conditions, consumers have access to fewer goods and services at higher prices and/or lower quality, reducing consumer surplus and their welfare.

As Henry Hansmann, professor emeritus of law at Yale University, has argued, the nonprofit form exists in part as a solution to cases in which the conditions for a competitive market generating an efficient outcome do not exist.[18] Hansmann identifies higher education as one such market. For a competitive market to maximize consumer welfare, the variety of conditions that need to hold include perfect information, low barriers to entry and exit, no transaction costs, many producers, and fairly homogeneous products. In higher education, many of these conditions do not hold. Usually, consumers (i.e., students) get a bachelor's degree only once, and they often don't know the value of what they have gotten until many years later.

Hansmann suggests that the nonprofit form can be useful when the services provided are complex and difficult to evaluate. Parents and students may not be able to effectively evaluate the quality of the educational services offered and therefore would benefit from being able to trust the producer, in this case the higher-education institution. Under these conditions, students' decisions about what to buy do not effectively discipline the market and encourage efficiency. In addition, there are concerns that students may not value the same things as their parents, who (at least in some cases) are paying the bills. The preferences of nineteen- to twenty-three-year-olds while in college may not lead to the highest-quality education, but instead to more amenities and programs that would more appropriately be considered consumption rather than investment. This situation is more similar to Hansmann's example of why some forms of expenditures, such as donations to charities around the world where someone else is receiving the goods and services, will not be supplied optimally through a for-profit firm. In the same way that a contributor cannot be sure that some child in another country has received the services promised (immunizations, food, clean water, etc.), parents may not be able to evaluate the education that their children are receiving. If supplied by a for-profit firm, there is little way to ensure that the firm will deliver on its promises and put the interests of its students first rather than just seeking to increase its profits. If a college is set up as a nonprofit, this temptation does not exist to nearly the same extent.[19]

Because most colleges are set up as nonprofits (either private or public) as a result of market failures, a simple application of the idea that competition maximizes consumer welfare does not apply. If the concept of efficiency is to be used to evaluate anticompetitive behavior in the higher-education sector, the notion would need to be considered within a more complicated situation than just a perfectly competitive market today. Higher-education institutions are firms that maximize an objective function that includes a variety of activities, including education and research, which they carry out over time. For example, they are devoted not just to educating current students, but future ones as well. In addition, when students receive an education, they are not only investing in themselves but generating externalities for the economy and the society within which they exist. Maximizing efficiency in the market for higher education would involve taking the intertemporal issues into account at the same time as the externalities, and any anticompetitive activities would have to be evaluated within this framework. Anticompetitive behavior that would reduce efficiency and consumer welfare in a perfectly competitive market for fairly homogenous goods and services may not have the same impact in the marketplace for higher education.[20]

HAVE THE JUSTICE DEPARTMENT'S ACTIONS IMPROVED EFFICIENCY?

Current antitrust laws do not deal well with the market imperfections of the higher-education sector in the United States. Nor do they clearly recognize the federal government's role in promoting greater college access and affordability. As a result, we have conflicting government interventions working at cross-purposes. The Justice Department's interventions seem to be motivated by concerns that higher education has become too expensive and increasing competition will lead to lower prices and/or higher quality, as it would in a perfectly competitive industry. College leaders, in contrast, believe that many of the activities that the Department of Justice has challenged were and are designed to protect access to a college degree for low- and middle-income students, and the public benefits as a result.

The Department of Justice views these policies as restricting competition among colleges and universities that otherwise would lead to lower prices. But while this might be the case for some students, it will put others at a disadvantage, and doing so may undermine the quality of the education offered, as well as undermine other government goals. It has been shown that the increased competition that has resulted from the merit aid arms race, along with rising income inequality, have led to increased costs and average prices rather than reductions, as colleges and universities compete for both students and faculty by spending on a variety of programs. Higher average prices, along with increases in "sticker prices," leave low- and even middle-income students worse off, requiring them to either take on more debt or engage in activities that make it harder for them to graduate, such as working long hours or going part time.

Given this reality, there are several alternative paths forward to allow greater collaboration across American higher education in service of public objectives. One strategy is to take antitrust laws as they are and more effectively argue that allowing collaboration among colleges would increase efficiency. This approach would involve recognizing that the market for higher education is not a perfectly competitive market where straightforward competition leads to efficiency gains. Instead, it is a market with imperfect information and a variety of other market failures that make the conditions for increasing efficiency more complicated than just enforcing competition among perfectly competitive for-profit firms.

Because of the ways in which higher education deviates from a perfectly competitive market, there are arguments that could be made to defend cooperative actions that otherwise would seem to violate antitrust laws to increase the allocation of resources to need-based financial aid on efficiency grounds. One argument would be that higher education is an associative good, meaning that the value of the service to an individual depends on the other individuals who are partaking of it.[21] Exactly how this occurs may matter, but peer effects are one possibility.[22] For example, students might all learn more from being around other similarly academically accomplished students with a variety of life experiences. Prioritizing need-based aid would help ensure that the most talented students can attend each institution, regardless of their family incomes, while also serving to increase diversity on campuses and in classrooms and therefore benefit all students. In past cases challenging colleges' affirmative action policies in admissions decisions, the US Supreme Court recognized that there are educational benefits to having a diverse student body.[23] Previous Supreme Court decisions affirming that diversity is a compelling state interest provide one possibility for an efficiency defense of policies that otherwise might be considered to violate antitrust laws.

Take early decision, for example. A 2006 *Yale Law Journal* article makes the case that early decision programs violate antitrust laws for very different reasons than those motivating the Department of Justice's investigation.[24] While the Justice Department worries that early decision disadvantages the (mostly privileged) students who take advantage of it, even though they agreed to the conditions when they applied early, the article argues that these policies disadvantage low-income students and students of color, reducing the diversity of the student body. Given that the courts have determined that diversity is a compelling state interest by increasing the educational benefits for all, early decision reduces efficiency, and eliminating it could be justified on these grounds, the article states. This is a good example of how there is more than one way to interpret how antitrust laws affect higher education.

Another possible justification for allowing collaboration across colleges and universities on efficiency grounds is to address the financial market imperfections that exist. If capital markets were perfect, families could borrow and invest in higher education for their children and everyone would have equal access. Higher-income families could choose to pay out of current income and assets, while lower-income families could borrow and invest in their children, who would then pay back their debt out of higher future earnings. But capital markets do not work perfectly for a variety of reasons, and not all students, particularly low-income and first-generation ones, will have access to adequate loan markets. Schools that offer need-based financial aid and then fundraise from their graduates is a partial solution to this problem.[25] By encouraging the allocation of resources to need-based aid, some of the inefficiencies of the higher-education market where capital markets are imperfect are again reduced, and therefore allowing cooperation to increase need-based aid could be justified on efficiency grounds.[26]

Arthur Okun, in *Equality and Efficiency: The Big Tradeoff*, makes the case that dealing with this capital market imperfection in the higher-education sector by encouraging greater need-based aid and college access on the part of lower-income students is one of the ways that we can actually increase both efficiency and equality without requiring the usual trade-off between these two objectives.[27] Both the capital market imperfection and diversity arguments could justify cooperative actions to increase need-based financial aid solely on efficiency grounds.[28]

In critiquing the Justice Department's stance on antitrust in higher education, college leaders can point to the Court of Appeals decision in the MIT case that ruled that the district court did not adequately consider the social benefits that the university argued the Ivy Overlap Group provided. But changing the Justice Department's interpretation of the law seems unlikely. The appeals court gave MIT the chance to win its case and force the agency to change its position, but the university agreed to settle the case instead. If anything, the Justice Department's position appears to have hardened since then. Under both the Obama and Trump administrations, Justice Department officials have objected to even the mere hint that colleges might work together to limit the spread of non-need-based aid.

Recognizing that winning the Justice Department over is a long shot, college leaders could seek an exemption from Congress for higher-education institutions under the antitrust laws. But providing colleges with a blanket exemption is not an adequate solution because there is no guarantee that colleges would follow through and limit their use of non-need-based aid. The refusal of many need-blind colleges to join the 568 Presidents Group shows how reluctant many schools are to give up the freedom they have to use their aid as a tool to compete for students. And even if colleges did agree to reduce their spending on non-need-based aid, there's no guarantee that they would reallocate the savings to need-based financial aid. Institutions could choose to spend the resources saved on other ways to attract affluent students, including serving better food, building fancier dorms, or providing even more-lavish amenities than they currently do.

If Congress gives higher education an exemption from antitrust laws, that exemption must come with increased regulation. Higher-education institutions are not only organized as nonprofits but receive significant public subsidies. This is true of both private and public colleges and universities. It is completely reasonable that the government, both federal and state, should require certain behaviors or outcomes in exchange for these subsidies. If subsidies are justified on the grounds that young people should have access to higher education regardless of their family income, then the subsidies should be conditioned on schools accomplishing this end. Equity and equal opportunity are legitimate interests of government since our society places value on them and pure market economies do not generate either under all circumstances. If colleges and universities use available subsidies to improve the quality of their education, but that education is primarily available to high-income students, the subsidies are not accomplishing their intended purpose.

Higher-education institutions have historically been trusted to serve the public good with little regulation and significant autonomy. Over the last few decades, these institutions have lost much of the public trust, both because of rising costs and the increased importance of receiving an education. The drivers of these trends are closely related to the increasing income inequality in the United States over the last forty years.[29] One does not have to look any further than the COVID-19 crisis to see the importance of higher education. The health outcomes and job and earnings outcomes are highly correlated with educational attainment. Those with more education have fared significantly better than those without.

One of the public's goals in the education sector has traditionally been greater equity or equal opportunity, not just efficiency. Access to opportunity in life depends importantly on education in the United States, but education is not equally available. K–12 education, while hardly equal, is at least a right for all children, but this is not the case with regard to higher education. And while college access has significantly increased during the twentieth century, the importance of higher education to future earnings has also increased, and degree attainment still depends importantly on income and race. These inequities are tied in large part to income and the rising cost of higher education for many families. Greater equality of opportunity to higher education and all its benefits, a goal of public policy, could be accomplished by tying access to public subsidies to outcomes desired by policy makers. Exempting colleges and universities from antitrust laws to allow them to accomplish these ends can be justified on equity as well as efficiency grounds. The solution to Winston's part-church, part–car dealer dilemma is not enforcement of antitrust laws, but exemption combined with appropriate subsidies and regulation.

One option would be to offer an exemption to colleges that meet full need and want to coordinate with other institutions to avoid competing through merit aid for higher-income students. The current exemption under section 568 is limited to colleges that are need-blind in the admissions process. Few schools meet this condition, and the exemption has not worked to encourage collaboration. Since many institutions are arguing that there is a collective action problem with regard to merit aid and it is difficult to unilaterally disarm, allowing an exemption for a larger group of schools—those that meet full need, regardless of whether they are need-blind or take financial need into account when admitting a limited number of applicants—is more likely to succeed. Limiting the exemption to colleges and universities that meet full need would exclude institutions that gap students and thereby encourage excessive borrowing on the part of students and their families.

Appropriate regulation is needed because otherwise any resources freed up through cooperation to limit merit aid in fact could be spent on other programs to compete for higher-income students. The incentives to compete for wealthy students are strong, as is clear from the behavior of the better-endowed colleges and universities that do not rely on merit aid. Lawmakers should consider requiring some minimum representation of lower-income students in the student body. Such a change could justify both access to the antitrust exemption and the subsidies that colleges and universities currently receive from federal policies, including access to federal financial aid funds and special tax treatment. Limiting the use of financial aid dollars to meet financial need would not be adequate on its own since schools could still decide to spend available resources on other items than financial aid.

Good public policy is, of course, not a given. But strengthening the economy while also contributing to greater equity should be in all our interests and gain bipartisan support.

Rather than trying to make arguments for how to treat higher education differently within existing antitrust laws, it makes more sense to recognize the country's interests in encouraging certain outcomes in the higher-education sector and to determine the most effective way to accomplish these goals.

Part 3. How Enrollment Management Works to Limit College Access and Affordability

CHAPTER 6

Finding the "Right" Students

The Student List Business and Enrollment Management[*]

Ozan Jaquette, Karina Salazar, and Patricia Martín

Enrollment management consulting firms play a central role in the recruiting process for many colleges and universities, helping the institutions identify prospective students to pursue and developing admissions and financial aid strategies to compete for them.

The first step in the recruiting process is identifying promising high school students. While name-brand institutions, such as those in the Ivy League, are flooded with applications from top students, most colleges aren't so lucky. They often work with enrollment management consultants to discover promising prospects who can be convinced to enroll.

However, colleges do not know who these prospects are, where they are, or how to contact them. That's where the student list business comes in. The student list business is a matchmaking intermediary connecting colleges and universities to prospective students.

For decades, the College Board, the parent company of the SAT and Advanced Placement (AP) exams, and ACT have dominated the student list business because of their enormous databases of test takers. ACT and the

College Board encourage students to permit the testing agencies to share with colleges their names and contact information, as well as other details about their academic records. Colleges then purchase names from these student lists, often with advice and counsel from the enrollment management consultants that they hire to guide them through the process. Many colleges even outsource this activity entirely to the enrollment management firms, giving these private companies a huge amount of influence in shaping the institutions' incoming classes.

The College Board and ACT have made it substantially easier over the years for the colleges and their consultants to find students whose families can afford to pay full freight by including search filters in their student list products that allow colleges to target prospects. Colleges, for example, can filter for students within small geographic areas, including particular ZIP codes, making it possible for public and private nonprofit universities to concentrate their recruiting in areas that are overwhelmingly white and affluent.

As competition for top students and wealthy ones has become even more intense over the past decade, the College Board and ACT, to a lesser extent, have introduced new search filters based on statistical models that have made it easier for selective colleges and their enrollment management consultants to zero in on the types of prospects they covet. For example, the College Board has introduced geodemographic search filters that allow colleges and their consultants to target prospects based on the college-going behavior and socioeconomic characteristics of the schools they attend and the census-tract level neighborhoods in which they live.[1] Unsurprisingly, the neighborhood and high school clusters are highly correlated with race and income, which can result in redlining, systematically avoiding recruiting students in communities that are made up predominantly of lower-income Black and/or Latinx residents. And even when selective institutions use these filters to specifically target students of color, they tend to search for ones with high standardized test scores living in wealthy communities and attending wealthy high schools.

Until recently, the relationship between enrollment management firms and the standardized admissions testing agencies have been mutually beneficial when it comes to the student list business. But over time, there has been a blurring of the line between student list vendors and enrollment management consultants. For one thing, both testing agencies have used their position in the student list markets to offer enrollment management consulting services themselves. Colleges that pay for the College Board's Enrollment Planning Service, for instance, receive enrollment management consulting services and obtain data about prospects not included in purchased lists, which can help them make more efficient and effective decisions about recruiting interventions.[2]

For another thing, EAB, a giant enrollment management company, has recently become one of the most important players in the student list business based on a series of strategic acquisitions that it has made. Whereas the College Board and ACT have historically sold student names at a per-prospect price to any accredited college or university, EAB requires colleges to purchase expensive software or consulting services in exchange for access to its proprietary database of prospective students. As a result, only the firm's clients have access to the unique student lists that the firm compiles, giving these institutions a competitive recruiting advantage over other institutions.

EAB's sudden prominence in the student list business is even more significant because it comes at a time when the College Board and ACT face an existential threat: the "test optional" movement. During the 2010s, more than one thousand colleges decided to go test optional for at least a subset of their students, although the vast majority of highly selective public and private colleges and universities continued to require applicants to submit their test scores.[3] However, the COVID-19 pandemic changed the equation. The inability of millions of high school students to sit for the SAT and ACT exams in the pandemic's first years forced nearly all four-year colleges, including the most elite, to stop requiring students to submit their scores.[4] Assuming that most of these institutions remain test optional moving forward, the College Board and ACT databases will contain a shrinking share of prospective college students, undermining their competitive advantage in the domain of coverage.

Will the demise of the SAT and ACT allow EAB and potentially other enrollment management firms that follow its lead—including its largest competitor, Ruffalo Noel Levitz, with its RNL Prospective Student Network—to gain control of the market for student names?[5] Such a development, in which companies maintain proprietary databases available only to their clients, would give these private for-profit firms an extraordinary level of sway over colleges' student recruitment efforts.

There is a better way. We propose the creation of a "public option" student list product developed by a consortium of states based on data from statewide longitudinal data systems. The names of students who opt in would be provided free to eligible postsecondary institutions, thereby eliminating the rationale for efficient name buys that target some prospects but not others. The overriding goal of such a system would be equity of opportunity for all students.

INVESTIGATING THE STUDENT LIST BUSINESS

To understand just how much clout enrollment management companies have gained in shaping colleges' recruiting practices, it is crucial to understand how the student list business works and how it is evolving. But that was not our focus when we first started this project.

Much of our prior work focused on the recruiting priorities of public flagship and research universities.[6] In 2019, we published "Recruiting the Out-of-State University," which analyzed off-campus recruiting visits by public research universities and showed the extent to which many of these institutions, in the face of state disinvestment, focus on recruiting wealthy out-of-state students.[7]

We intended to expand on that work when we issued in February 2020 public-record requests to ninety-three public universities in five states to collect quantifiable data about the institutions' student list purchases from the College Board and ACT. Our requests sought two pieces of information: the deidentified student list data and the "order summary," which shows the specified search criteria to determine which prospects are included in the lists. Our goal was to understand whether the recruiting efforts of these universities were representative of their surrounding communities. Thus, we initially assumed that the set of prospects included versus excluded for student list purchases was a function of individual university enrollment preferences.

But as we started to receive responses to our public records requests, we were surprised by the extent to which public universities outsource student list purchases to enrollment management consulting firms. In these cases, we were usually unable to obtain the requested records. Furthermore, public records officers often could not identify university employees who knew about student list purchases because of high employee turnover on their campuses.

Over time, we realized that the most problematic aspects of student lists—particularly which prospects are excluded from student list purchases—are functions of student list products themselves and the broader market for student list data, which includes student list sellers, aggregators, and enrollment management consulting firms. Therefore, instead of focusing on the behavior of colleges and universities that purchase student lists, we decided to investigate dynamics in the market for student list data and the student list products created by this market.

Although colleges are the primary customers of student list products, we cannot understand the student list business without understanding the role of enrollment management consulting firms. Because recruiting students has become more sophisticated and competitive over the past twenty years, a growing number of colleges and universities have hired private enrollment management consultants to develop and/or implement recruiting campaigns.

In general, the relationship between enrollment management firms and the standardized admissions testing agencies that dominate the student list business has been mutually beneficial. A core service that these firms provide is making recommendations to colleges about student list purchases. Many colleges empower these companies to make purchases on their behalf. In addition, data from student lists are a key input into the predictive models and recruiting interventions (e.g., email, mail, and social media) that the consultancies market to colleges. Over the years, College Board and ACT student list products have made it easier for institutions to find affluent students with high SAT or ACT scores who will help raise these institutions' rankings and revenue.

Theoretical Framework

While the market for student list data has been primarily controlled and shaped by the College Board and ACT for decades, it has become surprisingly dynamic. For example, technological advances in the twenty-first century have yielded new sources of student list data—leading to entry by new firms—and have been incorporated into existing student list products in troubling ways. Within the past five years, there have been a surge in acquisitions and a blurring of distinctions between student list vendors and enrollment management consultants, and the test-optional movement threatens the College Board and ACT oligopoly. This box introduces concepts from sociological theories of organizational behavior that enable us to analyze these dynamics.

Resource Dependence Theory

Our analysis of the market for student list data draws from resource dependence theory, one of several theories of organizational behavior that provides insight into "make or buy" decisions by firms, which we refer to as "in-house" (make) or "contract-out" (buy) decisions.[8] Resource dependence theory begins with the assumption that organizations require resources from the external environment to survive. The central concept of resource dependence theory is dependence, as defined by the sociologist Richard Marc Emerson in 1962.[9] Actor *A* depends on Actor *B* to the extent that *B* controls goals important to *A*—values that *A* cannot obtain outside the *A-B* relationship. Resource dependence theory states that an external resource provider has power over an organization to the extent that (1) the resource is essential for organizational operations, (2) few alternative sources of the resource exist, and (3) the external organization has discretion over how the resource is allocated.

As one example of dependence, colleges and universities depend on the stable flow of prospect contact information to achieve enrollment goals. The dependence of a college on a particular student list vendor is more significant when there are few suppliers for some pools of names. This action characterizes the long-standing oligopoly market structure of the student loan business, where the College Board and ACT capitalize on their market power by forcing customers (colleges) to pay higher prices (e.g., fifty cents per name) than they would pay in a competitive market. While College Board and ACT each owns a unique set of names, every institution has the right to buy these names at a set price. By contrast, dependence on the supplier of unique names increases if the supplier has discretion over which universities have access to those names, as in the example of EAB restricting access to a pool of prospects to those colleges that have signed consulting and/or subscription contracts with the enrollment management company.

In their influential work on resource dependence theory, Jeffrey Pfeffer and Gerald R. Salancik describe strategies organizations may deploy in response to the problem of dependence on a particular resource (including compliance, resource diversification, cooptation, professional associations, and acquisitions).[10] While the choice of strategy is contextual, resource dependence theory recommends choosing "the least-constraining device [action] to govern relations with your exchange partners that will allow you to minimize uncertainty and dependence and maximize your autonomy."[11] For example, one strategy is finding an alternative supplier of the same resource, such as a different student list vendor, to reduce reliance on a particular provider. *Resource diversification* is the strategy of reducing reliance on a resource by finding substitute resources. For example, a university may reduce dependence on names by using behavioral-based marketing to identify/target leads and by using brand marketing to grow inquiries. *Cooptation* is the strategy of socializing external resource providers to the goals of the organization through shared participation in organizational activities. For example, enrollment management consulting firms depend principally on colleges. If a firm places a consultant in a vice president of enrollment management position at the college, it becomes more likely that the college will retain the consulting firm.

Acquisitions, the "most resource-intensive means" of exerting control over the external environment, have received little attention from higher-education scholars.[12] However, they are quite common in the market for student list data. *Vertical integration* refers to whether two distinct activities in the input/output value chain of an organization are done by two organizations (contract-out approach) or done by one organization (in-house approach). A *vertical acquisition* occurs when an organization acquires an organization at adjacent stages in the value chain. For instance, "furniture manufacturers may merge (backward) with lumber companies or (forward) with furniture distributors or showrooms."[13] In the market for student list data, consider college search websites, which generate student list data by asking prospective students to enter information about their background and college preferences. For simplicity, assume that the market consists of two activities: building websites and selling data to colleges looking for names. A firm that specializes in building college search websites may acquire a firm with the capacity to sell names to colleges to complete both activities in house.

Somewhere between contracting-out and vertical acquisitions is the strategy of forming *alliances*, which are "agreements between two or more organizations to pursue joint objectives through a coordination of activities."[14] Alliances are less costly than acquisitions and can be mutually beneficial when each organization performs an activity that is an essential input for the other organizations.

A *horizontal acquisition* occurs when two firms that perform similar activities merge. For example, an enrollment management firm may acquire one of its competitors. Horizontal mergers increase market share and reduce competition, potentially enabling the acquiring firm to charge higher prices. More generally, larger firms can exert influence on their external environment, including the ability to control suppliers, buyers, and regulators.[15]

New Institutional Theory

Whereas resource dependence theory provides insight into the decisions of firms within an industry, a new institutional theory provides insight into macrostructural forces that shape organizational behavior. In their seminal work, "Institutionalized Organizations: Formal Structure as Myth and Ceremony," John W. Meyer and Brian Rowan argue that organizations survive not by superior performance (efficiency) but by appearing legitimate to external stakeholders.[16] Legitimacy is defined as conforming to recognized, accepted standards. An organization has legitimacy if external actors view it as an accepted member of a particular type of organization. In turn, gaining/maintaining legitimacy depends on adopting practices deemed appropriate for a particular type of organization. Thus, Meyer and Rowan define *institutions* as taken-for-granted ideas about appropriate practices. *Institutionalization* is the process by which ideas about appropriate practices "come to take on a rule-like status in social thought and action."[17]

Because all organizations within a population (research universities, for example) are beholden to the same expectations from the external environment, the institutionalization of a practice results in *isomorphism*, defined as the process by which organizations within a population adopt the same processes, policies, and structures.[18] Whereas early adoption of an innovation is motivated by substantive rationale, later adoption is motivated by legitimacy considerations.[19] The diffusion of the SAT and ACT exams is a textbook example of isomorphism. Once the leading public and private colleges and universities adopted the SAT or ACT as an admissions requirement, other colleges followed suit. In turn, the institutionalization of the college entrance exam compelled college-going high school students to take either the SAT or the ACT.

A subsequent wave of empirical scholarship from new institutional theory examined *deinstitutionalization*—the conditions and processes by which institutions die. Examples include the conglomerate firm as an organizational form and lifetime employment in Japan.[20] Deinstitutionalization is caused by macro forces in the external environment, including technological change, social movements, and political mobilization.[21] With respect to technology, the sociologist Gerald F. Davis states that "underlying the shifts in forms of finance and production were advances in information and communication technologies that substantially expanded the range of possible organizational structures and repertoires."[22] David Karen, another sociologist, describes political mobilization as "involving a collective effort on the part of individuals who are excluded from some critical resource [such as access to higher education] to change existing patterns of institutionalized behavior."[23]

SYSTEMATIC EXCLUSION

The student list products sold by testing agencies perpetuate racial and socioeconomic disparities because they predominantly include those who have taken standardized college admissions tests.[24] Rates of test-taking differ across race and class, yielding systemic inequality as to who is included in the underlying databases and, in turn, whom colleges recruit. Communities of color that have been historically underrepresented in higher education are less likely to be in the College Board/ACT student list databases because of lower test-taking rates, which may be partly due to concerns among students of color that standardized tests have been designed in ways that are biased against them.[25]

In addition, the student list products include search filters to help colleges find the types of students they most desire, often disadvantaging low-income students and students of color. For example, the College Board student list filters encourage colleges to target prospects based on AP scores. However, Black, Latinx, and Native students are less likely than white students to attend high schools that offer substantial AP curricula.[26]

The College Board and ACT filters also allow colleges to specify ZIP codes in their purchase orders, making it possible for public and private nonprofit colleges and their consultants to buy lists that systematically exclude low-income communities and communities of color. ZIP codes are highly correlated with income and racial demographics. There is no equality-of-opportunity rationale for filtering for students who live in one ZIP code but not in a neighboring one.

Over the last decade, as competition for top students has intensified, the testing agencies have further catered to the enrollment management needs of colleges and their consultants by enabling colleges to target the prospects they covet with even greater precision. ACT has moved more modestly in this direction, adding an "Enrollment Predictor" that allows colleges to filter prospects based on their predicted probability of enrolling. The College Board has moved more aggressively, adding geodemographic filters that allow colleges to target prospects based on the socioeconomic demographics and historical college-going behavior of students from their high schools or neighborhoods.

GEODEMOGRAPHIC SEARCH FILTERS

Geodemographic search filters, which the College Board introduced with the creation of its Segment Analysis Service, are efficient tools of microtargeting, which we believe can, knowingly or unknowingly, result in racial redlining. Geodemography—now often referred to as "spatial big data"—is a branch of market reach that estimates the behavior of customers based on where they live.[27] According to the College Board:

> The basic tenet of geodemography is that people with similar cultural backgrounds, means, and perspectives naturally gravitate toward one another or form relatively homogeneous communities; in other words, birds of a feather flock together. When they are living in a community, people... share similar patterns of consumer behavior toward products, services, media, and promotions. The primary appeal of geodemography from the marketer's perspective is that, with just an address, s/he can begin to craft an image about a particular set of individuals based on the values, tastes, expectations, and behaviors associated with their geographic community.[28]

As this quote illustrates, geodemography is based on problematic assumptions. People with similar backgrounds do not "naturally gravitate toward one another." Rather, US neighborhoods and schools are racially segregated because of historic and ongoing systematic discrimination embedded in policy and law.[29] Product marketing decisions that are based on geodemography are likely to reinforce the race-based inequities in opportunity that have been fundamental to creating and maintaining racial segregation.

The College Board Segment Analysis Service allocates each of the United States's 33,000 high schools to one of twenty-nine high school clusters and allocates each of the country's 44,000 census tracts to one of thirty-three educational neighborhood clusters based on the college-going behavior and socioeconomic characteristics of the school or neighborhood.[30]

Customers of the Segment Analysis Service can purchase a list that contains prospects who scored within a particular range on the SAT, live in a particular set of metropolitan areas, and are associated with particular combinations of neighborhood and high school clusters. Segment neighborhood and high school clusters are highly correlated with both racial and income demographics. For example, according to a 2011 College Board table of "Neighborhood Cluster Sample Characteristics," the neighborhood cluster "EN:61" is 30 percent nonwhite and has a median income of $123,858, while the cluster "EN:71" is 97 percent nonwhite and has a median income of $42,661. Similarly, the high school cluster "HS:70" is 33 percent nonwhite and has a median income of $105,721, while the cluster "HS:71" is 98 percent nonwhite and has a median income of $43,391.[31]

As part of our research project, we analyzed eight student list orders that a public research university made using the College Board's geodemographic Segment Analysis Service filters. The university made the orders between February 2018 and April 2020, targeting students in the 2019–2023 high school graduating classes. They resulted in 131,562 purchased prospects. The orders focused on students living in large metropolitan areas with grade point averages (GPAs) of at least a B− and with PSAT or SAT scores ranging from a low of 1220–1240 to a high of 1,450. Each order also filtered particular combinations of neighborhood and high school clusters.[32]

We found that selected neighborhood and high school clusters tended to have a higher income and a lower percentage of nonwhite students than clusters that were not selected. For example, white and Asian students comprised 58 percent and 27 percent of the nearly 28,000 purchased prospects from the New York metropolitan area, respectively, even though white students make up only 30 percent of students in the public schools there, and Asians just 9 percent. Meanwhile, Black and Latinx students comprised only 1 percent and 8 percent of the purchased prospects from New York, even though together they make up about 60 percent of public-school students there. Furthermore, the purchased prospects lived in ZIP codes that were much more affluent, with an average median household income of $153,000, than the overall New York metropolitan area, where the average median household income is $91,000.[33]

Similarly, Black and Latinx students made up only 2 percent and 5 percent of the prospects that the university purchased from the Philadelphia metropolitan area, respectively, even though these students make up nearly half its public-school population. At the same time, wide income disparities existed across all metropolitan areas. In Washington, DC, for instance, the purchased prospects lived in ZIP codes with an average median household income of $164,000, compared to $114,000 for the metropolitan area as a whole.

To be fair, some research universities that we examined used the College Board filters to target Black and Latinx students with good grades and test scores as means to overcome the historical exclusion of students of color in higher education and promote racial diversity in college access. We found, however, that purchases targeting underrepresented minority students with relatively high standardized test scores tended to yield prospects who lived in wealthy communities and attended schools in wealthy communities. In New York, Philadelphia, and Chicago, the Black and Latinx prospects that the research universities purchased tended to attend predominantly white high schools. By contrast, the underrepresented minority prospect profiles purchased from Miami, Houston, and Atlanta tended to attend schools with larger shares of nonwhite students. However, even in these metropolitan areas, schools with at least one purchased prospect tended to have a lower enrollment of Black students than schools with no purchased prospects.

In recent years, the College Board has doubled down on geodemographic filters by adding three Environmental Attributes search filters to its Student Search Service. The new filters are Travel Rates (out of state), Travel Rates (distance from home), and AP Engagement Rates. Using out-of-state travel as an example, each high school is categorized as "low," "medium," or "high" in terms of the percentage of college students who attend an out-of-state college or university. In turn, a Student Search Service customer could purchase prospects who live in a particular metro area, with PSAT scores within some interval, and attend a high school with a "high" out-of-state travel rate, which is likely to be in an affluent area.

BLURRING BOUNDARIES

While the testing agencies have long catered their student list products toward the enrollment management needs of colleges and their consultants, in recent years there has been a blurring of the roles between student list vendors and enrollment management consultants.

Both the College Board and ACT, for example, have employed their oligopoly position in the student list market to enter the enrollment management consulting business. The two organizations took different routes, with the College Board entering the enrollment management market through internal development and ACT entering the market through acquisitions.

When colleges buy student lists from the College Board, they receive only a subset of the information that the agency has about each prospect. The College Board's Enrollment Planning Service gives colleges that become clients of its consulting services more-detailed data about these students, including data related to their academic achievement and where they are sending their test scores. The value proposition that Enrollment Planning Service makes to colleges is this: rather than buy lists from the College Board and work with a private enrollment management firm, purchase names and enrollment management consulting from the College Board and get access to prospect data that cannot be obtained from student lists and can help the institutions make more efficient and effective decisions about recruiting interventions.

ACT entered the enrollment management business by acquiring Eduventures, a market research and consulting firm "focused on innovations in higher education."[34] Eduventures came to ACT as part of its 2018 purchase of the National Research Center for College and University Admissions, which had acquired the firm two years earlier.[35] Under ACT, Eduventures offers "primary research, analysis, and advisory services to support decision-making throughout the student life cycle," from recruitment to student success.[36]

While the testing agencies now offer enrollment management consulting services, EAB, one of the largest enrollment management firms, has made a series of acquisitions over the past few years to make it a significant player in the student list business. EAB was able to make these purchases because it is owned by Vista Equity Partners, the largest private equity firm globally.

EAB took its first step into the student list business in 2019 when it acquired YouVisit, which the firm described as "the leading provider of virtual tour and interactive web content for higher education."[37] The purchase of YouVisit gave EAB a product that its clients could use to offer virtual tours on their websites. The product records the Internet Protocol (IP) addresses and the contact information of students who take the virtual tour. As a result, colleges obtain inquiries of prospective students who are interested enough in the institutions to take their tours.

In 2020, EAB acquired Cappex, a college and scholarship search website used by 1.5 million students each year.[38] Cappex was one of a number of companies that emerged in the 2000s that sell student list data to colleges based on survey data that students voluntary submit when they visit these websites in the hopes of finding a good college match or scholarship. The Cappex deal allowed EAB to provide its clients with the proprietary student list data that Cappex generates. To the extent that Cappex users do not take standardized admissions tests, the company provides names that cannot be purchased from the College Board or ACT. The acquisition of Cappex "will enable EAB partners to identify and engage prospective students who do not interact with schools through the traditional channels, such as campus visits or standardized tests," Chris Marett, the president of EAB Enrollment Services, said in a press release announcing the purchase. "By expanding schools' inquiry pools, we can help institutions grow and diversify their student populations."[39]

The Cappex and YouVisit acquisitions—now fully integrated within the EAB platform—are synergistic, in that prospects searching for colleges on Cappex are served the virtual tours of EAB clients. Therefore, purchasing Cappex increased the value of the YouVisit virtual tour asset, in that it steers a steady stream of prospects to the virtual tours of colleges that are EAB's clients.

Those acquisitions helped EAB gain a foothold in the student list business. But the enrollment management firm took its biggest leap in 2021, when it became the exclusive reseller of a recruiting platform that gives its clients a huge advantage in connecting to millions of students who conduct their college searches using Naviance, popular software that high schools purchase for their students to use. Under a deal that it made with PowerSchool, which was another subsidiary of Vista Equity Partners at the time, EAB became the exclusive reseller for the next decade of the Intersect student recruitment platform.[40] Intersect is the only platform that gives colleges the ability to send targeted advertisements to Naviance users, encouraging them to apply to their institutions.[41]

More than ten million students and 40 percent of US high schools use Naviance to research colleges, request recommendations, and submit transcripts and applications.[42] As with the College Board and ACT student list products, colleges that use Intersect decide which students to target with their recruiting messages by filtering based on criteria such as geographic location, "academic ability," intended major, and whether a student used Naviance to "research competitor institutions."[43]

Having access to these students has become more crucial for colleges over the last several years as more and more of these colleges have gone test optional, meaning that they don't require applicants to submit test scores. As fewer high school students take SAT and ACT exams, colleges face pressure to pay for Intersect to reach students who have chosen not to take these tests. For example, a University of Utah procurement justification for Intersect states that "there is a unique group of prospective students who are only in the PowerSchool Naviance platform."[44]

EAB pays PowerSchool, one of the largest providers of education software in North America, $32 million annually to be the exclusive reseller of Intersect. EAB has rebundled Intersect—along with Cappex and YouVisit—into Enroll360, which connects college clients with a unique, proprietary database of prospects that cannot be obtained from other enrollment management consulting firms or other student list vendors. In announcing the rollout of Enroll360, Michael Koppenheffer, EAB's vice president of marketing programs, stated:

> We spent the last couple of years creating *a connected recruitment ecosystem* that allows enrollment leaders to keep pace with students as they pursue these increasingly digital journeys to college. *This work led us to join forces with several leading companies: Cappex, Intersect, Wisr, and You-Visit*.... Individually, each solution can solve important challenges at various stages of the enrollment funnel.... By bringing these capabilities together, our vision is to reinvent how enrollment leaders reach their goals.[45]

Koppenheffer illustrates the advantages of Enroll360 with a vignette that conveys both the unique database of prospects that EAB controls and the ability for its college clients to get these prospects over time and across multiple platforms:

> Imagine a high school student today. Let's call her "Emma."... Fast forward to Emma's junior year. She has begun to think more seriously about college and like many of her peers, she turns to Google to explore options. Emma quickly comes across *Cappex*, where she's prompted to fill out her ideal college location—close to her hometown in Rhode Island—and her intended major—computer engineering.
>
> After connecting with her counselor during her senior year, Emma has narrowed down her list of schools to five and enters her shortlist in *Naviance*. From there, she explores your university's website and comes across a link to your *virtual tour*. Since she won't be able to visit in-person, she and her mom tour your campus from their kitchen table. Emma can picture herself picnicking in the campus quad and participating in the lab featured during the tour of the engineering building. After the tour, she starts to see Instagram ads for your school depicting students in that same lab. And after receiving an email from your school with an invite to apply via a personalized application, she applies.

> Emma is admitted to four of her five top schools, including yours. But to help her decide where to enroll, she wants to hear what student life is actually like. Through *Wisr,* Emma connects one-on-one with Kayleigh, a current junior and student ambassador at your institution studying computer engineering.[46]

As the example shows, EAB is first and foremost an enrollment management firm that is helping its college clients recruit and enroll students. Through its acquisitions and partnerships, EAB has obtained proprietary control over a key input—student names. Other enrollment management consulting firms can buy names from the College Board, ACT, and other vendors on behalf of clients, but they do not have access to EAB's proprietary database. By contrast, EAB can buy names from student list vendors and integrate these names with the proprietary ones in its database. Whereas the College Board and ACT use their oligopoly position in the supply of names to charge oligopoly prices, EAB can use the market power that it has gained in the supply of names—and the software-of-service products built on top of these names (Enroll360)—to attract new college clients and to extract more revenue from each client.

In exchange, EAB essentially promises to funnel prospective students to colleges that pay for these products. For example, EAB's promotional material states that "Intersect is the preeminent provider of high-intent student inquiries and candidates for colleges" and "80 percent of high school students who connect with a college through Intersect apply to that institution."[47] EAB's press release for Enroll360 states that "students [who are] included in EAB Search campaigns and take a virtual tour are 3.5x as likely to apply and 10x more likely to deposit." And when colleges combine Cappex with "Intersect's High Intent Inquiries," they will achieve "a 16 percent increase in enrollments," the press release promises.[48]

AN EXISTENTIAL THREAT

EAB's move to become a major player in the student list market received a boost from an unlikely source: the COVID-19 pandemic, which shook up the business like never before. For decades, nearly all selective colleges required applicants to submit SAT or ACT scores.[49] But over the last twenty years, a broad social movement of well-organized coalitions developed, calling on colleges to stop requiring students to submit their test scores. Research backed up the test-optional movement's main critique of the standardized admissions exams: that they are racially and socioeconomically biased and that they are not good predictors of student success, undermining their legitimacy.[50]

While the movement gained some traction in the years immediately preceding the arrival of COVID-19, the frequent cancellation of SAT and ACT exams during the first two years of the pandemic pushed most four-year colleges to stop requiring the tests.

As of November 2022, more than 1,750 colleges were not requiring applicants to submit scores, and another eighty-five chose to stop considering test scores at all, going fully "test blind" in admissions, according to FairTest.[51] The organization, which promotes test-optional policies, has surveyed those colleges and found that nearly 80 percent of them plan to make these policies permanent, a development that would serve as an existential threat to the College Board and ACT.

Although the pandemic complicates the interpretation of these trends, scholarship on organizational behavior suggests that test optional has been institutionalized as the "new normal."[52] How will deinstitutionalization of the SAT and ACT affect the student list business? As fewer colleges require applicants to submit test scores, fewer high school students will take these tests. In turn, the College Board and ACT databases will contain a shrinking share of prospective college students, undermining their competitive advantage in the domain of coverage.

The College Board and ACT have been trying to counteract these trends by convincing states to require their high school students to take the tests to qualify for high school graduation.[53] But this strategy is unlikely to offset the long-term decline in test-takers. The College Board can sell the names of AP test-takers, but fewer students take AP classes than take the SATs, and there is obvious racial and socioeconomic inequality in terms of the availability of AP curricula in different high schools. In other words, unless the momentum driving highly selective colleges to test optional and test-blind admissions reverses, the oligopoly that the College Board and ACT have maintained over the student list business is likely to collapse.

The deinstitutionalization of the SAT and ACT exams will undoubtedly benefit EAB and other enrollment management firms, like Ruffalo Noel

Levitz, that try to stay competitive by offering their own student list products. But the EAB model raises questions for policy makers. Should access to a substantial share of college-going high school students be restricted to the clients of a private firm? And should private firms be able to funnel prospective students toward their own clients and away from other colleges?

A PUBLIC OPTION IS NEEDED

Student lists play an essential role in the college access process because the US higher-education market is structured as a national voucher system that depends on providers to go out and find students. Unfortunately, the contemporary student list business is characterized by the systematic exclusion of underrepresented students, the likely death of the college entrance exam, and the looming takeover by the corporate and private equity interests that control enrollment management firms. Is this the best we can do?

We propose a public option student list product, oriented around the goal of equality of opportunity for students. Our concept is inspired by the example of national voter databases that US political parties use in political campaigns. The basic inputs for these databases are voter files, essentially free public records collected by local and state governments. Data firms, working for the political parties, layer on additional information, such as income levels and purchasing patterns, "to create detailed profiles of voters."[54]

The way that political campaign managers use voter data to inform political campaigns is strikingly similar to the way that enrollment managers utilize student lists to inform "recruiting campaigns." However, voter files—the basic input to national voter databases—are free, public records. By contrast, the basic inputs for student lists—contact information, academic achievement, and college preferences—are proprietary, with the College Board charging fifty cents per name in 2021.[55]

Under our proposal, a consortium of states would develop a national student-list product based on data from statewide longitudinal student data systems. Students and their parents would have the opportunity to opt in or opt out of such systems. Colleges would receive the names of students who opt in for free. The public-option student lists also would include students' contact information and the codes of the high schools that they attend, as well as their high school academic records, including their GPA and the courses that they have taken. In addition, colleges would receive the students' demographic information, as well as their responses to a short survey about their college preferences, including what subject they are planning to pursue as a major.

Several product features are essential for the public option to compete with private-sector products. First, the public option will serve as a viable alternative only to the extent that it includes a high share of states and a high share of prospects from these states. Second, just as the College Board and ACT student list products enable colleges to reach out to prospects early in their college search process, the public option should enable colleges to obtain the names of sophomores and juniors who have opted in, a product feature that requires timely data. Third, the public option must possess data quality on par with the College Board and ACT student lists, meaning that the data need to be accurate and complete, without missing fields. Fourth, students opting in to the public option should be required to complete a brief questionnaire to provide data that enrollment professionals value but is not included in high school administrative data, such as their intended majors, how far away from home they want to be, and whether they prefer to go to a public or private college.

A robust, reliable public student list product would improve college access and equality of opportunity in a number of ways. For one thing, students would not be excluded from name buys because they did not take a particular standardized exam. For another, the public option would not include search filters that help selective colleges microtarget the "right" students in the "right" neighborhoods and high schools, and often result in the systematic exclusion of underrepresented students. Colleges value those types of search filters, in part, because the College Board and ACT charge a high price for names. By offering names for free, the public option eliminates the incentive for efficient name buys that target very particular prospects while excluding others. We believe that offering free names will result in more recruiting interventions directed at underrecruited student populations. That is important because prior research shows that these students tend to be the most responsive to attention from colleges and universities.[56]

In offering our proposal, we fully recognize that using statewide longitudinal student data systems to create a national public list product would face formidable political and technical challenges. The most significant political questions are: Who will pay for, develop, and maintain the system? State laws currently restrict sharing statewide longitudinal data, and some state policy makers may be concerned about participating in a system that would facilitate student brain-drain to out-of-state universities. On the technical front, it would be quite a feat to create a timely database that incorporates contact information, transcript data, and demographic information, with data drawn from many states and many schools and districts within each state.

In short, creating such a public option would be difficult. Alternatively, we can do nothing and allow for-profit interests to take control of the student list business and steer prospective students to their college clients, further deepening a college access crisis that we already face in this country for low-income students and students of color. Under those circumstances, how can we *not* act?

CHAPTER 7

Words Without Actions

The Troubled Relationship Between Enrollment Management and Diversity

Peter Schmidt

The college administrators gathered in a Disney World conference room were basking in the glow of the Magic Kingdom. Holding positions that entrusted them to promote diversity, they received nothing but praise and encouragement from speaker after speaker at the twenty-first annual National Conference on Race and Ethnicity in American Higher Education. They expected those good feelings to continue when Evelyn Hu-DeHart, the director of Brown University's Center for the Study of Race and Ethnicity in America, stepped to the podium. She began pleasantly enough, observing how the conference's location had given its roughly two thousand attendees easy opportunities to slip off to enjoy Disney World's amusements.

Then, however, Ms. Hu-DeHart stunned her audience by lifting the curtain on her profession. She told the administrators that they had gotten where they were by selling out the students whom they claimed to care about. Their employers had covered their registration and travel costs to reward them for accepting higher education's status quo and not making waves by demanding greater equity and more Black and Hispanic representation, she said.

"Let's face it: diversity has created jobs for all of us. It is a career. It is an industry," she said. "We do what we need to keep our jobs."

She then honed in on the chief diversity officers in the room, accusing them of diverting attention from the failures of presidents and provosts responsible for campus diversity and making their institutions appear more concerned with diversity than actually is the case.

"You all are covering up," she alleged. "You all are complicit in this," and will remain so "as long as we keep doing our job the way we are told to do it," helping colleges pursue an ideal of diversity rooted in a business-driven desire to have different types of people on campuses rather than pursuing justice for those whom higher education historically has excluded.

Her remarks initially met polite applause interspersed with a few loud cheers. As this 2008 conference progressed, however, it became clear she had sparked a firestorm.[1]

College diversity officers tend to see themselves as both advocates for social justice and agents of positive change at their institutions. They generally characterize enrollment management and related admissions and financial-aid practices as tools for ensuring that Black, Latino, Native American, and low-income students are well represented on campus.

When minority enrollments either dwindle or remain low, the administrators' go-to response typically involves pointing fingers at things that they can't do much about. They blame competition from better-funded colleges that offer prospective students more financial aid, or gaps between various student populations' college preparation rooted in inequalities in our society and K–12 schools, or headwinds generated by economic or demographic trends. Those who work at public colleges frequently also fault state governments for not allocating to their institutions sufficient tax-dollar subsidies to hold down tuition and remain affordable.

The conference's attendees weren't happy about being accused of covering up their institutions' failures to enroll more minority students. They objected to being described as willing participants in institutional efforts to pair public statements of noble purpose—as embodied in mission statements professing concern for diversity, equity, and the common good—with the private pursuit of selfish ends such as attaining greater wealth and prestige for their colleges and job security for themselves.

The stinging truth, however, is that rather than looking after the powerless, college administrators often seem focused on appeasing those in power. Many college leaders are far more concerned with catering to whatever populations will increase their institutions' revenue and rankings, which generally reward colleges for becoming more exclusive, than they are about providing opportunity to Black, Latino, Native American, and low-income students.

Enrollment management, despite being heralded as a means to promote campus diversity, has far too often brought more precision to efforts to benefit our society's haves and neglect its have-nots in ways that serve colleges' interests. To the extent that colleges have pursued diversity, many have done so largely in a narrow, cosmetic sense, more focused on assuring white parents that their children would interact with students from different backgrounds than on helping to provide opportunity to historically oppressed populations.

Those conference attendees who'd been thinking otherwise had traveled to Disney World from their own lands of make-believe.

COMPETING AND HIDDEN PRIORITIES

Enrollment management experts often speak of this enterprise as having an iron triangle of three broad goals: bringing in tuition revenue, raising an institution's profile, and increasing student diversity on campus. Pursuing one goal tends to come at the expense of at least one other, even though colleges often seek to balance them and generally give lip service to pursuing all three.

Enrollment managers project an image of their field as being deeply concerned with college access and diversity, and many indeed seem to care deeply about social justice and the well-being of students who are Black, Latino, Native American, low income, or first generation. A fall 2014 survey of undergraduate enrollment and admissions office leaders at 338 nonprofit four-year colleges found that racial and ethnic diversity ranked high on their agenda—not nearly as high as enrolling students with outstanding test scores and grades, but well above improving rankings.[2] College admissions experts say that enrollment leaders feel tremendous outsider pressure to increase diversity and would pursue it more aggressively if left to their own devices.[3]

But having values is one thing; sticking one's neck out for them is another. And enrollment managers work in environments that constantly demand that they compromise their principles and be willing to turn away members of disadvantaged populations in order to maintain or increase their institutions' wealth and prestige.[4] Nearly all the steps they take to improve their institutions' rankings undermine diversity, and those who won't neglect diversity in pursuit of these other objectives run the risk of being replaced. Missing net revenue goals or overseeing a drop in the rankings is much more likely to get them fired than failing to meet diversity objectives, which can be blamed on forces beyond their control.[5]

Many enrollment managers protest that it's unfair to blame them for their colleges' lack of low-income and underrepresented minority students. They describe themselves as torn between competing institutional priorities set by others further up the chain of command, and blame their institutions' presidents, trustees, and faculty members for pushing them to focus on status and selectivity to the detriment of diversity.[6] For their part, college leaders, boards, and even professors at selective colleges operate in a higher-education environment that has been steeped in an enrollment management mindset for decades, where an institution's success is measured by how well it is ranked by *U.S. News & World Report.*

As the writer Paul Tough has observed in his book *The Years That Matter Most*, college leaders' desire to advertise their institution's diversity and generosity with financial aid inevitably comes into conflict with the pressure on them to maintain tuition revenue and chase higher rankings, "and the place on each campus where that conflict plays out is the admissions office."[7] In his book *The Chosen*, an extensively researched history of admissions at Harvard, Yale, and Princeton, the sociologist Jerome Karabel posited that elite colleges retain only those admissions policies that serve their institutional interests, and the admissions system that they build around that goal requires "discretion so that gatekeepers would be free to do what they wished and opacity so that how they used their discretion would not be subject to public scrutiny."[8]

When selective colleges say they are pursuing diversity, it's important to keep in mind that the concept is not synonymous with "access," "equal opportunity," "minority enrollment," or the promotion of social justice—at least in any way that administrators will openly admit. Even before its 2023 decision *Students for Fair Admissions (SFFA) Inc v. Presidents and Fellows of Harvard College* and *SFFA v. University of North Carolina*, prohibiting colleges from using racial preferences in admissions, the US Supreme Court had barred colleges from using affirmative action for the sake of promoting social justice in its 1978 case *Regents of the University of California v. Bakke.* It also had forbidden colleges from setting aside a specific number of seats for minority group members or awarding scholarships specifically to recruit students of color. As a result, colleges have publicly spoken of diversity mainly as an educational imperative realized by enrolling enough students from different backgrounds for all to benefit from access to new perspectives, a justification that the Supreme Court had previously endorsed in its *Bakke* ruling. This is an amorphous concept that encompasses diversity by race, ethnicity, class, gender, geographic origin, and/or life experience, and it can be used to justify the inclusion—or exclusion—of just about any student.

Because the concept of diversity is so amorphous, it has fit perfectly with enrollment management because it has given colleges the freedom to pursue their strategic objectives as they wish. For example, college leaders may have preferred to increase the campus's diversity by enrolling a wealthy international student over a low-income minority one since that individual wouldn't need any institutional aid to attend. As Karabel indicates, maintaining gatekeepers' discretion is seen as paramount. Any effort that limits that discretion and forces colleges to *actually* be more diverse is seen as a threat.

The upshot is that many colleges that have given lip service to the pursuit of socioeconomic and racial diversity quietly operate enrollment management systems that have kept their student bodies disproportionately white and wealthy. This issue has not just been with private colleges. Several recent studies suggest that public universities' embrace of enrollment management since the late 1990s has led to a significant retrenchment in racial and socioeconomic diversity at those institutions.[9] The privatization of selective public universities has made the whole higher-education system even more stratified than before—pushing more and more low-income and minority students into nonselective four-year institutions and community colleges, where they have far less chance of graduating.

Allowing selective colleges to pursue diversity through race-conscious admissions has largely failed to produce greater equity in higher education. The system gave enrollment managers and other college officials far too much autonomy to define diversity in any way they saw fit. In the wake of the

Supreme Court's recent decision prohibiting the use of affirmative action in college admissions, civil rights advocates and liberal activists now must push federal and state lawmakers to take bolder action to reform selective college admissions to make these institutions both more socioeconomically and racially diverse.

The solutions needed—from banning legacy admissions, in which colleges reserve a certain number of seats for the children or family of alumni, to erecting firewalls between the admissions office and the offices of financial aid and development, to promoting "percentage plans," which provide admissions guarantees to public universities based on high school class rank—all have one thing in common: they give enrollment managers *less* discretion, not more. If progress is to be made, enrollment management needs to be reined in, or at least reoriented, to serve a far greater public purpose.

THE ORIGINS OF THE CONCEPT OF DIVERSITY

To understand how we got here, we need to go back. The period from the late 1940s through the 1970s was marked by a dramatic expansion in college access for low-income and working-class students set into motion by the GI Bill of 1944 and the Higher Education Act of 1965, which created federal student aid programs to help financially needy students gain access to college.

In addition, the end of legally mandated college segregation, the civil rights movement, and the urban unrest of the 1960s pushed the nation's most elite colleges and universities to make enrolling economically disadvantaged Black students a top priority for the first time. These highly selective institutions embraced affirmative action in the late 1960s for the sake of becoming more racially integrated and offering hope for progress to African Americans. Colleges also expanded their affirmative-action efforts to include Latino and Native American students out of the same desire to promote social justice and social mobility.

But these efforts to become more racially and socioeconomically diverse were relatively short-lived. The first major obstacle to selective colleges' efforts to enroll and graduate more minority students was practical. The nation's paucity of Black high school students who could meet these institutions' admissions standards prompted the colleges to begin adopting race-conscious admission policies in the 1960s. By as early as 1970, however, they were confronting the limits of their ability to graduate minority students from economically disadvantaged homes. Administrators typically responded to these challenges by retreating from efforts to recruit students from that population rather than seeking to strengthen support services to give these students a better chance of succeeding.

"We cannot accept the victims of social disaster, however deserving of promise they once might have been, or however romantically or emotionally an advocate (or a society) might plead for him," Harvard's admissions dean wrote at the time. The share of Harvard's Black students who came from lower-income backgrounds dropped from nearly 40 percent in 1969 to 25 percent in 1973. As other selective colleges reached the same conclusion, they began to compete intensely for a much narrower share of the Black and Latino population: middle-class students from high schools with strong academic profiles.[10] When even some of those students struggled to graduate, college leaders began changing how they spoke about disadvantage, no longer characterizing poverty as a necessary element of it and speaking of membership in certain racial and ethnic groups as a disadvantage in itself.[11]

The next challenge came on the legal front, from conservatives and libertarian activists who sought to halt or even roll back the court-imposed desegregation and integration of education underway since the 1950s. They had watched advocates of the racial integration of education make great strides since the Supreme Court's 1954 *Brown v. Board of Education* ruling. That decision had overturned the court's notorious 1896 *Plessy v. Ferguson* decision, which held that racially "separate but equal" public accommodations could be reconciled with the Fourteenth Amendment's Equal Protection Clause. Although the *Brown* decision focused on public elementary and secondary schools, its conclusion that racially segregated educational accommodations are inherently unequal, and thus violate the individual right to equal protection enshrined under the Fourteenth Amendment, spurred both court-ordered and voluntary integration efforts at all education levels.

The opponents of such racial desegregation and integration efforts gained traction in their fight against them by coopting the same individual rights–based logic used by the other side. They argued that the equal-protection rights of white students were being trampled by overly zealous efforts to remedy past discrimination, especially in situations where that discrimination had not actually been mandated by policy or law. Their first major legal victories helping to turn the tide came at the K–12 level, most notably with the Supreme Court's 1974 *Milliken v. Bradley* decision involving metropolitan Detroit, which held that suburban school districts could not be compelled to remedy any racial segregation of urban schools not caused by their own actions.

The fight against affirmative action in higher education began with a lawsuit filed by Allan P. Bakke, a former marine officer who had been rejected by the University of California at Davis's medical school. Despite never being found guilty of racial discrimination, the university had adopted a quota system ensuring minority students a predetermined share of seats in each entering class.[12]

The opposing sides in the *Regents of the University of California v. Bakke* case presented it to the Supreme Court in 1977 as hinging on the question of whether the US Constitution permits colleges to favor minority applicants to remedy societal discrimination. Four liberal justices believed that it did, given the nation's historically rooted inequalities, and were willing to uphold the medical school's use of quotas. Four conservative justices disagreed, arguing that it would be folly for courts to let colleges continue trying to sort out which racial and ethnic groups were owed favorable treatment at the expense of others to remedy historical injustices.

The ninth member of the court, Justice Lewis Powell, was too conservative in ideology to accept the remedial justification but too conservative in temperament to sign a decision requiring huge changes in higher education. In cobbling together a compromise opinion, he seized on a rationale that colleges and other higher-education associations had introduced into the Supreme Court's deliberations mainly through friend-of-the-court briefs: diversity's importance to education. Up until this case, college leaders had said little about the importance of diversity, and they presented the argument in their briefs without offering empirical evidence to back it up. Meanwhile, the rationale had played little role in most of the other justices' opinions. Nevertheless, Powell's compromise opinion rejected the use of admissions quotas as too heavy-handed but stated that the government had a compelling interest in letting colleges consider applicants' race and ethnicity as a "plus" factor to derive diversity's educational benefits.[13]

The Supreme Court's 1978 *Bakke* ruling had the effect of ensuring that any college that had not been racially segregated in the past would be under no legal obligation to increase minority enrollments, and in fact would put itself in legal jeopardy if it tried to do so through a heavy-handed consideration of applicants' race. Considering applicants' race as more than a thumb on the scale, as well as using race-conscious admissions policies to remedy societal discrimination, thus were taken off the table. The only exceptions were those covered by court orders requiring the desegregation of public colleges that had been racially exclusive under Jim Crow.[14]

The *Bakke* ruling replaced an affirmative-action rationale grounded in history with one grounded in educational theory. It also helped establish *diversity* as a buzzword and goal in higher education, the business community, and elsewhere. The ruling gave those who pulled the levers of power an excuse to stop doing the hard work of remedying current and past discrimination and instead seek only to have enrollments or workforces that loosely reflected the diversity of American society.[15] The decision also raised questions that colleges and the courts would struggle henceforth to resolve: What exactly constitutes a "plus" factor? What are the purported educational benefits that colleges seek from diversity, and do they truly exist? What populations does a college need to enroll to achieve such benefits, and in what numbers?

Eventually, it became clear just how amorphous the concept of "diversity" was. Pursuing diversity could be used to justify sincere efforts to promote equal opportunity and social justice. But it also could be used as an excuse to retreat from such efforts. When colleges' desire to be seen as diverse came into conflict with their pursuit of money and prestige, many sought to reconcile the two by defining *diversity* in narrow terms that minimized any associated financial costs or potential erosion of their reputation and ranking. They'd compete aggressively for the limited populations of Black or Latino students with outstanding SAT scores or financially well-off parents, while largely ignoring others. And they withheld admissions offers or financial aid from low-income white students, whose contribution to diversity would be invisible to the naked eye.[16]

Colleges might have viewed themselves as contributing to campus "diversity" by enrolling a Saudi prince, a Swedish soccer player, or the child of a multimillionaire who lives in an especially remote part of Montana, based on small numbers of similar people on campus and the assumption that many of their students have not been around such people before. Historically Black colleges sometimes fostered educational diversity by enrolling white students. Programs in fields traditionally dominated by women, such as nursing, promoted diversity by enrolling men.[17] Although colleges cannot technically count Black or Latino international students in tracking and reporting their enrollments from racial and ethnic minority groups in the United States, such students do help contribute to perceived levels of racial and ethnic diversity on campus. A substantial share of selective colleges reported assigning increased importance to international diversity when surveyed in the wake of a 2013 Supreme Court decision that emphasized the need for strict judicial scrutiny of race-conscious admissions policies.[18]

Barred by *Bakke* from explicitly using racial preferences to help bring about social justice, and embarrassed by their past failures to retain minority students from disadvantaged backgrounds who had arrived at college poorly prepared, selective colleges generally shifted their efforts away from enrolling economically disadvantaged minority students. They increasingly competed for well-prepared minority applicants, mainly from the disproportionately small share of minority families in the middle and upper middle classes. They also sought out other populations of Black and Latino students whose particular circumstances had spared them some of the disadvantages endured by others, such as biracial students and immigrants (or their children) who had arrived in the United States relatively wealthy or well educated. By 1999, a year in which immigrants accounted for 3 percent of the nation's Black population, immigrants accounted for 9 percent—and the children of immigrants, about 25 percent—of Black freshmen entering one heavily studied set of twenty-eight selective colleges. About two-fifths of Black students at four Ivy League universities—Columbia, Princeton, the University of Pennsylvania, and Yale—were either immigrants or the children of immigrants.[19]

The question of how to view the admission of relatively wealthy immigrants who are Black is a loaded one. On the one hand, they're often subjected to the same discrimination experienced by African Americans in general. An upper-middle-class Black professional from Jamaica or an African country has as much reason to fear encounters with police as working-class Black descendants of slaves. On the other hand, it's hard to say how much credit colleges deserve for accessibility when their Black enrollment numbers are padded with students who came from backgrounds that spared them hardships experienced by African Americans whose families have been here for centuries. The law professor Lani Guinier triggered an uproar at a 2003 reunion of Harvard's Black alumni by calling diversity there "a question of aesthetics" because a majority of the university's Black students are immigrants, the children of immigrants, or the children of biracial couples.[20] Black students who protested Cornell University's racial climate in 2017 complained that its Black population on campus "disproportionately represents international or first-generation African or Caribbean students." They demanded that Cornell define underrepresented Black students as only those whose families have been in this country more than two generations.[21]

The frustrations expressed by the Cornell protestors were at root about a system that essentially values diversity as an academic concept, rather than one trying to make up for past discrimination or to promote social justice or social mobility. Under enrollment management's iron triangle, choosing more-affluent Black immigrants over Black students from less-privileged backgrounds was a no-brainer. Enrolling these students, who might not need financial aid, allowed selective colleges to achieve greater diversity without reducing net revenue. And because these students tend to be well educated and were unlikely to drop out for financial reasons, they posed little risk to colleges' rankings and prestige.

ENROLLMENT MANAGEMENT AND THE RETREAT FROM EQUITY

Even as the Supreme Court heard the *Bakke* case, four-year colleges' priorities were changing. As noted earlier, selective colleges made great strides in the decades following World War II toward making higher education more accessible. But by the late 1970s, sagging enrollments, a souring economy, and growing antitax sentiment put enormous pressure on colleges' budgets, prompting selective colleges to retreat from commitments to equity that had carried high price tags and obliged them to take in large numbers of financially needy students.

The country's rightward shift in politics, culminating in Ronald Reagan's presidential victory in 1981, made the colleges' retreat easier. Pushing for substantial cuts in federal student aid spending, the Reagan administration argued that the primary responsibility for paying for college should rest with students and their families. As a result, government-backed student loans replaced grants as the main form of federal assistance for students to help pay for college. The view that going to college was more of a private than public good took hold among many federal and state policy makers, who cut back government support and increasingly left colleges to their own devices to raise revenue.

By the late 1980s, many private colleges had substantially raised their prices and began embracing enrollment management as a path away from financial trouble. That meant that these institutions removed whatever firewalls had stood between their admissions and financial aid offices, and began awarding financial aid strategically as a means of aggressively competing for students who were wealthy or exceptionally academically talented. The debut of the *U.S. News* rankings in the 1980s accelerated this process by creating purportedly objective measures of institutional quality closely tied to how successfully colleges competed for students who had high SAT scores or families wealthy enough to donate large sums. Colleges that didn't award financial aid based on strategic considerations risked reputationally falling behind those that did. The enrollment management industry's emergence in the 1980s created a supply of well-paid private consultants who encouraged private, and then later public, higher-education institutions to award institutional aid based on considerations other than financial need to help increase net revenues and rise up the rankings.

Enrollment management represented an excellent mechanism for shrouding potentially unpopular decisions in opacity. With it, administrators could treat various policies and practices as knobs that could be adjusted to get specific results—including a desired racial, ethnic, and socioeconomic mix of students—that had little obvious connection to the means used to achieve them.[22] They didn't need to publicly admit wanting to reduce the enrollment of financially needy students because enrollment management let them achieve the same result by pursuing more palatable stated objectives, such as increases in the average SAT scores of entering freshmen or in out-of-state enrollments.[23] Enrollment management's predictive tools helped colleges tweak marketing and recruitment practices to target some population segments while skirting others. These tools also let enrollment managers recalibrate the balance between need-based and merit-based aid to attract the students they most desired, who all too often were upper-middle-class white students with high SAT scores.[24]

Under the *Brown* decision and various lower-court decisions and federal civil-rights laws that it helped inspire, colleges were prohibited from engaging in outright, formalized discrimination based on race, ethnicity, or sex. But nothing in the law precluded them from engaging in outright discrimination based solely on economic status. At least as a legal matter, low-income students remained fair game for exclusion. Because the nation's Black, Latino, and Native American populations were disproportionately low income, they inevitably were hurt most by systemic discrimination against the working class and poor unless they were somehow shielded from it by race-conscious admission or financial-aid policies.[25]

Tweaks by a college to increase its revenue or improve its *U.S. News* ranking tended to erode enrollments of populations that were socioeconomically disadvantaged by definition, such as low-income or first-generation students, or disproportionately likely to be disadvantaged, such as students who were Black, Latino, Native American, or members of certain Asian American ethnic groups. Conversely, efforts to increase enrollments from these populations tended to produce declines in revenues and rankings, which were tied to institutional wealth and academic selectivity.[26] Unwilling or unable to expand to accommodate big enrollment increases, colleges characterized some forms of diversity as in a zero-sum competition with others, arguing that low-income, first-generation, and minority students all were vying for limited seats in freshman classes or funds from a limited financial-aid pool.[27] Robert J. Massa, a former vice president for enrollment at Dickinson College, recalled in a recent interview that when he took that post in 1999, the college had low Black and Latino enrollments but exceptionally high enrollments of low-income, first-generation white students from that state. "We needed to balance that," he said, and the college did so by redirecting resources toward minority recruitment at the expense of its enrollments of socioeconomically disadvantaged white students.[28]

The embrace of enrollment management by public universities, which have long provided low-income and working-class students a gateway to the middle class or higher, has been especially damaging for higher-education equity. Public university leaders say that they've adopted the enrollment management strategies of their private college counterparts out of necessity. State disinvestment has left their institutions scrambling to find alternative revenue sources, such as affluent out-of-state students, who generally pay more than in-state students even after receiving tuition discounts. But less talked about is the fact that wealthy out-of-state students often provide an additional benefit to these institutions: they tend to come with the high standardized test scores that the *U.S. News* rankings reward. For many selective public universities, raising revenue and rankings go hand in hand.

Several recent studies suggest that public universities' increasingly aggressive pursuit of out-of-state students has come at the expense of low-income and minority students. In a study published in 2019, for example, researchers at the University of California at Los Angeles examined the recruitment priorities of fifteen public research universities by sending them public-records requests and scouring university admissions website data for listings of the high schools that the institutions' recruiters visited. They found that twelve of the fifteen made more out-of-state than in-state recruitment visits—seven made more than twice as many—and their out-of-state visits were concentrated in affluent communities within major metropolitan areas. Most of these universities were significantly less likely to visit out-of-state public high schools with a high percentage of Black, Latino, and Native American students, even after controlling for factors such as enrollment size and student achievement. "In contrast to rhetoric from university leaders, our findings suggest strong socioeconomic and racial biases in the enrollment priorities of many public research universities," the report said.[29]

A recent study by the Education Trust found that six-tenths of the nation's 101 most selective public universities have experienced a decline in Black students' relative share of enrollment over the past twenty years. "While a handful of institutions have been able to improve, access at the overwhelming majority of institutions has gotten worse," said the Education Trust's report on its findings. "Overall, these selective public institutions are regressing toward segregation."[30]

The net result of the use of enrollment management over the past several decades has been a hardening in the stratification of the nation's higher-education system. The children of the wealthy and highly educated—a population that is disproportionately white as a result of structural barriers and longstanding racial and ethnic discrimination—are tracked toward prestigious four-year and advanced degrees that confer status and wealth. The children of disadvantaged segments of the population—Black, Latino, Native American, and low-income families—are increasingly tracked away from college entirely or into community colleges and nonselective four-year institutions, where they face uncertain prospects of earning academic credentials that will ever land them a decent job.[31]

In terms of gaining *any* access to higher education, our nation's Black, Latino, and Native American populations have, in fact, made significant strides. Their share of all postsecondary enrollment has been growing at a time when technological change has made education beyond high school a prerequisite for doing a rising share of low-wage and blue-collar jobs.[32] However, more than seven-tenths of the growth in absolute numbers of Black and Latino individuals going on to postsecondary education since the mid-1990s has been at the nation's 3,250 open-access, two- and four-year colleges. Meanwhile, more than eight-tenths of white enrollment growth had been at the nation's 468 most selective colleges, where white students remain overrepresented and where their share of overall enrollment has declined much less than their share of the nation's college-aged population.[33]

Largely as a result of this stratification, these minority populations have lost ground when it comes to their relative access to the bachelor's degrees that are increasingly a prerequisite for good jobs. The gap in bachelor's degree attainment between white students and Black and Latino students increased from 15 percentage points in 1980 to 21 percentage points as of 2015.[34]

Much of the widening of the gap stems from the lower graduation rates at the less-selective institutions where Black and Latino students are disproportionately relegated, regardless of academic potential. One recent analysis of federal data by the Georgetown University Center on Education and the Workforce found that a Black or Latino student who scores at least 1000 on the SAT has an 81 percent chance of graduating if enrolled at a selective college but only a 46 percent chance of graduating if enrolled at an open-access college. Only about 33 percent of Latinos and 26 percent of Black students who start at a two-year college get any postsecondary credential within six years, and just 9 percent of Black students and 11 percent of Latino students who start at such a school earn a bachelor's degree within six years.[35]

Black, Latino, or Native Americans might still be completely absent at most colleges—or at least represent even smaller shares of enrollments than they do today—if not for their past successes in mounting legal challenges to discriminatory admissions policies and in protesting and lobbying for greater access. Their progress has come sporadically, often in response to some event, such as a highly publicized racist incident, that enabled them to mobilize enough political pressure on colleges to counterbalance that which routinely comes from powerful defenders of the racial status quo.[36] At other times, the interests of low-income and minority students almost always take a back seat to colleges' desire to cater to populations that represent sure sources of revenue. This has especially been the case during economic downturns, but it has increasingly become the norm as more and more colleges have embraced enrollment management. Market forces and an increasingly competitive market for students have ramped up pressure on colleges to serve families that are wealthy enough to donate and pay full tuition.[37]

AFFIRMATIVE ACTION FOR THE WEALTHY

Affirmative action opponents have succeeded in persuading much of the public that minority students who attend selective colleges are there because they have received unfair advantages, while white students at these institutions are there based on their merits. This is a myth. In fact, researchers have found that at the 146 most selective colleges, white students who enroll despite failing to meet the institution's advertised admissions standards far outnumber Black, Latinx, and Native American students whose race or ethnicity tip the scales in their favor.[38]

Many seats in the entering classes of the most exclusive colleges are taken by affluent white students who entered through side doors, with their family's cash and connections enabling them to bypass the regular competitive process and receive preference over better-qualified applicants. A recent study found that 43 percent of white applicants that Harvard admitted received preferential treatment in the admissions process either because they were athletes, family members of alumni, the children of faculty, or they had ties to donors.[39] One key advantage that white wealthy families have over others are the legacy preferences that selective colleges routinely provide applicants if their parents or relatives are alumni. Research has shown that legacies are far more likely than other applicants to come from families at the top of the income scale.[40] And colleges have been known to reserve seats for the children of alumni who have made substantial donations to these institutions.

Just how big an edge does legacy status confer on applicants? According to a 2011 analysis of data from thirty highly selective colleges, prospective students whose relatives were alumni had a 23.3 percentage point advantage over other applicants in terms of the likelihood of being admitted. That bump nearly doubled to 45.1 percentage points if their parents were the alumni in question.[41]

Selective colleges defend the use of legacy preferences by saying that they strengthen the sense of community and build greater alumni loyalty. In addition, enrollment managers like enrolling legacy students because they are very likely to enroll if admitted, boosting a college's "yield" rate, and they don't typically need financial aid, increasing its net revenue.

Still, college leaders are aware of how controversial legacy preferences are and, as a result, they are not exactly transparent about the favoritism that they show to alumni.[42] Case in point: in a 2019 editorial, the *Tufts Daily* student newspaper took the university's administration to task for hypocrisy for quietly holding an annual matriculation-day reception for legacy admits and their families, even as other students went through orientation programs described as exploring the "impact of power and privilege." The editorial alleged that "wealth and heritage remain a ticket into Tufts University." Noting that university administrators had omitted any mention of the legacy student reception from the event listings in that year's orientation guide, the editorial concluded: "Worse, they seek to bury it, because they know it is wrong."[43]

Also troubling is the extent to which college presidents, trustees, government relations officials, and other administrators inappropriately lobby admissions offices on behalf of the offspring of family, friends, business associates, public officials, and other well-connected and deep-pocketed individuals, as well as donors. While it's hardly a secret that colleges reserve seats for the progeny of big donors, few admissions directors are as candid as Middlebury College's dean of enrollment services was when he told the *New York*

Times that "every admissions office in the country is paying attention to families' ability to make a major donation."[44]

Examining 1,950 pages of emails that it received under open-records laws from thirteen public universities, the *Chronicle of Higher Education* found that "university trustees and some presidents inquire routinely about the fates of individual applicants."[45] High-profile scandals that have occurred at the University of California at Los Angeles, the University of Illinois at Urbana-Champaign, and the University of Texas at Austin make clear how readily college admissions offices bend the rules when pressure is applied from leadership.[46] These universities were found to have run "shadow admissions systems" where applicants' qualifications mattered less than their parents' clout.[47]

In response to the scandals, the three universities adopted new rules aimed to prevent—or at least limit—such blatant meddling and favoritism in the admissions process. The University of Illinois at Urbana-Champaign, for example, "created an admissions log requiring admissions officials to note information about all inquiries except those made by an applicant or his or her parents, guardians, or high-school counselor," according to the *Chronicle*.[48] Such policies, and stronger ones, are needed nationwide to guard against this type of corruption.

CONFRONTING IDEOLOGICAL LIMITS

The affirmative action debate—a product and continuing reflection of our nation's deep racial divisions—imposed artificial, ideologically motivated limits on any consideration of reforms in college admissions that would increase selective colleges' enrollments of underrepresented minority students. It not only led to legal restrictions on how much colleges could consider applicants' race, but also hindered promising alternative means of potentially achieving greater socioeconomic diversity.

Pursuing the vague goal of achieving greater diversity mostly allowed selective public and private colleges to pursue their strategic objectives as they wished. They could appear altruistic without having to do the hard work of actually making their campuses accessible and affordable for low-income and minority students. While some colleges have strived to make their campuses more racially and socioeconomically diverse, many more have used enrollment management tools to keep their campuses predominantly white and wealthy.

Colleges' overriding goal in the fight over affirmative action has been to preserve their autonomy to enroll whomever they choose. Any efforts to limit that autonomy and force colleges to be more equitable have been seen as threats. Take, for example, percentage plans, admissions guarantees based on high-school class rank. These admissions guarantees emerged in the years following the 1978 *Bakke* decision as the libertarian and conservative assault on the use of affirmative action in college admissions intensified.

Although the *Bakke* decision had left race-conscious admissions policies alive in the federal courts based on their educational rationale, it did not preclude later efforts to abolish them through legislation, ballot measures, or the actions of college governing boards. Since the mid-1990s, opponents of these policies made substantial progress on all three fronts. Public universities were barred from using race- or ethnicity-based admission preferences under resolutions adopted by the governing boards of the University of California and Florida university systems, state laws enacted in Idaho and New Hampshire, and state ballot measures passed in Arizona, California, Michigan, Nebraska, and Washington State.[49] In response to many of these actions, state policy makers scrambled to come up with race-neutral means of ensuring diverse enrollment. Texas lawmakers adopted a measure guaranteeing in-state students in the top 10 percent of their high-school class admission to the public university of their choice. The governing boards of the University of California and Florida's public universities adopted similar guarantees, covering students in the top 4 percent and top 20 percent of their high-school class, respectively.[50]

By exploiting the stark disparities in Texas high school enrollment to generate diversity, Texas's top 10 percent plan has made the University of Texas at Austin nearly as diverse racially and ethnically, and far more diverse geographically and socioeconomically, than it had been previously. The plan forced the flagship campus to take far more low-income students from both rural and urban areas and many fewer affluent students from the suburbs and private schools.[51]

As Paul Tough writes in *The Years That Matter Most*, the secret of the Texas plan's success in making the flagship more socioeconomically diverse is that it effectively curtailed the university's ability to use "the tools of enrollment management" to recruit two-thirds of its incoming class because those seats are reserved for those who are automatically admitted. The admissions office retains discretion over the remaining third of the class and uses it to recruit the same types of students that other selective public universities are increasingly pursuing: "mostly wealthy and mostly white, packed with full-paying students with high SAT scores."[52]

The percentage plan also forced the University of Texas at Austin to create student support services to help those automatic admits who were not as academically prepared as their more-privileged classmates and who might feel isolated on the sprawling campus. These support services have been extremely effective in raising student retention and graduation rates. From 2012 to 2018, four-year graduation rates rose from 40 percent to 61 percent for students with family incomes low enough to receive Pell Grants; from 37 percent to 58 percent for Black students; and from 43 percent to 64 percent for Latino students.[53]

Despite the promise that they offer of making public universities more diverse socioeconomically, percentage plans have had few champions. Many liberal activists and civil rights groups, including some who initially supported these plans as a promising means for achieving enrollment diversity, have opposed them out of fear that any remaining judicial support for race-conscious admissions would be undermined if the plans were seen as a viable alternative to affirmative action.[54] To be fair, the ability of percentage plans to maintain racial diversity at public universities depends on the demographics of the states in which they are employed. The plans work best in racially and ethnically diverse states that have large numbers of high schools with predominantly minority enrollments. They wouldn't bring greater racial diversity to public universities in overwhelmingly white states, but they could bring more socioeconomic and geographic diversity.

The higher-education establishment has also resisted percentage plans—but for less altruistic reasons. Percentage plans take away colleges' discretion to admit whomever they want, and, as the University of Texas at Austin example shows, force universities to do the hard work of serving students who don't come from privilege.

It's perfectly understandable that civil rights advocates and liberal activists have fought so hard over the decades to try to protect the use of affirmative action in admissions from the continual onslaught that libertarian and conservative groups have waged. But now that the battle over the use of racial preferences in higher education is over, they must push policy makers to carry out reforms in admissions and financial aid that will make colleges both more socioeconomically and racially diverse. Nothing prevents the federal government and states from using their power over the purse strings to prod selective colleges to reform their enrollment management practices to promote diversity and better serve the public good.

Federal and state policy makers need to recognize that they can no longer put blind trust in enrollment managers and college leaders to live up to their institutions' mission statements. These administrations need *less* discretion, not more. A good start is the building of institutional firewalls precluding inappropriate interference in admissions policies by the wealthy or powerful and the administrative offices charged with placating them. Decisions related to academic standards and enrollment composition should not be getting made by administrators concerned with alumni relations, development, or political lobbying. There needs to be a ban on legacy admissions and much more use of admissions guarantees based on class rank, which bring both transparency and fairness to the process and promote diversity by identifying students who excelled in the face of disadvantage. And there must be a far greater effort to ensure that colleges use their institutional aid to meet financial need rather than to pursue privileged students.

Otherwise, a huge chasm will remain between colleges' rhetoric in support of diversity and their actual deeds.

CHAPTER 8

The Dangerous Game of Financial Aid Leveraging

Stephen J. Burd

In 2011, Clemson University's longtime goal of becoming a top twenty public university in the *U.S. News & World Report* rankings hit a snag. James Barker had set that goal a decade earlier when he became Clemson's president, and his administration had been laser-focused on achieving it since.[1] "It is the thing around which almost everything revolves for the president's office," Catherine Watt, a university official, said in a speech at the Association for Institutional Research's annual forum in 2009.[2]

In her talk, met at times with gasps from the audience for its unusual candor, Watt laid out Clemson's strategy for climbing up the rankings. Under Barker's leadership, the university stopped admitting freshmen who were not in the top third of their high school class because *U.S. News* rewards colleges for greater selectivity; ran a campaign to get graduates to send the university $5 apiece to artificially inflate its alumni giving rate, another key metric; and failed the university's competitors in the reputational survey that weighs heavily in the rankings. "We have walked the fine line between illegal, unethical, and really interesting," Watt said.[3]

By decade's end, Barker had gotten Clemson close to the goal. But ever-increasing competition from the school's rivals slowed its momentum.

Clemson officials struggled to yield admitted applicants, forcing the school to accept more students than they wanted. A rising acceptance rate—the share of applicants admitted—threatened to jeopardize the university's progress in the rankings. Things took a turn for the worse in the fall of 2011, when the school missed its enrollment target by three hundred students despite admitting nearly two-thirds of applicants.[4]

Desperate, Clemson turned to outside enrollment management consultants for help. Huron Education provided the type of advice that such consultants typically do. The company recommended that Clemson create "a new organizational structure for enrollment management to elevate its importance within the university" and focus financial aid on "the most academically talented admitted students." The university's Board of Trustees embraced Huron's recommendations and "directed the administration to move forward immediately," the consulting company boasted.[5]

Clemson moved quickly to change its financial aid policies. In the fall of 2012, the university increased spending on non-need-based "merit" aid by more than $6 million, bringing the total to $17 million after adjusting for inflation. Between 2012 and 2019, the university's annual spending on non-need-based aid to relatively affluent students grew nearly 160 percent, to about $28 million. The share of non-needy freshmen receiving institutional aid, mostly in the form of discounts off tuition, increased from about one-in-five to one-in-three, with the average annual award doubling to more than $6,000.[6]

As Huron promised, Clemson's generosity with non-need-based aid helped the university lower its acceptance rate and improve its yield. And the average SAT scores of its incoming class rose by about 80 percentage points.[7] But were these "improvements" worth the cost? By its own standards, Clemson is still not a top twenty public university (Clemson tied for thirty-one in the most recent rankings).[8] And, more consequently, the changes were made largely on the backs of low- and lower-middle-income students—many of whom are students of color—who have benefited little from the university's generosity with tuition discounts to non-needy students.

In fact, these financially needy students have seen the cost of attending Clemson rise substantially since 2012. Not only has Clemson's list price increased significantly, but the university now meets, on average, just 52 percent of the financial needs of its freshmen student aid recipients, about

20 percentage points less than it covered in 2010.[9] As a result, financially needy students are facing much larger funding gaps to attend Clemson than their counterparts did a decade ago.

In the fall of 2019, for example, Clemson freshmen from families making $30,000 or less paid an average net price—the amount of money that students and their parents have to pay after all grant and scholarship aid is deducted from the list price—of $13,744, representing nearly half or more of their families' yearly earnings. Those from families making between $30,001 and $48,000 were on the hook for $16,650.[10]

How exactly are cash-strapped families supposed to come up with this money each year while their children are in college? The university has a solution, courtesy of Parent PLUS Loans, a federal program created in 1980 to help middle- and upper-middle-income students afford expensive colleges by allowing them to borrow up to the cost of attendance.[11] Unlike federal student loans, which are strictly limited to $5,500 to $7,500 per year for most students under the age of twenty-four, parents can borrow up to the full cost of attendance of the school, regardless of their income. To obtain the loans, they only need to pass a lax adverse credit history check that does not assess whether the borrower will be able to repay the debt. In other words, the families of low- and lower-middle-income students who are admitted to Clemson are finding that they often have little choice but to take out hefty PLUS Loans they are unlikely to be able to repay.

In fall 2019, Clemson families borrowed nearly $44 million in PLUS Loans. Of that total, four-fifths went to the families of financially needy students.[12] Meanwhile, the US Department of Education's College Scorecard indicates that 40 percent of PLUS Loan borrowers whose children graduated from Clemson in 2019 and 2020 were the families of students who received Pell Grants, the federal government's primary source of aid for low-income students. These families borrowed a median of $23,749 in PLUS debt while their children were in college.[13]

For low-income families with few assets, borrowing PLUS Loans is a very risky proposition. Like federal student loans, Parent PLUS debt generally cannot be discharged in bankruptcy, and the loans are subject to the government's extraordinary debt collection powers, including wage garnishment and partial offsets of defaulted borrowers' Social Security benefits.[14]

Back in 2009, Watt had shocked her audience with her candor about Clemson's enrollment management strategies. "We have favored merit over access in a poor state," Watt said. "We are more elite, more white, more privileged."[15] Her statement remains true today, if not even more so. What's changed, however, is that Clemson now is leaving many families of students who do not meet those criteria in harm's way, loaded down with PLUS Loan debt they can't afford.

PART OF THE GAME PLAN

Unfortunately, the financial aid strategies that Clemson has pursued are hardly unique. An analysis that we at the nonpartisan think tank New America conducted for this book examined institutional financial aid data at 575 selective private and public colleges and universities over a twenty-year period and found that as these colleges have focused their institutional grant aid on wealthier students, low-income students have increasingly turned to risky Parent PLUS Loans to fund the difference.[16]

In fact, leaving low- and lower-middle-income students with substantial amounts of unmet need and encouraging their families to take out Parent PLUS Loans is part and parcel of the financial aid leveraging strategies that private enrollment management firms, such as EAB, Ruffalo Noel Levitz (RNL), and Huron, have been pushing colleges to use in awarding institutional aid.

Under these strategies, institutional aid is not used to meet financial need. With enrollment managers primarily focused on increasing colleges' net revenue and rankings, covering low-income students' financial need is considered wasteful. Instead, enrollment managers use financial aid leveraging to determine the precise price points that it will take to enroll different groups of students without spending a dollar more than needed. At selective colleges, the largest discounts go to the students they want most: typically, the best applicants and those who otherwise can pay full freight and help boost the institutions' bottom line.[17]

"Aid leveraging is an analytical tool that enables admissions and financial aid administrators to estimate the amount of financial aid (regardless of formal need formulas) that would be necessary to increase the probability that a student with a specified set of characteristics would enroll," Donald Hossler wrote in 2000, when he was Indiana University at Bloomington's vice chancellor of enrollment services. "This approach raises tuition and uses large portions of the increase to provide financial aid to prospective college students in order to induce them to matriculate," he explained. "Although these financial aid inducements might be used to meet student financial need, the intent behind the strategy is to use the award as a merit award that will help individual campuses more effectively 'court' or recruit students with higher grades, with more talent, or with lower levels of financial need."[18]

We found that selective public and private colleges and universities spent nearly $101 billion of their own financial aid dollars on students who lack financial need between 2000 and 2020. About $1 out of every $4 of institutional aid that these institutions awarded went to non-needy students, those whom the federal government deems able to afford college without its help.

Selective colleges' use of non-need-based aid to recruit relatively affluent students skyrocketed over the past two decades from an inflation-adjusted $2 billion annually in 2000 to over $8 billion yearly by 2020. Breaking those figures down by college sector, our analysis found the following:

- The 307 selective private colleges increased the annual amount they spent on non-need-based aid to $4.9 billion, from about $1.4 billion.
- The 268 selective public universities increased the yearly amount they spent on non-need-based aid to $3.3 billion, from $931 million.

To be clear, many selective colleges use these financial aid leveraging strategies for only a subset of their students, and some may use a portion of the additional revenue that they receive from recruiting affluent students to boost need-based aid. And some colleges have used these strategies to recruit high-achieving students of color to increase the diversity of their institutions' students.[19]

However, the country's largest private enrollment management firms aggressively market financial aid leveraging or optimization products that are designed to help colleges use all their aid to pursue the most desirable prospective students.[20] As EAB states in its marketing material, "Our Financial Aid Optimization program ensures that every dollar you commit to aid is used to further your enrollment and net tuition revenue goals."[21] Our analysis suggests that while most selective colleges initially used financial aid leveraging for just a subset of their students, more and more public and private four-year colleges are increasingly spending the bulk of their aid for these purposes.

The data show that spending on non-need-based aid has escalated rapidly since 2013, as the country recovered from the financial crisis that had started six years earlier, when the economy fell into a deep recession and credit crunch. In fact, more than half the $101 billion that selective colleges spent on non-need-based aid since 2000 was awarded from 2013 to 2020. In recent years, the schools' spending on non-need-based aid has outpaced need-based aid spending.

The spending surge has been especially dramatic at public universities. While it took from 2000 to 2015 for selective public universities to increase their yearly spending on non-need-based aid from just under $1 billion to $2 billion in inflation-adjusted numbers, it took them only five more years to reach $3 billion. It seems clear that the substantial cutbacks that state legislators made in per-student spending during the Great Recession pushed many more public universities to embrace enrollment management and leverage their financial aid. With state spending still lagging during the recovery and enrollment growth slowing, these institutions became more determined to use their aid to pursue wealthy out-of-state students with decent standardized test scores, who could help them raise their revenue and rise up the rankings.[22]

In addition, the emergence of EAB as an eight-hundred-pound gorilla in the consulting business, after it purchased the enrollment management firm Royall & Co. for $850 million in 2014, appears to have raised the stakes.[23] EAB, now owned by two private equity firms, has grown its business by marketing products that encourage colleges to use all their aid to find "the right students," as the company suggestively states on its website.[24] The company's competitors were either already offering similar products or felt compelled to follow suit.

In his book *The Debt Trap*, the *Wall Street Journal*'s Josh Mitchell explains the role that the enrollment management companies play in financial aid leveraging:

> Firms like Ruffalo Noel Levitz help schools determine how much to discount for each student to make as much money as possible overall. The firms use hundreds of variables—including race, home address, SAT scores, parental education level and wealth, and even how many times the student visited

> campus during recruiting—to gauge each student's "price sensitivity." That phrase refers to how much his or her family might be willing and able to pay. The firms study the behavior of the past three years of freshman classes and then suggest, down to the dollar, what the school should charge students of different characteristics.[25]

At colleges that work with consultants to leverage their aid, a portion of this money will go to financially needy students. But seldom will these funds come close to meeting these students' need. To put it bluntly, at these institutions, leaving low-income students with large funding gaps is part of the game plan to get the students that they want the most.

Indeed, our analysis found that at the same time that selective colleges accelerated their spending on non-need-based aid, they left low-income and other financially needy students with greater amounts of unmet need. Between 2000 and 2020, the average amount of financial need these colleges covered of their freshman student aid recipients dropped substantially: from 90 percent to 85 percent at private colleges and from 74 percent to 65 percent at public universities. A deeper dive into the data reveals that over this time period:

- Nearly two-thirds of selective public universities decreased the amount of financial need they covered by an average of 18 percentage points.
- Nearly three-fifths of selective private colleges decreased the amount of financial need they covered by an average of 11 percentage points.

And our analysis found that many of these institutions are encouraging low- and lower-middle-income families to borrow PLUS Loans to cover their funding gaps. Unsurprisingly, the families of Pell recipients attending expensive private colleges take out larger debt loads than their counterparts at public universities. But at public universities, generally a larger share of Pell recipients' families borrow these loans as follows:

- At nearly two in five selective public universities, the families of Pell Grant recipients made up more than half of PLUS Loan borrowers, and at more than three in four, they made up more than 40 percent. At one in four selective private colleges, these families made up more than half of PLUS Loan borrowers, and at about three in five, they made up more than 40 percent.

- At selective private colleges, Pell recipients' families with PLUS Loans borrowed a median debt load of $26,003.[26] At public universities, these families borrowed a median debt load of $12,445.[27]

For colleges, Parent PLUS Loans represent easy credit that they can offer low-income families to cover their funding gaps.[28] PLUS Loans are readily available so long as potential borrowers don't have bad credit. And because colleges are not held accountable if borrowers go into default on this debt, their administrators have the luxury of not having to worry about how hazardous these loans may be for the families borrowing them. As a 2019 Urban Institute report stated, the Parent PLUS Loan program is "a no-strings attached revenue source for colleges and universities, with the risk shared only by parents and the government," which loses money if borrowers default.[29]

To make matters worse, low-income families are not always aware of the risks that they take on when they borrow PLUS Loans, which have higher interest rates and origination fees than federal loans and offer less flexible repayment options. Incredibly, many colleges include PLUS debt in the aid packages that they offer students without fully explaining the terms of these loans. A 2022 analysis of financial-aid-award letters that the US Government Accountability Office conducted estimated that 31 percent of a nationally representative sample of 176 colleges included PLUS Loans directly in "their financial aid offers," making it appear that parents don't have any choice but to borrow the loans if their child wishes to attend the school. And 21 percent of the colleges "did not list key details" in the award letters about how PLUS Loans "differ from student loans."[30] Keeping students and their families in the dark about PLUS Loans' potential hazards appears to be another trick that enrollment management firms encourage colleges to play to entice students to come to the schools.

Despite the tens of billions of dollars that the federal government spends on financial aid to help low-income students afford college, neither the US Department of Education nor Congress has taken a serious look at how colleges are putting low-income families at financial risk. Higher-education policy makers simply have not come to grips with the dramatic transformation that has occurred over the past four decades in the ways that colleges use their institutional aid.

HOW FINANCIAL AID USED TO WORK

To understand how far the country has strayed in how financial aid is used, it's instructive to go back to the 1950s, decades before the enrollment management industry existed. At that time, a group of private college leaders made a bold decision to limit competition among their schools by agreeing to devote their aid to students who could not afford to go to college without the help.

Prior to World War II, such considerations weren't relevant since only a small share of high school graduates pursued higher education, and most private college students came from upper-class families.[31] But the federal government changed the equation in 1944 with the passage of the GI Bill of Rights, which provided World War II veterans with funds to attend the college of their choice. Within a few years, the number of undergraduates nearly doubled, with veterans accounting for about half of enrollments.[32] Suddenly selective private colleges were opening their doors to less-advantaged students.

To try to prevent bidding wars, private college leaders recognized that they needed to become more systematic in their use of student aid. The newly created College Scholarship Service (CSS), an affiliate of the organization now known as the College Board, developed in 1954 a standard need-based methodology that private colleges were to use to award their aid. The methodology made this determination based largely on a family's annual income and assets, as well as the number of children. The formula also considered how much savings a family would need for retirement and medical expenses.

These selective private college leaders had "a rather powerful and attractive vision of the role of financial aid in U.S. higher education, a vision of such coherence and force that it might well be termed 'an ideology,' " the higher-education experts Michael S. McPherson and Morton Owen Schapiro wrote in their 1998 book *The Student Aid Game*.[33] This vision held that colleges would use financial aid to meet their students' financial need. At the same time, these colleges would admit the most meritorious students, regardless of their families' income.

One of the methodology's overriding goals was to ensure that students with families in similar financial circumstances would receive consistent financial aid packages, no matter which college they attended. To accomplish this aim, the organization supported the creation of Overlap Groups, which were made up of groups of selective private colleges that generally received applications from the same students. About 150 colleges participated in the Overlap Groups throughout the country. Colleges in these groups generally forged common financial aid policies, including banning non-need-based aid.[34]

The most prominent group, known as the Ivy Overlap Group, consisted of the eight Ivy League schools and the Massachusetts Institute of Technology (MIT). The Ivy Overlap Group agreed on common aid offers for the promising applicants who had been admitted to more than one of the institutions. The universities' leaders said that this high level of cooperation was needed to preserve institutional aid for those who truly needed it.

The CSS's efforts were so successful that Congress used its methodology as a model when it designed the federal student aid programs. With the passage of the Higher Education Act in 1965, the government made an informal pact with colleges that each would complement the other in using financial aid to open the doors of college to those who otherwise could not afford to attend. It was thought that, working together, the federal government and colleges could fully cover students' financial need and make higher education accessible to all students.

Meanwhile, college officials built firewalls between their schools' admissions and financial aid offices to ensure that aid dollars would be devoted to meeting need.[35] While these firewalls may have had some leaks, many financial aid administrators felt that these boundaries were essential for maintaining the sanctity of need-based aid.

THE RISE OF ENROLLMENT MANAGEMENT

But while the vision that colleges should admit students regardless of family income and fully meet financial need was powerful, it proved difficult to realize. Private colleges that lacked the endowments of Ivy League schools often fell short. And by the late 1970s, private colleges' commitment to this model wavered as they struggled financially and the college-age population declined.

Boston College (BC), for example, was hurting. With enrollment down and hundreds of students leaving the school each year without graduating, the Catholic liberal arts college was heavily in debt and on the brink of bankruptcy.[36] To deal with these crises, BC's president put Jack Maguire, a physics professor, in charge of admissions. In a 1976 article that Maguire wrote for the college's alumni magazine, he argued that the school would be better off using its financial aid strategically to "yield the best possible mix of students at a reasonable expense" than trying to meet the full financial need of its students.[37]

In the influential article, he introduced the phrase "enrollment management" to show how colleges "through conscientious planning and measured decision-making" could "exert significant influence over [their] destiny." Such efforts required colleges to break down the barriers that existed between the admissions and financial aid offices. "Boston College," he wrote, "has recently been on the leading edge of the growing movement to reduce fragmentation by systematizing and integrating these fields into one grand design."[38]

Maguire's efforts were so successful that he left BC in the early 1980s to start a private consulting company to help other colleges embrace this new field of enrollment management and use their financial aid strategically. But Maguire Associates had the field to itself for only a short while. Soon competing consulting companies, such as Noel-Levitz, which later became Ruffalo Noel Levitz, and Royall & Co., which later became EAB, emerged to help spread these practices to private colleges nationwide.[39]

OPENING THE FLOODGATES

BC was hardly the only selective private college to reconsider its need-based aid policies. Throughout the 1980s, many private colleges started using financial aid to pursue more-affluent students. The US Justice Department gave this shift a boost in 1991 when it charged the Ivy Overlap Group members with violating federal antitrust laws for coordinating common aid awards for applicants to more than one of the institutions.[40] (For more information on the Justice Department's lawsuit against the Ivy Overlap Group and its views on antitrust in higher education, see chapter 5.)

CSS had supported the creation of the Overlap Groups in the 1950s to ensure the use of its methodology in awarding institutional aid. The collapse of the Overlap Groups took those guardrails off and encouraged private colleges to use financial aid strategically to gain competitive advantage, or at least to avoid being put at a competitive disadvantage.

Selective private colleges had many incentives to use non-need-based aid to compete for affluent students, but none more so than the *U.S. News* rankings, which came to prominence in the late 1980s. It didn't take long for the colleges to see that the quickest way to rise up the rankings—and build their prestige and fortunes—was to use their aid to entice wealthy students with good grades and high SAT scores to enroll. Washington University in St. Louis's meteoric rise into the elite ranks of the listings provided a powerful example of how to get ahead.[41] Awarding generous amounts of non-need-based aid to wealthy, high-achieving students helped transform the school from being a college that attracted mostly local students who commuted to campus into one of the country's top-ranked universities.[42]

It's no coincidence that the country's wealthiest and most exclusive private colleges started at the top of the *U.S. News* rankings and remain there today. These are the Ivy League colleges, MIT, and Stanford, as well as the most elite liberal arts colleges, such as Amherst, Swarthmore, and Williams. These institutions tend to admit students regardless of financial need and meet their students' full need, although they generally enroll a relatively small number of low-income students. These schools are flooded with applications from "the best and brightest students," and therefore they do not have to use non-need-based aid to entice top students to enroll. But to protect their flanks, they generally have adopted generous financial aid policies that enable them to provide need-based aid to students from affluent families. At Princeton, for instance, students from families making up to $300,000 annually now qualify for need-based aid.[43]

The selective private colleges that most aggressively use their financial aid strategically are those striving to join this pantheon of colleges and universities, or come as close as they can. Initially, these striving private colleges tried to outbid their competitors by providing larger and larger scholarships to the most desirable students. But over the years, they have adopted far more sophisticated strategies. With enrollment management consultants' help, they use their financial aid to pursue students while protecting their institutions' bottom line. The aim is not just to use tuition discounts to get the best students, but to increase their net revenue as well.

But why would a college provide discounts to wealthier students? Doesn't that work at cross-purposes with raising revenue? While there's a cost, colleges find it worthwhile because providing four $5,000 discounts to otherwise "full-pay" students is much more lucrative for the institutions than spending $20,000 on one low-income student.[44] These students will not only pay more overall in tuition than the low-income student, but they will also pay the full price for nontuition expenses, such as room and board, books, and food. And they and their parents may eventually become generous donors as well. In addition, colleges know that offering these so-called merit scholarships is an effective marketing tool. Students and their families love being offered scholarships because they see it as a reward for hard work, when schools actually award these discounts to improve their bottom line.[45]

These practices almost always come at the expense of low- and lower-middle-income students, who are left with large funding gaps. Compounding the problem, financial aid leveraging is most effective when colleges jack up their sticker prices so they can provide larger discounts to the students whom they covet the most.[46] Kevin Crockett, a senior executive with RNL who previously served as the company's president, came clean about this in a 2015 interview with the *New York Times Magazine.* "I've got to have enough room under the top-line sticker price," Crockett stated. "A school that charges $50,000 is able to offer a huge range of inducements to different sorts of students: some could pay $10,000, others $30,000 or $40,000. And a handful can pay the full price."[47] Inflating the sticker price to offer larger discounts to affluent students leaves financially needy ones with even larger funding gaps.

As noted earlier, the enormous growth of non-need-based aid at selective private colleges since 2000 was accompanied by a downward shift in the average amount of financial need the schools covered. As a result, low-income students generally were left with larger funding gaps. In the fall of 2020, more than 80 percent of the selective private colleges that we analyzed charged freshmen from families with annual incomes of $30,000 or less an average net price of more than $10,000, and more than one-third required these students to come up with $20,000 or more. Sixteen schools left the lowest-income students on the hook for $30,000 or more, with the University of Miami charging them an average net price of over $44,000.[48] Low-income families have few options other than taking out PLUS Loans to cover these costs.

In 2021, the *Wall Street Journal* ran an exposé about how Baylor University, which charges the lowest-income freshmen an average net price of about $28,000, has been "steering parents into no-limit federal loans to cover rising tuition, leaving many poor and middle-class families with debt they can't repay." The article cited College Scorecard data showing that about 47 percent of PLUS Loan borrowers whose children graduated from Baylor in 2018 and 2019 were the parents of Pell recipients. They borrowed a median of $43,500 in PLUS debt while their children were in college. Meanwhile, the Scorecard data showed that "only about a quarter of Baylor parents paid down any of what they originally borrowed after two years."[49]

Confronted by the journalists, Linda Livingstone, Baylor's president, acknowledged that the university had "admitted students who really couldn't afford Baylor." She said that the university is working harder now to ensure that families are fully aware of the costs of attending before making admissions decisions. "My heart goes out to families that are in that situation," she said.

Livingstone's sympathy provides cold comfort for the families who were encouraged to take on this debt. And even if Baylor changes its ways, it's hard to see how much of a difference can be made without a wholesale rejection of the financial aid leveraging strategies that the giant enrollment management firms promote.

CRISIS POINT

It's bad enough that private colleges engage in aid leveraging practices that put low-income families' financial well-being in jeopardy. What makes this a true crisis is that public universities, which educate about 70 percent of undergraduates at four-year colleges, have gotten in on the act as well.[50]

Over the past two decades, state disinvestment and institutional status-seeking have worked hand in hand to encourage public universities to adopt the enrollment management tactics of private colleges. With the help of enrollment management consultants, many public universities have hiked up their prices and provided tuition discounts and merit scholarships to lure affluent out-of-state students with good grades and standardized test scores to their campuses to increase their revenue and climb up the rankings.

The fact that many selective public universities now engage in the same harmful financial aid leveraging practices as private colleges stands in stark contrast to how these once-low-cost institutions long operated. For generations, public universities had an entirely different mission than private colleges. In fact, the federal government spurred states to create public universities in the second half of the nineteenth century expressly to serve those who had been shut out of elite private colleges: "the industrial classes."[51]

In most regions of the country, states heavily subsidized public universities to keep the cost of attending low for their citizens. These institutions were generally accessible for students regardless of family income, and they didn't award much aid. Instead, the schools relied on the federal government to provide need-based aid to low-income students.

But by the late 1980s, this low-tuition, low-aid approach was no longer working as effectively as it had been. States started to pull back funding for public universities, especially during recessions. Unable or unwilling to raise taxes to increase revenue and facing ever-growing health-care and public safety costs, state policy makers left public universities with little choice but to jack up tuition. As their institutions' price tags increased and Pell Grant funding stagnated, public university leaders realized that they couldn't stay out of the student aid game anymore.

At first, public universities primarily used their aid to meet students' financial need. In the fall of 1995, the schools spent about $1.5 billion on financial aid, with 55 percent going to need-based aid.[52] But public university officials were far less committed to need-based aid than private college leaders had been because they hadn't taken part in its creation. And it didn't take long for enrollment management firms, recognizing a lucrative market when they saw it, to push selective public universities to embrace enrollment management. It wasn't a hard sell. By 2000, the 268 public universities that we analyzed spent nearly $1 billion annually on non-need-based aid, more than half of the institutional aid that they awarded that year.

Why are so many public universities using their financial aid for strategic purposes rather than for helping students who can't afford to attend without the aid? The reason is simple. Using financial aid to attract affluent out-of-state students provides public universities with a relatively quick and easy way to address the most pressing challenges that they face. Leveraging financial aid helps them increase revenue, fill classrooms and dormitories, and boost prestige.

For public universities, there's been no greater challenge than state disinvestment, which accelerated during the financial crisis. Funding levels have not recovered since. According to the Center on Budget and Policy

Priorities, state higher-education spending fell by more than $3.4 billion nationally between 2008 and 2019. Per-student funding fell in thirty-seven states. Six states—Alabama, Arizona, Louisiana, Oklahoma, Mississippi, and Pennsylvania—reduced funding per student by more than 30 percent.[53] Declining state funding left public universities looking for alternative revenue sources, such as affluent out-of-state students. The allure of these students is obvious: even with discounts, they pay more than in-state students.

Using non-need-based aid to lure out-of-state students is also attractive to public universities in states where the number of high school graduates is shrinking. The biggest declines have been in the Northeast and the Midwest.[54]

Practical concerns such as maximizing revenue and filling classrooms are only part of the equation. As many have said, prestige is the coin of the realm at our nation's colleges. And that is as true today for selective public universities as it has always been for elite private colleges. For schools like Miami University of Ohio and the University of Alabama, there's been no more important goal than rising up the *U.S. News* national university rankings, where public universities compete fiercely with elite private universities for the top one hundred spots.[55] These institutions annually spend tens of millions of dollars—and in the case of the University of Alabama, more than $150 million—to reel in top students who have the impressive SAT scores that *U.S. News* loves. Rising up the *U.S. News* rankings enhances the schools' reputation and marketability with the upscale students they most desire.

To be clear, the goals of increasing revenue, raising prestige, and filling classrooms are not mutually exclusive. Many selective public universities try to achieve these goals simultaneously. And just as with private colleges, the more that public universities use their financial aid strategically, the more pressure there is for their competitors to join the fray.

To be sure, there are still many public universities that haven't embraced enrollment management. But these institutions tend to be located in a small number of states. In 2020, for example, nearly half of the eighty selective public universities that we examined that devoted less than 20 percent of their aid to non-needy students were located in just four states—California, North Carolina, Texas, and Washington. These states have one thing in common: they generally keep their public universities affordable, particularly for low-income, in-state students.[56]

As more and more public universities leverage their financial aid, they are leaving low-income students with larger funding gaps. In 2008–2009, only a quarter of the 268 public universities that we examined charged their lowest income in-state freshmen an average net price of more than $10,000.[57] By the fall of 2020, more than half did. Seventeen schools left these students on the hook for $15,000 or more, with both Penn State and Christopher Newport University leaving them with funding gaps of more than $20,000.[58]

Parent PLUS Loan borrowing has grown enormously at these institutions over the past two decades. According to the Century Foundation, annual PLUS Loan disbursements at public universities increased by nearly 300 percent between 2000 and 2017, from $2 billion to almost $8 billion.[59] The foundation analyzed data from the Education Department's College Scorecard and found that the families of Penn State students hold about $1.4 billion in outstanding Parent PLUS debt, and the families of University of Alabama students carry nearly $700 million.[60]

The rapid escalation of PLUS Loan borrowing at once-low-cost public universities should be a concern in and of itself. But policy makers could be forgiven if they assumed that these loans were going exclusively to middle- and upper-middle-income families who needed extra help sending their children to out-of-state public universities. Helping such families overcome liquidity constraints was, after all, the purpose of the Parent PLUS program.

But the College Scorecard data tell a different—and much scarier—story. Many public universities, like Clemson, are doing exactly what the *Wall Street Journal* discovered Baylor doing: leveraging aid and leaving low-income families with little choice but to take on large PLUS Loans to cover the hefty funding gaps they are left with as a result.

THE NEXT SUBPRIME BUBBLE?

That low-income families—and particularly those of color—are taking on an alarming amount of Parent PLUS Loan debt is not exactly news. New America's Rachel Fishman was the first to put a spotlight on this alarming development in a report that she wrote in 2018. She explained how discriminatory federal housing and lending policies had prevented most Black families from building wealth, forcing them to be more reliant on debt financing for college than white families. "Given the enormous collection powers of the federal government, the Parent PLUS Loan is becoming predatory for Black PLUS borrowers who are more likely to be low-income and low-wealth, and who will likely struggle to repay," she wrote.[61]

More recent data show these problems have only gotten worse. A 2022 report from Georgetown University Law School's Center on Poverty and Inequality found that the share of students whose families annually earned under $30,000 and borrowed PLUS Loans grew from fewer than one in ten in 2008 to one in five in 2018. The increase was sharpest for low-income Black students. The share of Black undergraduates whose families had annual incomes of less than $30,000 and borrowed PLUS "nearly tripled," from 18 percent to a shocking 44 percent.[62]

A 2022 report from the Century Foundation had similar findings: "Because low-income families, and especially Black and Latino/a parents, are disproportionately taking out Parent PLUS Loans, their heavy use and the unfavorable terms and conditions exacerbate the racial wealth gap." The country "needs a larger reckoning" with "the lasting damage that college-related debt burdens cause families, especially families of color," the report argued.[63]

These reports show the extent of the crisis that these families, the government, and taxpayers may face in the not-too-distant future. It's hard to see how encouraging low-income families to take on debt that they probably can't repay will end in anything but disaster, unless the government takes decisive action to contain the damage.

Because these two reports rely mostly on national student loan data, their explanations for how we got into this crisis are a little thin. Without better understanding the origins of the crisis, policy makers won't know how to solve it or prevent it from recurring. What's happened is no accident, and this outcome wasn't inevitable. Loading low-income families with PLUS debt is part of the deliberate financial aid leveraging strategies that the country's largest enrollment management firms have sold colleges. These firms and their clients need to be held to account.

PUTTING THE BRAKES ON FINANCIAL AID LEVERAGING

A potential subprime PLUS Loan disaster is looming, but federal policy makers are not going to be able to head it off unless they acknowledge that the way they think about financial aid is outdated. As the higher-education expert Jon H. Oberg wrote in chapter 4 of this book, Education Department officials need "to familiarize themselves with the theory and practice of enrollment management" and financial aid leveraging. They also need to send program reviewers to review the aid practices of colleges at which low-income students make up a disproportionately large share of PLUS Loan borrowers.

Congress must conduct its own investigation into the roots of the crisis and how to resolve it. Lawmakers need to bring the leaders of the giant enrollment management firms to Capitol Hill to testify about the financial aid leveraging products that they market. Federal policy makers not only have a right to know how these firms' leveraging algorithms work to enhance or undermine the goals of federal student aid, but also have an obligation to find out.[64]

To limit the damage that these firms have caused, the Education Department should forgive the PLUS Loans of low-income families who clearly will not be able to pay them back. It doesn't make sense to try to collect on debt that has little hope of being repaid. But heading off a Parent PLUS Loan crisis is not enough. Policy makers must prevent a possible recurrence by forbidding colleges from packaging PLUS Loans and requiring them to use a standardized award letter that clearly lays out how much families will be on the hook for after all grant and scholarship is awarded. They also need to tighten the PLUS Loan eligibility requirements, while increasing federal loan limits for low-income students whose families would no longer be eligible to take on this debt, and they must penalize colleges if too many of their former students' families struggle to repay PLUS debt.[65] Congress must also increase the government's investment in Historically Black Colleges and Universities and other minority-serving institutions that will suffer disproportionately from a tightening of PLUS Loan eligibility requirements.[66]

All these proposals deal with the crisis at hand. But a more ambitious federal effort is needed to rein in enrollment management and put the brakes on financial aid leveraging for good.

The federal government clearly has a compelling interest in curbing these harmful practices. It spends tens of billions of dollars annually through the federal Pell Grant program trying to keep college accessible for low-income students. But Pell Grants have a design flaw: they make no demands on the colleges that receive them to do their part to help low-income students.

The federal campus-based aid programs—the Supplemental Education Opportunity Grant (SEOG) program and College Work-Study—are many magnitudes smaller than the Pell Grant program, but they require colleges to partially match money that they receive from these programs.

Congress should use the Campus-Based Aid programs to change the incentives that have driven selective colleges to put low-income families in harm's way. Congress must first scrap the Campus-Based Aid programs' long-outdated funding formulas, which provide a disproportionate share of funding to wealthy colleges that serve few low-income students. Lawmakers also need to substantially boost funding for these programs, something that they haven't done for decades.

Under this plan, the only selective colleges that would be automatically eligible for funding from the Campus-Based Aid programs are those that enroll a large share of Pell Grant recipients and do a good job of meeting their financial need. Others would have to submit action plans to the Education Department, showing how they would ratchet up the amount of financial need that they cover, in order to continue receiving funding. Selective colleges that do a good job of meeting financial need but enroll few low-income students would have to commit to becoming more socioeconomically diverse. Those colleges that fail to live up to their promises would forfeit their funding allocations. These funds would then go to nonselective colleges, which tend to have small endowments and serve large numbers of low-income students, to help them do a better job of meeting their students' financial needs.

Meanwhile, Congress would cut off federal financial aid eligibility for any college that fails to meet at least a minimum amount—such as two-thirds—of their students' financial needs. This would be an extreme approach, but one worth adopting to stop these institutions from continuing to undermine national college access goals. Since the proposal's aim is to improve colleges' practices rather than to punish them, schools that miss the cutoff would have at least two additional years to come into compliance. Any savings that the government derives from this proposal would be redirected into the Campus-Based Aid programs.

Making such significant changes to the federal student aid programs would face heated opposition from college leaders and lobbyists. Previous efforts to make the Campus-Based Aid funding formulas more equitable have failed. But the higher-education associations' victories in those battles have come at a cost, as the funding for these programs has remained stagnant for a very long time. The proposal aims to breathe new life into these programs by giving them a critical role to play in changing the incentives that drive higher education. The sooner those misguided and harmful incentives change, the better.

CHAPTER 9

Gapping Through College

Beth Zasloff

As a high school senior in Red Hook, Brooklyn, Joanne Bresilien knew that pursuing a bachelor's degree would be a battle against scarcity and low expectations. Joanne's guidance counselor did not seem to believe that she would be able to succeed at a selective college because she has a learning disability. And Joanne knew that it was going to be a big financial struggle to pay for college. Her mother, who raised her two children on her own, supported them with a monthly disability check.

But Joanne was determined to attend a selective residential college, where she hoped to find a path to a fulfilling career. As a result, she ignored the list of community colleges that her guidance counselor made for her. Instead she turned to Tarik Bell, the director of youth services at the Red Hook Initiative (RHI), a community-based nonprofit in Joanne's industrial waterfront neighborhood. "Tarik actually understands me, and how I learn. And we came up with a different list," she said.

At the top was Ithaca College, a highly regarded private nonprofit college in New York State's Finger Lakes region. The college had a program in exercise science and teacher education, so Joanne could pursue her goal, inspired by an internship at her high school, of becoming a physical education teacher. Joanne also saw Ithaca as a place where she would receive the academic support she needed. "It was important that I stay in a smaller environment, where I know the teacher and the teacher knows me," she explained.

Ithaca costs $64,000 annually to attend, but Joanne understood that financial aid could bring a private college with an astronomical price tag within reach for low-income students. Throughout the month of February, she wound her way through the Kafkaesque combination of bureaucratic requirements and disclosure of intimate details that defines the financial aid application process. Although the process is designed for parents, Joanne, like many of her peers, had to manage it herself: her mother, an immigrant from Haiti, could offer little in the way of logistical support. In March, Joanne started to hear back from colleges. One rejection followed another.

Then, in April, Joanne opened her email to find an acceptance from Ithaca. Finally, it felt like the puzzle pieces were falling into place. "I was really excited. I was like, 'Oh, everything is going great!'" In her eagerness, she immediately paid the $400 deposit to hold her spot, with help from funds from the RHI.

Joanne's financial aid award letter arrived about a week later. At first, the financial aid package that Ithaca offered looked amazingly generous: the college had awarded her $30,000 in scholarship aid, and federal and state government grants covered another $13,000. But after reviewing the letter with Tarik at the RHI, Joanne realized that she would need to come up with the overwhelming sum of $21,000 to make her first year at Ithaca possible. About a third of that amount could be covered through work-study and federal student loans, as Ithaca recommended. But that still left her with a funding gap of nearly $14,000.

Joanne felt as though she were standing at the edge of a precipice as she tried to make sense of the choices ahead. Was it even possible for her to secure scholarships or borrow enough to build a bridge to the college of her dreams? And was the promise of a bachelor's degree and pathway to a meaningful career worth the risk that a family with almost nothing could be dragged into a downward spiral of debt? At one point, Joanne remembered, "I ended up breaking down and crying because I wasn't sure whether or not I could go or what I was supposed to do. That was the hardest thing for me, because I wanted to go to college."

LEAVING LOW-INCOME STUDENTS IN THE LURCH

Joanne's predicament was the result of the widespread practice known as "financial aid gapping," when colleges fail to meet the full financial need of the students they accept. Gapping has seen a dramatic rise in the last two decades. According to the financial aid expert Mark Kantrowitz, the average gap at private colleges is $16,000, an increase of 43 percent since 2008. At state colleges and public universities, the rise is even steeper: the average gap has increased 72 percent, to $11,000, since then.[1]

This precipitous growth in gapping disproportionately affects the most vulnerable families in the United States, who are asked to take on a far greater financial risk than those who are more affluent. Each year, according to a 2011 analysis that the Education Trust conducted of US Department of Education data, low-income families must "pay or borrow an amount equivalent to nearly three-quarters of their family income for just one child to attend a four-year college. In contrast, middle-class students must finance the equivalent of 27 percent of their family income to go to college, while high-income students must finance just 14 percent."[2]

Why aren't colleges giving more grant aid to the low-income students they admit? One reason is scarcity: at a time when college costs have skyrocketed and state funding has been cut, only a small number of colleges can afford to meet the full financial need of all the students they accept. But disinvesting in the futures of low-income students is also an institutional choice.

In the enrollment management practice known as *financial aid leveraging*, colleges devote a significant portion of their financial aid dollars toward non-need-based aid, which is popularly—but not always accurately—known as "merit aid," to attract students whose standardized test scores will help colleges rise in the rankings and whose families can otherwise afford to pay full freight. Financial aid leveraging helps colleges determine the exact amount of tuition discount necessary to beat the competition for an affluent student, and the size of the gap that they can get away with in the financial aid packages that they offer for students with high levels of financial need. The worst kind of offer is known in the industry as "admit-deny," an acceptance followed by an aid package that is so inadequate that it is meant to discourage a low-income student from attending. This disgraceful and potentially hazardous practice enables a college to falsely claim that it is opening its doors to all.

The rise in competition for affluent students means that colleges with missions that include fostering diversity and equity increasingly direct their financial aid resources toward the mostly white and well-to-do. There is a popular misconception that low-income students fare much better in financial aid than the middle class. This idea is fueled by the national obsession with the most elite and prosperous colleges and universities, which, with the help of the federal government and states, are able to provide full rides to the relatively small number of low-income students they tend to enroll. In reality, many selective colleges, including some with sizable endowments, are choosing to use their financial aid to pursue the students they most desire—the "best and brightest," as well as the wealthiest—to rise in the *U.S. News & World Report* rankings and increase their revenue. Other schools, with minuscule endowments, are struggling to stay afloat and look to students with money as life preservers. The result is that many low-income students are left adrift. Even public universities, created as a means to broaden college access for low- and middle-income Americans, are increasingly using aid to attract the affluent. Recent research has shown that public universities are spending billions of dollars annually on students who lack financial need.[3]

In college searches riddled with complex questions about value and cost, non-need-based aid creates choices for families with means. Scores of books and blogs are devoted to helping parents claim their share from the merit aid pot. "The best way to increase your family's chance of capturing a price cut is to understand the motivation behind the pricing discrimination that routinely happens behind closed doors on college campuses," Lynn O'Shaughnessy writes in her book *The College Solutions: A Guide for Everyone Looking for the Right School at the Right Price.*[4] Gapping, merit aid's unfortunate corollary, means fewer and worse options for low-income students, who often apply for aid with insufficient guidance and without parental support.

For a high school senior from a family with means, a financial aid award letter with a merit scholarship is a kind of courtship offer. "Evidently, they believed in me a little more than I did in myself," a student posted on the online forum *College Confidential*, describing her excitement about the $20,000 in non-need-based aid that came with her early acceptance to Ithaca. The student, who applied the same year as Joanne, concluded that while her grade point average (GPA) of 3.49 was considered low at her competitive suburban high school, "I think all of this proves that Ithaca really is a place that genuinely cares about seeing people as more than just numbers." Joanne found a different kind of message in her financial aid award letter, which made her question whether the college really wanted her. Over the months that followed, she would hold onto her own determination to believe in herself within a system that undervalued her future and asks the most of those who have the least.

Amid debates over college affordability, the voices of low-income students are often unheard, their stories reduced to grim statistics. I came into contact with Joanne, along with other students whose experiences are recounted in the chapter, through the RHI, which is driven by the idea of empowering youth and offers young people support from mentors and peers, employment in RHI's programs and expansive community farm, and a "college access pipeline."[5] I reached out to RHI to explore the impact of financial aid gapping on a community invested in overcoming systemic inequity and helping students create their own futures.

Joanne shared her experiences with me as a way to convey what it feels like to forge ahead on a path to a four-year degree while carrying the weight of a gap in aid. Joanne's struggles underline the need for a sharp change in colleges' financial aid policies and practices.

A "$14,000 MOUNTAIN TO CLIMB"

When I first talked to her, Joanne lived with her mother and younger brother, William, in Brooklyn's largest public housing development, the Red Hook Houses, which in 2019 still awaited repairs seven years after its devastation from Hurricane Sandy. Red Hook is a storied neighborhood whose history is defined by inequality and competing visions for the public good. Most notorious is its lack of access to public transportation: in the 1950s, the Brooklyn Queens Expressway bisected the neighborhood, connecting the Brooklyn Bridge with the Brooklyn Battery Tunnel but cutting off the subway for the working class Italian immigrants who were then Red Hook's main residents.[6] Wealthy New Yorkers are increasingly attracted to Red Hook's cobblestone streets, gourmet food scene, and views of the Statue of Liberty, and today, the median price to purchase a home in Red Hook is over $1 million. But almost half of Red Hook's residents live below the poverty level and lack access to equitable education, housing, and employment opportunities.

Joanne was well aware that very few of her neighbors in the Red Hook Houses had a bachelor's degree—only 5 percent, according to the Social Science Research Council's Measure of America, which creates metrics to understand the "distribution of well-being and opportunity in America."[7] She also knew that a bachelor's degree was key to economic mobility and a fulfilling career. Determined to get help to be admitted to a four-year school, Joanne had begun participating in RHI's college preparatory workshops and high school events.

Now, Joanne faced a crucial next challenge in the complex, high-stakes game of college admissions: understanding the terms of her financial aid award. Her first reaction on looking at her financial aid award letter had been confusion. At the top of the page was the college's cost of attendance for the first year: $64,158. The letter indicated that the "Estimated Family Contribution," the amount the federal government deemed her family able to pay based on her federal financial aid application, was just $141. But Joanne could not understand whether the college was meeting her approximately $64,000 in need. "I wasn't sure what I had to pay out of pocket, what they were telling me to pay," she remembered.

Joanne was not alone in finding her aid package difficult to decipher. There is no standardized form or set of terms for colleges to use to help students make sense of different types of aid and understand how much tuition they will be responsible for in their first year. An analysis that the DC-based New America think tank and the Boston-based nonprofit uAspire performed on thousands of financial aid award letters revealed that not only do colleges offer insufficient aid, but also that award letters overwhelmingly lack clarity and transparency. "It is exceedingly difficult for students and families to make a financially-informed college decision," the study, entitled "Decoding the Cost of College," concluded.[8]

More often than not, the lack of clarity in financial aid award letters is no accident. Many enrollment managers seek to make colleges appear more affordable than they actually are in order to entice students to enroll. Some schools deliberately do not include the annual cost of attendance that students must pay on the award letter, leaving students flying blind when evaluating the aid being offered. The study found that this omission is surprisingly widespread and showed how hazardous it can be, especially for low-income and working-class students who can't afford college without receiving significant amounts of financial aid.[9]

In a field of confusing financial aid letters, the one that Ithaca sent to Joanne at least laid out the actual costs to attend the college. At the top of the page, the "Cost of Attendance" chart broke down tuition and fees ($45,274), room and board ($15,570), books ($1,200), personal expenses, and a $67 federal student loan origination fee, adding up to a total of $64,158. But Ithaca employed another trick that many colleges use to downplay the costs that students will ultimately pay to go to college: grouping grants and loans together, as well as work-study, without including explanations of the various forms of aid to help students differentiate among them. Grants and scholarships are known in the financial aid world as "gift aid," as they do not have to be repaid. In contrast, student loans need to be paid back over a period of years after borrowers graduate from school, with interest charged. Failure to repay the loans comes with severe penalties, such as losing access to credit and having wages garnished. While these distinctions may seem obvious to adults who have gone to college, teenagers often do not understand them and may believe that all the financial aid being offered is gift aid—a misconception that some enrollment managers are only too willing to exploit when designing their schools' aid award letters.

Joanne was luckier than many lower-income students because she had Tarik to help her understand the terms of the various types of financial aid that Ithaca had grouped together. First, they looked at the money that she would not have to pay back. Ithaca was offering Joanne $30,000 in tuition discounts and scholarships. The package also included about $13,000 in federal and state grants, close to the maximum offered in each category.

Along with this $43,000 total in gift aid, Joanne's package included a $1,900 Federal Work-Study award, $3,500 in federal direct subsidized loans, and $2,000 in federal direct unsubsidized loans. Work-study, Tarik explained, was money that Joanne could earn through a part-time job while she was enrolled—it was not money she was being given, nor was she guaranteed a job. The federal direct subsidized and unsubsidized loans were student loans that she would need to begin repaying after she graduated, with one important distinction: the subsidized loans, which are offered based on need, would not accrue interest while she was in school, while the interest that she owed on the unsubsidized loans would grow during her years in college. Together, those types of federal aid are considered in financial aid parlance as "self-help," and they are meant to help students finance their education in ways that are not too burdensome. Work-study hours are limited so that they are manageable with full-time course loads, and the annual and total amounts of federal loans that students can receive are capped to prevent overborrowing.

The most dangerous and misleading line in Joanne's aid award letter was the $13,898 listed as Federal PLUS Loans. This line appeared between "Federal Work-Study" and "Federal Subsidized loans," disguising the fact that this is a very different kind of loan than the others, and it should never be included under the category of "aid." Labeling PLUS Loans as student aid is simply not accurate. For undergraduates, PLUS Loans go to parents rather than students, and parents must apply for them. Even worse, these loans are the most potentially hazardous ones that the federal government offers, and parents, particularly those who are low income, need to carefully consider the risks of borrowing them. The "Decoding the Cost of College" report explains what those risks are:

> Unlike federal student loans, which come with strict borrowing limits, Parent PLUS Loans are capped at the total Cost of Attendance (minus other aid), allowing some parents to borrow up to tens of thousands of dollars year after year. Unlike federal student loans, parents must apply for PLUS. But eligibility is based only on credit history and not on an ability to repay the loan. Parent PLUS Loans also come with a higher origination fee and interest rate than federal student loans and are not eligible for most income-driven repayment plans.
>
> Given the potential for the accumulation of debt beyond a parent's ability to repay, and the federal government's ability to garnish wages, Social Security, and tax refunds to pay it back if the parent defaults, it is vital that families receive accurate and complete information about Parent PLUS Loans when choosing a college.[10]

Ithaca is hardly alone in grouping PLUS Loans with other forms of aid in its financial aid award letters. The authors of "Decoding the Cost of College" found that 15 percent of the 128 colleges that they examined included Parent

PLUS Loans "as part of the 'award.'"[11] Packaging PLUS Loans is yet another way that enrollment managers try to make schools look cheaper than they are, without giving applicants and their parents the "accurate and complete information" that they need to evaluate their options. Joanne's case illustrates this well. By including PLUS Loans as part of Joanne's aid award, Ithaca, in effect, was suggesting that Joanne's mother, who supported two kids on her own with a monthly disability check, should apply for a loan that, if approved, could lead her to ultimately run up over $56,000 in debt to pay Joanne's tuition over four years.

It was the college that fell short in meeting Joanne's need with grant and scholarship aid, and, unfortunately, her funding gap is fairly typical for a low-income student attending a four-year college.[12] At Ithaca, ranked number 12 for "best value" among "Regional Universities North" in the all-important *U.S. News* rankings, families earning $0–$30,000 must pay an average price of about $20,000 after all grants and scholarship funding are taken into account.[13]

That a typical low-income student assumes this much risk to attend a four-year college does not mean that it is advisable, and usually Tarik would have tried to steer a student toward a different choice. For the RHI teenagers whom he typically works with, the safest option is a school within the City University of New York (CUNY) system, where two-year community colleges annually cost around $5,000, and four-year colleges about $7,000. But many of these students do not have the standardized test scores to qualify them for admission to CUNY's most selective schools, and community colleges' low graduation rates and commuter campuses make them less appealing to students in search of economic mobility and the kind of self-discovery that is typical of the traditional college experience. Public university options, originally designed to make college accessible to all, are now largely out of reach for low-income students without significant financial aid: within the State University of New York (SUNY), the annual cost of attendance for a four-year residential college is over $25,000.

Helping low-income students find affordable four-year choices requires specialized knowledge of the pathways designed for economically disadvantaged students, as well as private colleges, with track records of offering generous amounts of need-based aid. For students in New York State, some of the best options can be found through college opportunity programs that offer full tuition and academic support to participants: the Educational Opportunity Program at SUNY schools, SEEK at CUNY, and the Higher Education Opportunity Program (HEOP) at private colleges, all of which provide preparatory summer bridge programs before students begin their first year, as well as mentorship and peer-support structures through graduation.

Very high achievers may find pathways and support through national nonprofits that match low-income students with the elite colleges that will pay their way, like Questbridge and Posse, which have their own rigorous application processes and relationships with cohorts of highly selective schools. Joanne's brother, William, was selected as a scholar by Cloudpeak, a small nonprofit that helps place low-income students at elite colleges that are need-blind in admissions and that meet the full financial need of the students they admit. William was one of twenty sixteen-year-olds who were selected for a high school research internship at Rockefeller University, and he knew that he wanted to continue on a science path: "Biology, chemistry, physics, they're all very interesting to me," he told me. But although William was intellectually ambitious, his college application process was focused on affordability. "Aid was the most important thing," he said. "I don't have to be able to go to a prestigious school. I just have to be able to afford it."

At the most-selective colleges and universities, aid and prestige usually go hand in hand. It is the most wealthy, elite schools that have billion- or multi-billion-dollar endowments that enable them to pay the way of the low-income students that they admit. The prestige of these schools also means that the top earner families in the United States scramble for a spot that will cost them over $70,000 per year. But the fact that hyperelite schools are affordable for low-income students does not mean that they are well represented there. A 2016 study by the Equality of Opportunity Project (now known as Opportunity Insights) has a host of findings that reveal the vast income inequality among young people being groomed for leadership at these august institutions. For example, at thirty-eight elite public and private nonprofit colleges and universities, there are a larger share of students who come from families in the top 1 percent, earning over $630,000 per year, than from families in the bottom 60 percent, making less than $65,000 a year.[14]

The vast majority of low-income students seek college options elsewhere and find a field that is increasingly uneven. Much as they do in elementary and secondary education, low-income students generally go to the colleges with the least resources, be they community colleges, regional state schools, or nonselective or barely selective private nonprofit four-year colleges. These schools generally have worse outcomes than wealthier schools because they cannot afford to provide the types of support to their students that more-affluent institutions can.

Deija Boynes, who graduated high school the same year as Joanne, had initially doubted that college was for her. Although she loved to write and valued her school community, "I just felt like high school was hard enough," she remembered. But with encouragement from her teachers and from mentors at the RHI, Deija began to imagine her future and to believe in her own abilities. "I made a decision that I wanted to be a social worker, and I knew I had to go to college," she said. Deija had attended schools in Red Hook since kindergarten and dreamed of going to a different state. Georgia State University and Clark Atlanta were her first choices. During the wait, Deija said, "I was very nervous. I doubted myself a lot. I didn't really think that I would get accepted to any school." In the spring, Cazenovia College, a selective college in central New York, admitted Deija through HEOP, and that summer, she traveled there to begin the intensive summer bridge program.

For Joanne, Ithaca seemed like the right match in so many ways—a selective private college that would provide her with a residential campus experience and a bachelor of arts degree in the field of her choice that could be followed by a master of arts, and then a career as a New York City public school teacher. Joanne desperately wanted to go and called Ithaca's financial aid office for help. The college directed her to the studentaid.gov website for loan information. But beyond that, Ithaca's financial aid office offered no other guidance or financial support in her quest to make the college affordable, she said.

In the summer months between receiving her financial aid package and the early September deadline for tuition payment, she scrambled to figure out if and how she could make Ithaca work. With support from Tarik and her counselor, Juan Tejada, at the RHI, she applied for additional scholarships from community organizations but had no success.

The last pathway open to Joanne was the route that Ithaca's financial aid office steered her toward: having her mother apply for a Parent PLUS Loan to fill the $14,000 funding gap. This was a choice that carried enormous risk for Joanne's family. Unlike the $5,500 in federal subsidized and unsubsidized student loans in Joanne's aid package, this loan would be in Joanne's mother's name, not Joanne's. Even if the family agreed that Joanne would be responsible for repayment, it was her mother who would face the consequences of default, including the possibility that the federal government could garnish her wages and even seize a substantial share of her Social Security payments.

The prospect that Joanne's mother could be approved for a loan that she did not have the ability to repay is part of the inherent risk of the Parent PLUS Loan program. Eligibility for PLUS Loans is determined only by a check for adverse credit history, not by parents' income or assets—and the openness of access comes with dangers. The program was created in 1980 to help middle- and upper-middle-income families afford high-cost colleges. But with dramatic increases in college tuition for all and colleges using their aid to attract more-affluent students, PLUS Loans have become an all-too-common way for colleges to fill low-income students' funding gaps. Together with federal student loans, as New America's Rachel Fishman wrote in a 2018 report entitled "The Wealth Gap PLUS Debt," they "are driving an intergenerational accumulation of debt that burdens the neediest families."[15]

Fishman's report centers on the especially harmful effects of Parent PLUS Loans for Black borrowers, who have been hit hardest by the student debt crisis. As a result of decades of policies that have prevented Black families from building wealth, they rely more heavily on debt to finance higher education than members of other racial and ethnic groups, and they are disproportionately at risk of default.[16] A 2020 study by the New York City Department of Consumer Protection found that there are twice the number of student loan borrowers with debt in collections in predominantly Black and Brown neighborhoods (16 percent) in New York City as compared with predominantly white and Asian neighborhoods (8 percent).[17] Nationally, more than half of Black male borrowers default on a loan within twelve years of college matriculation, according to the progressive think tank Demos.[18] The Parent PLUS Loan program adds to this danger. "Given the enormous collection powers of the federal government, the Parent PLUS Loan is becoming predatory for

Black PLUS borrowers who are more likely to be low-income and low-wealth, and who will likely struggle to repay," Fishman wrote.[19]

Recalling this moment in Joanne's process, Tarik expressed the painful ambivalence that he felt about her family assuming more debt to get Joanne to Ithaca. "It came down to making a tough decision, like 'Can we do this? Are we willing to do this?'" Finally, Tarik said, "We decided that we were just going to increase the loans and take it on the chin for year one." In addition to accepting the $5,500 in subsidized and unsubsidized federal student loans, Joanne's mother was approved for the $14,000 PLUS Loan that Ithaca had recommended. Although the loan was officially in Joanne's mother's name, the family agreed that it would be Joanne's responsibility to pay it back from her future earnings.

For Tarik, helping Joanne make this decision came with the depressingly persistent feeling that colleges didn't really want the type of students that he served. After navigating the complex, intensive, and soul-baring demands of the American college application process, it was always jarring to face a message that college was "something that should only be accessed if you have money to pay for it," Tarik reflected. "It feels transactional. It doesn't feel personal."

That feeling of being seen and desired, which meant so much to the merit aid recipient who posted online about her acceptance to Ithaca, is lost on a low-income student facing a decision about whether to take on dangerous levels of debt. "It almost feels like these young people are being asked if they want it bad enough," Tarik said, adding, "Here's this young lady, who's so full of life, full of love, so focused on becoming a physical educator, and now we have this huge $14,000 mountain to climb."

PUTTING EVERYTHING ON THE LINE

Ithaca College's campus sits on South Hill, overlooking downtown Ithaca, Cornell University, and Cayuga Lake. The college was founded in 1892 as a music conservatory, and its modern campus was built in the 1960s, when the institution expanded to include schools of communications, business, humanities, music, and health sciences. The year that Joanne began as a student in the School of Health Sciences and Human Performance, Ithaca's student body was comprised of about 6,000 undergraduates. Like most selective colleges in the Northeast, it has overwhelmingly white and higher-income students. As a low-income student of color, Joanne found herself in a small minority: 72 percent of students are white and only 6 percent are Black; 58 percent have parents from the top 20 percent of earners, and only 4.2 percent from the bottom 20 percent.[20]

Joanne had a difficult fall adjusting to life on campus, away from family and the supports she relied on. "It was stressful in the beginning, because I had to do everything on my own," she said.

Joanne's financial aid gap shaped her first year in ways that she knew were invisible to many others on campus. For the first couple of months, Joanne's anxiety about the $19,000 in loans—$3,500 in federal subsidized loans, $1,500 in federal unsubsidized loans, and about $14,000 in PLUS Loans—that she and her mother had taken out made it difficult for her to invest herself fully in the college experience that she had worked so hard to achieve. "I was just worried because I didn't totally understand at that point what it meant to have loans out," she said. "I didn't know if I had to pay them off by the time I was done with the first year, or if I had to wait until after four years."

Joanne relied on frequent contact with her mentors at the RHI to help her understand her loans. Joanne, who enjoys math, found some calm from working through a spreadsheet with Tarik and making sense of which loans she would need to pay when.

On campus, Joanne felt the absence of people who could help her to understand and manage her aid. The financial aid office, which ideally would have provided counseling, was not a place where Joanne felt like she could find help. "It's a big thing known on the campus, where the financial aid office is the cleanest and the nicest, because there are no students in it," she said.

Tarik found it hard to see the students he loved fall through the cracks in a system that felt uncaring. Winter break of her first year brought distressing news for Deija Boynes, who had finished her first semester at Cazenovia College. While back home in Brooklyn, she received a call informing her that she owed $6,000 for the semester and could not return to school until she paid it. Deija had been accepted as an HEOP scholar with a scholarship that would cover tuition, as well as room and board. But at summer's end, the school had discovered that Deija's parents' taxes had been improperly filed. Deija had indicated on her Free Application for Federal Student Aid (FAFSA) form that her parents were married, but her mother, following the advice of a tax office, had filed as head of household. Deija, without understanding how this issue would affect her scholarship, completed her first semester at Cazenovia, and consequently, she was charged a balance not covered by aid.

An unpaid college bill with no degree is a major roadblock for a low-income student. Not only was Deija unable to return to school, but Cazenovia would not release her transcripts unless her bill was paid, preventing her from transferring her credits to another college. This practice of withholding transcripts because of an unpaid balance is common among colleges, and it leads to a dangerous trap for people unable to pay a debt or complete a degree that will increase their earning potential. When we spoke, close to a year after Deija left college, she was working at the fast-food restaurant Chipotle and looking for a way to get back on track. "Me and my parents, we're trying to get it fixed," she said. "Every time I get paid, I try to put at least $50 on it."

At Ithaca, Joanne's anxiety was driven by an understanding of the high stakes of making errors and a sense of operating without a safety net. Although she had chosen Ithaca because she believed that it would offer her the support she needed, she felt keenly aware that campus resources were not designed for a student from a background like hers. "A lot of the kids on campus, their parents are able to pay for them to go to college," she said, "so professors don't really understand that there are kids that don't have the same opportunity, and they have to take out loans."

Joanne's biggest academic struggle was in her anatomy class, a requirement for her major, where information was presented quickly for memorization, and this went against the grain of the way that she learned: "Every day is a new topic, so you don't have time to learn the topic you were taught the day before," she said. She recalled that her anatomy professor used to chastise the class when the students weren't paying attention by saying, "Do you realize your parents are the ones paying for you to go to college? Why are you wasting their money?" The professor's comment, which tapped into a cliché about college students as spoiled rich kids who don't understand the value of their education, made Joanne feel even more marginalized. "That always offended me, because my mom isn't able to pay for me to go to college," she said, adding, "I'm the one who has to take out the loans, and end up figuring out how to pay for it by the time I'm done."

Joanne knew the value of the class better than anyone: it was a necessary stepping stone toward her degree, her career, and ultimately, her ability to repay the thousands of dollars that she had borrowed to make her very presence in the lecture hall possible. This made it all the more frustrating when she was confronted with the suggestion that she just didn't care or wasn't trying hard enough. Joanne, an aspiring educator, had learned to self-advocate and to insist that the fact that she learned differently didn't mean that she couldn't achieve. She also knew that Ithaca had recognized her potential in admitting her, and that as a student with a disability, the college had a responsibility to provide her with appropriate support. Now, as a low-income student of color on a campus where most students were wealthy and white, she found herself facing intertwined assumptions about her character and capacity.

Each time Joanne visited her anatomy professor's office to seek help, she recalled, he would imply that she wasn't making enough effort. "Well, the numbers show that you're not doing well in my class, so it means that you're not studying enough, and you're not putting enough hours into this class," she remembers him saying. Finally, the professor advised Joanne to drop the class and take it again in the summer.

Although she felt vulnerable about revealing that she was a low-income student, Joanne explained that she couldn't afford to pay for a summer class. She remembers sensing, in her professor's reaction, that she was now set apart as different from her peers. "It just seemed like he looked at me a different way. He was like, 'Well, then get a job and pay for it.'" Joanne stayed quiet, but she wanted to argue back that it wasn't easy to find a job on campus—she had tried that year without luck—or to complete studies while working, or to pay again for a class that already stretched her far beyond her means. She also sensed, in his repeated urging to drop the class, that she was being dismissed as a student who wouldn't make it. "At one point it seemed that the lecture professor told all the other lab professors that I should drop the class, or that I wasn't going to pass, so they kind of paid less attention to me," she said.

But Joanne persisted. "Being me and being hardheaded, I just didn't listen." She sought help from her lab instructor, who taught the smaller section that was part of the class. "He definitely tried to help me a lot, and would put time into trying to help me figure out solutions," she stated.

When Joanne triumphed and passed the class, her lab instructor emailed her to say how happy he was and praised her good work. The lecture professor, cc'd on the email, responded too, with a note Joanne remembers as, "Wow, you passed the class, that's really good." Joanne felt irritated by the tone of surprise. "It was like, 'You didn't believe that I could do it, and now you're congratulating me because I did?' "

Finding people who understood her experience was crucial to staying afloat, and Joanne found her best support from professors who "understand that I learn differently, and sometimes I struggle." Joanne also depended on friends who shared her anxiety about student debt. "Some of my friends have more to pay than I do, so they understood what I was going through," she said.

As Joanne navigated life on Ithaca's manicured campus with the burden of mounting debt on her back, it came as a shock to discover that the college seemed to be handing money to students unencumbered by financial need. One day, an affluent friend made an offhand remark, as they were leaving the dorm together, that left Joanne reeling. "I have to go to the financial aid office, because I don't know why they're giving me an extra $14,000, and I don't need it," Joanne recalled her friend saying.

Hearing this number, the same amount as her gap, felt like a punch in the gut. Why, Joanne asked herself, did the financial aid office make it seem like they didn't have any more money to give out when they were giving out this money to students without need? "It just didn't sit right with me," she said. Joanne felt awkward with her friend and didn't know how to respond. "I didn't feel like I could tell her how my experience went because she just wouldn't understand."

What Joanne had picked up on was the uncomfortable reality still largely hidden from students despite its pervasiveness: in the logic of financial aid leveraging, the goal of aid is to secure revenue and prestige for a college, not to meet financial need. Joanne was correct in perceiving that her college gave significant aid to students who didn't need it. According to 2019–2020 institutional data, 24 percent of Ithaca College freshmen had no financial need and received an average non-need-based aid award of $17,000.[21] Offering scholarships and discounts is a key strategy to attract students who can pay, and gapping is part of the plan to reserve money for the students whom the college wants most.[22] For Joanne, hearing an example of this inequitable distribution of aid was an unnerving signal that the deck was stacked against her.

Joanne had chosen to attend Ithaca in a desire to move beyond her comfort zone and experience something new. The RHI had helped her develop the courage to strive. In encouraging Joanne to attend Ithaca, Tarik understood that she would struggle but also find opportunities to grow. In her first year at Ithaca, Joanne tapped her inner resources, sought the help she needed, and refused to give up. But she worried, as she awaited her aid package for the next year, about whether she would be able to build on this success.

In the spring, as Joanne was finishing her first year at Ithaca, her brother, William, received his college results, with good news: he had been admitted to Cornell University with a full scholarship through HEOP. It was a happy moment at home, even for their mother, who now faced the prospect of an empty nest. "There was a lot of crying involved, a lot of emotion involved," William said. He credited Joanne, saying that her decision to go to Ithaca had "paved the way for me to be able to go upstate."

Joanne's mother was also tremendously relieved that William's choice would be affordable. "They said they were committed to investing a certain amount in me," William said. "They waived everything they could waive—even the deposit fee."

Cornell, which has an endowment of over $7 billion, could afford to invest in William.[23] Like other Ivy League universities, it meets the full financial need of all the students it accepts. However, only about half of students in Cornell's freshman class applied for aid in 2019–2020. That suggests that the rest were paying Cornell's full cost of attendance, which was a staggering $78,000. It has no need to offer non-need-based aid to lure wealthy students or to gap the relatively small number of low-income students it admits.[24] Students from families with annual incomes of $20,000 or less per year make up only about 4 percent of its student body.[25]

Ithaca, by comparison, had a total endowment of $347.3 million in 2019. Like many other colleges, it has experienced an enrollment decline over the past decade, losing about seven hundred students. Ithaca was taking serious stock of its financial health even before the coronavirus pandemic decimated college budgets and spurred it to lay off 132 faculty members.[26]

But it would be a mistake to believe that the course that Ithaca and many of its peers have taken to engage in financial aid leveraging and leave low-income students with large financial aid gaps is inevitable because their endowments are a fraction of Cornell's. There are other selective private colleges with even smaller endowments than Ithaca's that do far better by their low-income students. Take Pitzer College, a small private liberal arts college in Claremont, California. The school, which has a total endowment of only $144 million, spends more than 99 percent of its institutional aid budget on need-based aid. And on average, the school meets 100 percent of its students' need.[27]

In the 2019–2020 academic year, the lowest-income freshmen at Pitzer paid an average net price of just $9,747 after all grant and scholarship aid was awarded, about half of what the lowest-income students paid at Ithaca that year.[28] And while one-quarter of Ithaca's freshmen received non-need-based aid awards, averaging about $17,000 per student, only six freshmen at Pitzer did, averaging just $5,000 each.[29]

The point is not to say that Pitzer is wonderful and Ithaca is terrible. After all, Ithaca enrolls many more Pell Grant recipients than Pitzer does.[30] But college leaders make choices with the resources they have, and these choices can have serious repercussions for the students they enroll, particularly for low-income students who have the most to gain from a college degree and are the most at risk.

The enrollment management strategies that Ithaca and so many other selective public and private colleges have embraced have created campus cultures that favor the rich and white. Wealthy students get the message that they are valued, while low-income students like Joanne are made to feel like second-class citizens who have to scrape and claw and put everything on the line for the chance of success.

It doesn't have to be this way. College financial aid practices and policies need to be reformed to make college more accessible and affordable for low-income students. Financial aid gapping narrows the field of good choices for low-income students and creates more perils on the obstacle-ridden path to college. If US colleges are to be engines of opportunity supported by federal subsidies, they should direct financial aid resources toward making college a solid stepping stone for low-income students instead of setting them and their families up to stumble into pits of debt.

Amid the large-scale systemic change that is necessary to make college affordable for all, colleges have an immediate responsibility to make the human-scale interventions that change lives. Low-income students need standardized financial aid award letters that clearly lay out students' financial aid options and help them understand the choices ahead. On campus, they need caring professionals who keep them on track in managing their aid and help them avoid crippling debt. They need counselors who give their families the benefit of the doubt, hear students' stories, and help them overcome hurdles instead of punishing them for missteps. Colleges need to value the students for whom the value of college means the most and widen the path toward a more equitable society.

Part 4. Recommendations for Reining in the Enrollment Management Industry

CHAPTER 10

Why National Price Controls Are Needed in Public Higher Education

Kevin Carey

Public higher education in this country used to offer a guarantee: students would pay the same low price to attend a given public university, without regard to their individual family's financial circumstances. State policies differed, but almost everyone got some version of this deal.

Universal low pricing didn't just make college accessible to people who couldn't afford it otherwise. It also broadened the constituency and political support for higher learning. It allowed public universities to bring people from different socioeconomic strata together, in a common place, for a common purpose. Twentieth-century middle-class prosperity was created, in part, because public colleges and universities were affordable.

Unfortunately, this guarantee no longer exists in many states. As this book has shown, enrollment management practices that were once solely the province of private colleges have been embraced by many public higher-education systems in their quest for greater revenue and prestige. The longtime promise of accessible public higher education for a common, affordable price is becoming obscured behind rising sticker prices and tuition bills that can be different for every undergraduate and vary for reasons that are hard for laypeople to understand.

Not only does this price variability make higher education less accessible for students from low- and middle-income families, it also undermines the role of higher education in building an inclusive, mutually supportive society. The more the forces of technology-driven disinformation and political extremism divide people into different ideological tribes and epistemological realities, the more important the unifying mission of public higher education becomes.

Action is needed now to reverse this troubling trend. The solution is an idea that has long been outside the bounds of polite policy discourse: national college price controls. Not price suggestions or guidelines or incentives, but tempered-steel bolts that can't be removed. There is, of course, a well-established and still active set of state-level price control regimes. But they are uncoordinated and steadily weakening in the face of state disinvestment in higher learning. Only federal action will do.

Historically, the Washington, DC, higher-education lobby has been able to bat aside any such policies. But decades of increasing college prices and the commensurate rise in student indebtedness have created so much anxiety and unhappiness in the general public that the political grounds on which the price control debate is taking place have shifted. Federal price controls are suddenly more viable than ever before.

SETTING PRICES AT PUBLICS

Enrollment management matters most at relatively high-priced selective colleges and universities. Expensive, selective public universities are also the most similar to private universities in their economic model, cultural positioning, and organizational aspirations. While nominally accountable to the public via state coordinating boards and publicly appointed trustees, these institutions are, in practice, highly independent. State subsidies and the commitments to undergraduate enrollment and pricing that go along with them are in many ways the only truly public thing about them. That's why enrollment management at public institutions is so troubling—if we're not careful, the publicness of public universities will steadily fade away.

The mechanisms of state price controlling vary.[1] In Florida, the legislature starts by setting tuition rates directly via statute, down to the penny per credit hour, and then allows its Board of Governors some discretion to make alterations. As a result, the tuition at the University of Florida and the University of Central Florida are almost identical. In neighboring Alabama, by contrast, the state doesn't control tuition at all. The University of Alabama and Auburn University set tuition as they like, probably during halftime. Most states are somewhere in between, delegating tuition authority to single-campus or multicampus governing boards. Size and structure matter: large states with multicampus systems tend to create intermediary governance bodies with tuition authority, while small states leave decisions to individual boards.

There is often an inverse correlation between the strength and centrality of a price-controlling authority and the level of the prices themselves. In 1980, Alabama public colleges and universities collected $2,412 in tuition per full-time equivalency (FTE) student.[2] Over the next forty years, that amount increased 424 percent in constant, inflation-adjusted dollars, to $12,633. Florida's tuition started at $1,701 in 1980, and it had increased by only 43 percent by 2020, barely one-tenth the rate of Alabama's increase.[3] In New York, where public universities are tightly controlled by the Board of Regents, tuition rose 123 percent.[4] In Michigan, where public universities pretty much do what they want, it rose 262 percent.[5] In states that combine centralized price setting and high prices, there is often a political story. Arizona's Republican lawmakers, for example, control tuition in the state's three-university system and chose to increase it significantly after the Great Recession as a means of avoiding their responsibility to raise state tax revenue.[6]

While the intergovernmental dynamics of state price controlling can be complex, they are all responsive to an underlying tension between the public's long-term interest in affordable, egalitarian higher education and the short-term financial interests of individual institutions. Some battles go this way and some go that, but over time, university financial interests are clearly winning. One can fairly point to many individual and collective actors to account for this. But the outcome was possible only because public colleges and universities exist in a hybrid state between the public and private sectors.

For government agencies like fire departments or public K–12 schools, the main questions for policy makers are determining how much money those agencies should spend and how to ensure consistently high-quality levels of public service. Budgeting and governance are the main debates. Quality can be a challenge to achieve in public agencies that are not subject to the competitive discipline of the free market, as the recent struggles to reform policing have shown. (This doesn't mean that policing should be privatized, but it does mean that changing public agencies is hard.)

For private-sector firms, the main public policy questions center on protecting consumers and workers and correcting for market failures. For some private firms, the government's proper role is limited to health and safety. Others exist in the public utility space and tend to be regulated by bipartisan boards that balance profits, prices, and the public interest. Consumer protection, workers' rights, and market failure prevention are always pitted against the ability of private-sector companies to purchase political influence and capture regulatory processes.

The challenge with thinking about enrollment management is that higher-education policy is all these things at once—public subsidy, direct government regulation, consumer protection, and market regulation mixed together. Public colleges and universities exist along a large section of the public-private continuum. Community colleges grew out of K–12 school systems and mostly behave like local government agencies providing free or nominally priced services. Public flagship and research universities mostly behave like enormous private businesses that happen to get an operating subsidy each year from the state education department. But none of these institutions are wholly public or wholly private, which creates a fundamental instability of position and identity that in turn creates the conditions for prices to rise.

The public institutions most likely to adopt the troubling aspects of enrollment management, moreover, occupy the most chaotic section of that unstable space. They are selective and independent enough to be unbound by most governmental limitations, but they generally don't have enough money or prestige to be stabilized by a semi-unassailable position atop the higher-education status hierarchy. This instability creates circumstances that can predictably lead responsible, professional, and well-intentioned university leaders to some variation of "I don't like it, but I'm not sure what else we can do."

For a growing number of these institutions, what they can do is hire an enrollment management consultant who will provide detailed, actionable advice about how the college can improve its marketing efforts to attract certain kinds of students. Having widened the funnel of prospects, the consultant will then provide tools for identifying, targeting, and recruiting students who present the optimal mix of personal and academic characteristics, likelihood of enrolling, and willingness to pay.

This process will be backed up by the same kind of sophisticated data analysis that airlines use to continually adjust the price of seats in the weeks and months before scheduled departure, with the goal of selling a certain number of seats, no more, no less, and maximizing the total amount of the fares paid. For colleges, the number of beds in the freshman dorm is the equivalent of the number of seats on the plane. The goal is to recruit as many first- and business-class passengers as possible—with the added complication that, unlike airlines, the college's reputation (and thus ability to market seats) is affected by what kind of people buy tickets. As enrollment decision days approach, colleges will fill in the unsold seats in the back, near the kitchen, by offering "scholarships" that are really just a label affixed to a discounted price.

There is a colorable argument to make that this process—*price discrimination*, in the economic vernacular—has the virtue of charging more money to wealthy people who might get a little extra legroom but are ultimately landing at the same destination at the same time. The problem is that enrollment management is completely opaque to the general public. Historical practice and popular culture have taught people that college financial aid is provided on an entirely different basis, with scholarships awarded for academic merit and financial need. The marketing dimension of enrollment management reinforces these misconceptions. This mismatch leaves students and parents increasingly vulnerable to making bad choices during the risky, confusing, and high-stakes college-search process, with consequences that can last a lifetime.

Fortunately, political conditions are currently ripe for reform. The biggest obstacle to the kind of changes that are needed is the political power of institutions that profit from continuing the current regime.

ENDING THE "ARMS RACE"

In 2021, President Joe Biden proposed and Congress considered federal legislation called America's College Promise (ACP), which would have provided every state with a grant of roughly $5,000 per community college student in exchange for states agreeing to set tuition prices at $0. ACP was an early casualty of the negotiations that eventually eliminated away all manner of subsidies for education and care. But the fact that it was seriously considered at all, and the specific way that it died, provide valuable lessons for future efforts to enact national college price controls.

Traditionally, the most important and influential organizations petitioning state and federal lawmakers for higher-education funding have been colleges and universities themselves. At the state level, that means pushing for maximizing operating subsidies and institution-level discretion over pricing. At the federal level, it means lobbying for maximizing research funding and student access to loans and grants that can be used to pay tuition. Econ 101 may have deservedly gained a reputation for teaching people just enough to be annoying and wrong on social media, but it still offers some important ideas, among them the fact that producers always grab a percentage of consumer price subsidies for themselves. Without federal price controls, part of each increase in GI Bill benefits, Pell Grants, and federal Stafford Loan limits ends up in the pockets of the people who run or own colleges and universities.

That's why the Washington, DC, higher-education lobby was no friend to ACP. Free college is just an unusually simple and powerful form of price controlling: one price of $0, or, if you prefer, no price at all. While the associations of community colleges were officially big supporters of ACP, some leaders of two-year institutions grumbled behind the scenes that the funding would do little to increase their capacity to educate students well.

Four-year institutions, meanwhile, were actively hostile to the idea, especially the most influential, selective, and wealthy private universities and flagship public universities that send many alumni to Capitol Hill. They proposed doubling the Pell Grant instead—more money, no price controls, predictable results. Privately, they told key congressional staffers that they would be happy to see the plan perish. Faced with the opportunity to help millions of racially and economically diverse community college students afford higher education while possibly setting a precedent that might someday affect their bottom lines, they swiftly said, "No."

A lot of people and institutions benefit from the way that higher education is currently financed. Confusion and obscurity create conditions where institutions can slip their hands in the pockets of students and taxpayers and steal away before anyone is the wiser. While the people who protect the interests of American public universities are smart enough to never say this in public, most of them don't want to be free. They'd rather be in the business of charging rich people a lot of money for an expensive and prestigious service because, with all that money and social capital swirling around, some of it lands with them.

The macropolitical conditions that led to the ACP, however, have not waned. Instead, they have strengthened. Beyond the specific necessity of an affordable higher education in an ultracompetitive modern labor market, and the need to help the victims of the $1.7 trillion student loan crisis in the United States, the reform movement is driven by the powerful emotional resonance of restoration. People sense, correctly, that the United States used to offer a good deal to young people in the form of affordable public colleges, and that that benefit was revoked for cruel and stupid reasons. They want back what was lost.

The word *free* also has a specific attraction. Zero is not like other numbers. Initial results from states that have put in place forms of free community college suggest that *free* drives enrollment decisions in a way that goes beyond the marginal dollars and cents involved.[7] Through financial-aid leveraging, enrollment management creates an almost infinite number of possible tuition prices while completely obscuring any consumer visibility into the price-setting process. This practice adds new layers of confusion to an experience that is already emotionally fraught and high-stakes for students and parents. Having public institutions set prices using literally the same algorithms that airlines use to maximize revenue from business travelers is a neoliberal nightmare come true. *Free* is sunlight that burns away the fog of price confusion.

That said, *free* is not the only option for national price controls. While some states have offered free public tuition in the past, many others had—and some continue to have—tuition schedules that are broadly affordable, allowing most or nearly all undergraduates to pay for college with a combination of parental contributions, savings, and work. There are valid distributional and resource arguments for using this approach, particularly if need-based grants continue to be available to defray living expenses. One could imagine a straightforward, graduated tuition schedule tied to household income. College would be free for many and affordable for all.

The key would be simplicity, affordability, and universality—a kind of federally mandated universal enrollment management disarmament for all public colleges and universities. Higher-education leaders would be able to opt out of an arms race that many institutions participate in reluctantly and few ultimately win. Without national price controls, the ability to obtain a public higher education will keep getting more uncertain and expensive and out of reach until we're left with a collection of public memorials to a time when everyone could afford a college degree.

CHAPTER 11

Cooperation for the Greater Good

Forging a New Covenant for Equitable Educational Results in Higher Education

Jerome A. Lucido

This book provides a thorough analysis, with ample critiques, of the process of enrollment management in higher education. It is a worthy topic for inquiry. If higher education is, in fact, managing enrollment, its results are heavily skewed in favor of the wealthy and powerful. As such, higher education's commitment to the public good can and should be called into question.

Indeed, this volume has documented how low- and lower-middle-income students and other populations, including those of Black, Latinx, and Native American heritage, have been disproportionately excluded from the pursuit of and benefits from higher education. Not only must the ideas, systems, and incentives that have given rise to these inequities be examined, they must also be changed for the good of the nation.

The need for change is both historical and contemporary. We must address the persistent systems that have privileged some and not others. Ample research has demonstrated that wealth distribution, health benefits, and civic participation vary directly with college completion.[1] Accordingly, the disparities that we see in higher education become reflected in the fundamental operation of a democratic and healthy society.

Principles of equity and fairness demand that we address these disparities, but if humanistic values are not enough, the dramatic demographic changes that this country is experiencing compel us to act. According to the Western Interstate Commission for Higher Education (WICHE), there will be a projected 11 percent decrease in high school graduates between 2025 and 2037. During the same period, it is expected that the percentage of low-income children will increase sharply as income inequality in the United States is also on the rise.[2] Further, demographic shifts will change the racial representation of prospective college students. The share of white students is expected to drop substantially, while there is projected to be a significant increase in Asian/Pacific Islander and Hispanic students. The changes demand that higher education become more inclusive.

A NEW COVENANT

The time has come to replace the current hypercompetitive enrollment environment that advantages those with advanced wealth and social capital to one that is based on cooperation for the greater good. Systemic change is needed for better results to be achieved. We cannot expect different results by doing the same things or by making marginal changes.

I am proposing in this chapter a three-part plan for making fundamental change. The centerpiece of this change is far greater cooperation among colleges and universities and between the federal government and each sector of nonprofit higher education. The plan calls for significant investment of new federal resources at the same time that it demands more equitable enrollment and graduation results from the campuses. Further, it drills down to the goals, plans, and strategies of campus presidents and enrollment leaders.

In short, a new covenant, or new social pact, is needed to redirect higher education to the service of a more fully and equitably educated population. This chapter describes how this change can take place. My objective is not to suggest that all the answers are here. The chapter lays a foundation based on collaborative research and years of higher-education experience to provide workable solutions. Additional ideas and approaches based on the premise of collective action and the needs of the nation will very likely be needed to ensure success.

WHY WE MUST CHANGE

Our colleges and universities, which act primarily on their own and with inadequate federal assistance, are failing to provide in a systematic way the educational results that are needed for a sound American future. In sum, we find a higher-education system that is out of balance, as it is:

- Struggling to meet educational missions while maximizing revenue and prestige;
- Known as the best in the world, yet caught in a spiral of costs and competition that undermines what may be its greatest legacy: the upward mobility and strength of the American people through education;
- Facing mistrust by state and national governments and flagging public confidence among those it is designed to serve;
- Awash in widespread doubts about the value of a college degree at the same time that the nation's long-term economic future depends on a more well educated population, and;
- Embedded in an overheated positional marketplace that encourages inefficiency and excess costs through the expansion of facilities, amenities, and non-need-based, merit-aid competition.

In other words, it is a system threatened by its own ambition and inflationary competition precisely at a time when it must refocus itself on its educational mission and on the public trust that it is chartered to pursue. While it is highly evident that these conditions apply to highly selective public and private institutions, make no mistake: the same forces drive institutions in every sector of higher education to place institutional benefit over the public good. The time for change is now.

Why is the higher-education system so out of balance with its purposes? College leaders respond to incentives that drive them to seek money and prestige at the expense of their institutions' mission to educate the population fairly and equitably for healthy and productive lives as workers, citizens, and leaders of future generations. These leaders act in this way not because they are driven by ego, although it is often said that prestige is the coin of the realm. More to the point, they respond rationally to public policy and external pressures to obtain the resources their colleges need to operate in a competitive marketplace.[3]

We are immersed in an era of academic capitalism.[4] Over the past several decades, politicians and policy makers redefined higher education as a private good, one to be purchased like any other product or service rather than as a fundamental builder of society. As a result, colleges have become highly dependent on the wealth and the buying power of students and families in the form of tuition dollars and payments for auxiliary services (food, housing, recreation, and health care). Expecting broad public benefit from a system that has become largely one of providing private goods paid for with private dollars is unreasonable on the surface of it. That is why it is so crucial to rebalance the public/private partnership.

Colleges and universities are chartered in the public interest and receive substantial tax benefits and other subsidies to act accordingly. However, public subsidies that aim to keep higher education accessible and affordable for lower-income students have not kept pace with rising college prices.[5] Moreover, the marketplace, replete with rankings, prestige hierarchies, and the resultant need to attract paying consumers, has overcome the public aspect of the equation. College presidents, for example, kowtow to rankings at the same time that they condemn them. At the same time, national and sector-wide higher-education organizations act as industry lobbying groups that promote institutional autonomy at the cost of educational policy that would benefit the nation. These conditions call for more effective public policy, including renewed public investment, coupled with institutional accountability and renewed collaboration between the federal government and institutions of higher education, both public and private.

And what of enrollment management? How higher education works and how enrollment management is conducted are tightly bound together. Enrollment management and enrollment managers are at the focal point of who enters and who completes higher education. Understanding what enrollment management is and how it works is key to designing what solutions should be considered and adopted.

ENROLLMENT MANAGEMENT AND ITS MULTIPLE MASTERS

Enrollment management is a philosophy of action, an organizing principle, and a set of operational strategies and tactics. Student enrollments and outcomes are fundamental to mission attainment and financial viability. Careful thought must be given and strategies must be invoked to plan for and achieve the desired levels of enrollment, characteristics of the student body, and outcomes for students. Using enrollment management strategies and tools enables institutions to have the student and financial resources necessary to produce the in- and out-of-classroom learning functions that are necessary in a high-quality higher-education experience. Toward this end, colleges create campuswide enrollment plans and operational divisions to carry them out. The latter include key enrollment-related services like admissions, financial aid, registration and records, and often institutional research and more, in order to recruit, retain, and graduate students. This makes good management sense. The rub comes when revenue goals, which are largely achieved via student tuition, and the drive for prestige, which is largely achieved via admission selectivity, overcome the educational imperative to educate future generations of Americans from all walks of life equitably and effectively.

A vivid example is the practice of financial aid leveraging, in which sophisticated algorithms are used to identify how much tuition and other costs each student or family is willing to pay at any given college. Championed by enrollment management consultants who sell this service as *the* way for colleges to maximize their revenue, aid leveraging relies upon a "profit maximization" model borrowed directly from the corporate world, and it is often applied absent the educational and social values that are almost invariably expressed in colleges' mission statements.

To what extent does enrollment management contribute to inequality in educational access and results? The answer depends on the charge that campus leaders give to their enrollment professionals, who decide which students to recruit, admit, and award student aid. When revenue goals and measures of prestige are the predominant objectives, as they all too often are, diversity, equity, and the needs of the nation take a back seat to institutional self-interest.

In this era of academic capitalism, there is no question that higher education is in a "positional arms race," where the perceived value of an entity is based on its position in the hierarchy relative to its competitors.[6] In such conditions, and within the context of enrollment management, colleges seek increased revenues from wealthy students who can pay. They also seek greater exclusivity in enrollments to climb in the rankings. Indeed, presidents are evaluated by watchful boards of trustees with an emphasis on financial sustainability and rankings. Have you yet heard of a president who was fired for a lack of campus diversity?

As a result, enrollment plans that reflect these dominant institutional impulses are created, and because the stakes are high, sophisticated tools, such as predictive analytics, are employed to determine who can pay for college, how much they can pay, who is likely to attend, and who is likely to graduate. The tools themselves are not the source of the problem. The same tools that can exclude disadvantaged students can identify students of promise and ability across all income levels and cultural backgrounds.[7] However, when these tools are employed in the service of exclusion, alongside other practices that advantage those with social and economic capital, remedies must be found.

A THREE-PART PLAN FOR RESULTS

The problems associated with the inequitable access, results, and benefits of higher education across American society must be addressed cooperatively and systemically across governments and institutions of higher education. In the remainder of this chapter, I am going to outline a three-part plan to fundamentally change the direction in which higher education has been heading. Accordingly, the following narrative is first devoted to changes in public policy. The discussion then turns to ways that higher education can and should act as an industry to produce greater educational attainment. Finally, the enrollment industry and enrollment practitioners are addressed in detail to find answers in policy and practice.

Part 1: Strengthening the Federal Role

The first step to altering the unequal results that we see in higher education is renewed and focused public investment in underserved students and in the institutions that predominantly serve them. Here, I call for enhancing the federal role through two proposals: one that directly benefits students from low- to lower-middle-income backgrounds and another that supports their success at the institutions at which they enroll.

1. DOUBLE THE PELL GRANT

As part of its plan to make college more accessible, the Biden administration has proposed doubling the maximum Pell Grant. This proposal should be a centerpiece of a new national covenant because doubling the Pell Grant is a direct subsidy to the students who need it most and would have an immediate beneficial impact in providing greater college access for low- and lower-middle-income students. The Pell Grant's purchasing power has dwindled over recent decades. Restoring the program's buying power will encourage more students to attend college, reduce the loan burden that they experience, lessen the financial aid burden on the colleges themselves, and contribute to college completion. In short, providing students greater financial resources through the Pell Grant program puts them in a better position to pay for college.

The many benefits that will accrue from enhancing the Pell Grant, however, come with one substantial drawback: the program comes with little institutional accountability. Colleges currently have only a modest incentive to recruit Pell recipients, who often require additional institutional aid. Further, colleges have little incentive to provide academic and social support to their enrolled Pell recipients, who often need these additional services to succeed, as the institutions do not receive any additional funding to do so. To achieve greater access and success, a companion approach is required.

2. CREATE A TITLE I PROGRAM FOR HIGHER EDUCATION

Because the Pell Grant program lacks incentives for colleges to admit and support low- and lower-middle-income students, doubling the maximum grant needs to be paired with a second federal effort that promotes student enrollment and success among this targeted population. My colleagues and I at the USC Center for Enrollment Research, Policy, and Practice, alongside researchers at the University of Wisconsin, are crafting a new program modeled after the Title 1 programs in K–12 education. While the existing Title 1 program provides financial assistance to K–12 schools that serve low-income students, a program adapted for higher education would provide incentives in the form of block grants to colleges and universities to enroll more low- and lower-middle-income students and increase their graduation rates.

Simply enrolling more low-income students is not enough. The data show that these students often need additional academic support to succeed in higher education. Currently, less than half (49 percent) of Pell Grant recipients who enroll in four-year colleges graduate within six years. At community colleges, less than one-third do so. Clearly, colleges must do a better job helping these students succeed. Too often, though, colleges have more incentive to steer away from these students than to provide them with the extra help they need.

Under our proposal, qualifying nonprofit institutions would receive an annual per-student subsidy for every Pell-eligible student that they attract and enroll. Research demonstrates that per-student subsidies of $500 to $1,000 would move the needle on educational attainment among these students.[8] Unlike Pell Grants and federal student loans, this new program would have teeth in the form of an accountability framework. Colleges would have to apply to participate by committing to programs of improvement in both the enrollment and success of Pell-eligible students. Only colleges with the best results would not be required to apply for grant renewal. Failure to achieve the stated goals would jeopardize or eliminate the block grant funds.

A major benefit of this program is that it would provide the most funding to colleges that already serve substantial numbers of low-income students but don't currently have enough resources to provide adequate support services to ensure that these students succeed. These institutions—public community colleges, the local and regional public four-year campuses, and many unsung small private colleges that do not have national name recognition—offer the greatest access to higher education via open or less selective admission policies and, therefore, the greatest prospects for social mobility. Federal assistance and leverage can best be applied to these schools.

Part 2: Higher Education and the Public Interest

Substantially increasing federal investment in higher education is only part of the solution. We will not be able to achieve the kind of fundamental change that is needed unless colleges step up in partnership with the federal government to embrace their mission to produce an educated population, one that is prepared to lead and comes from all walks of life. However, our colleges will succeed in this effort only if they act collectively to counter the forces and impulses that have led to inequitable educational results.

Spurred by an intense positional marketplace and confronted with insufficient public investment, American colleges and universities compete aggressively for student enrollments. But they do not compete equally across each segment of the population who could and would benefit from their services. Low-income, first-generation, and other historically marginalized groups see fewer college recruiters, are provided less information about applying to college, and receive far less encouragement to pursue higher education.[9] Selective colleges disproportionately recruit students from wealthier families, who can pay all or a substantial part of college costs, while simultaneously pursuing prestige in the form of rankings and exclusivity. This must change. New populations of students must be educated at the highest levels in order for our democracy and the fabric of our society to continue to stand.

This vital moment exists, sadly, at the same time that public perceptions about the efficacy of higher education are waning.[10] Some observers, scholars, and analysts, including many who have contributed to this volume, are convinced that if higher-education institutions do not act, the government should step in and make them do so. They may be right. The coercive power of government, including threats of reduced funding, elimination of favored tax status, and other disincentives, might be needed if the higher-education industry does not act on its own to improve results.

Instead of imposing a draconian and potentially destructive loss of autonomy, however, I suggest that this is the time for a collaborative agenda—one that begins with the two ambitious government programs outlined in this chapter. In turn, institutions must embrace their public responsibility to improve access and graduation rates. Simply stated, higher education must act collectively to serve and protect its public mission in equal measure to the efforts that it makes to promote, lobby, and compete for institutional gains.

This will be no easy task. Fear of antitrust scrutiny is commonly cited as a reason not to act cooperatively. Indeed, the fervor of the US Department of Justice in threatening antitrust litigation can be daunting. Only recently, for example, Department of Justice pressure led the National Association of College Admission Counseling (NACAC) to eliminate rules in its "Guide to Ethical Practice in College Admission" that barred colleges from actively recruiting other colleges' students to transfer and from poaching prospective students who have already committed to another college. The department's aggressive enforcement of federal antitrust laws in higher education discourages cooperation, confuses students, and is destructive to the continuity that students need at the higher-education level to persist through graduation.[11]

Nonetheless, there are many ways that higher education can behave that will not raise antitrust issues. Even more important, working together to gain an antitrust exemption for higher education is a key element of this plan and may be necessary to achieve a full measure of success. An example from the world of sports is instructive. The National Football League (NFL), which has such an exemption, cooperates in highly effective ways to allow small-market teams to compete as evenly as possible with large- and richer-market teams. By tempering competition that would hurt the league, costs to each team are reduced through salary caps, roster limitations, and consolidated marketing, while team competition stays focused on winning games through points scored on the field. Consider instead how the push for prestige and tuition dollars impacts the results of the higher-education system, leading to inflationary price tags and diverting the focus from public responsibility. We need to evaluate colleges' effectiveness by their educational results rather than ranking colleges based on inputs like admission rates and test scores. Surely the NFL, which thrives by creating a level playing field, does not have a more compelling public responsibility than higher education.[12]

Moreover, there is good legal reasoning for higher-education associations to band together to fight for such an exemption. In the 1991 Ivy Overlap Group case, the Department of Justice forced the Ivy League and other elite private universities to enact an agreement not to share information about the financial aid packages that they offer to common applicants. However, the Massachusetts Institute of Technology (MIT) refused to sign off on the agreement and instead fought the case on its own. While a federal district court sided with the Department of Justice, the appeals court looked more favorably on MIT's argument that the Overlap Group bolstered the government's mission of promoting college access for low-income students by preventing its members from engaging in costly bidding wars for students without financial need. "Overlap may in fact merely regulate competition in order to enhance it, while also deriving certain social benefits," the appeals court stated. "If the rule of reasoned analysis leads to this conclusion, then indeed Overlap will be beyond the scope of the prohibitions of the Sherman Act." While the department's action is often cited as a reason not to cooperate, the appeals court's decision provides a strong rationale for the reconsideration of cooperative arrangements.[13]

Fighting for an exemption from federal antitrust laws on the strength of the public good is an essential part of this plan because collective cooperation, goodwill, and shared purpose are crucial elements for achieving the far-reaching changes needed. Here are four additional steps that would go a long way toward advancing more equitable outcomes in how colleges recruit, admit, serve, and graduate students. The country's higher-education advocacy groups can lead the charge to persuade their members to take these steps in the interest of the nation and the industry.

1. PUBLICLY DECLARE THEIR COMMITMENT TO ADVANCING EQUITY AND INCLUSION

Acting collectively through state control boards, higher-education commissions, higher-education membership organizations, athletic conferences, and the like, colleges should declare their intent to educate leaders across society and to be more inclusive. Concretely, they should establish an action agenda to ensure the educational progress of low-income students and other groups who will shape the American future. This action agenda should include partnerships with federal and state agencies that provide enrollment and student support funding as well as with K–12 school systems, cooperation across sectors of higher education to facilitate transfer, and agreement on and the establishment of measurable progress goals. Local, regional, and national demographic trends lend themselves to tracking this kind of progress institutionally, by higher-education sector, by state, by region, and nationally. Colleges acting alone, and often in their own interest, have not and will not deliver the results that are needed.

2. MOVE AWAY FROM DESTRUCTIVE COMPETITION

With the possible exception of community colleges, overheated competition among institutions is a root cause of inequity that must be changed for progress to occur.[14] Among the many issues associated with higher education's positional marketplace are higher sticker prices, unmanageable funding gaps for needy students, public perceptions of inaccessibility and disconnectedness, and a lack of transparent public information about getting into and paying for college. Even more fundamental is how hypercompetition distorts institutional missions away from public-serving activities and toward those directed to the pursuit of prestige, which invariably and disproportionately benefits the wealthy and the well connected.

Colleges can take numerous steps to tamp down destructive competition while competing on equitable educational grounds. The overall goal of these efforts is to level the playing field by dismantling or discarding the structures that underpin disadvantage. To accomplish this, colleges should do all of the following:

- End their cooperation with publications that produce college rankings, which almost all higher-education leaders recognize as false and misleading;
- Roll back non-need-based merit aid in favor of supporting low- and lower-middle-income students who most need institutional support to afford to attend;
- End the practice of financial aid leveraging championed by corporate consultants and carried out in many campus enrollment programs, and;
- Close loopholes for donors, alumni, and influencers, who are already heavily advantaged in competing for admission.

Each of these steps can be carefully executed with collaboration, and each would be good-faith commitments to match the new federal funds described here. Some enrollment managers may argue, however, that rolling back merit aid would be impossible in tandem with ending the practice of financial aid leveraging, given that a primary objective of leveraging is to produce the revenue needed to increase spending on need-based student aid. It is true that some colleges use financial aid leveraging for this purpose. Far too often, though, aid leveraging is used to maximize net revenue without providing any additional benefit to financially needy students. More clearly stated, enrollment management tools that are capable of identifying needy students and the revenues to support them must not be weaponized for the sake of revenue maximization because doing so contributes directly to the social inequities that we seek to remedy. Principled application of these analytic techniques is needed, and consulting companies that aggressively market financial aid leveraging tools to colleges, as well as the campus enrollment managers that use them, need to be held to equitable practices.

3. ESTABLISH EQUITY AND DIVERSITY AS A FUNDAMENTAL ELEMENT OF INSTITUTIONAL EXCELLENCE

There is a persistent and false narrative that pursuing a more diverse and representative college population is detrimental to educational excellence. This narrative underlies the challenges that have been made to race-aware and holistic admissions, which equate standardized test scores with academic merit. Higher education must drive a stake into the heart of this anachronistic and pernicious idea. Study after study demonstrates that the benefits of educational diversity accrue to all students, institutions, and employers. This research consistently shows that learning and working in diverse environments expose students and employees to new ways of thinking and alternative perspectives that increase overall creativity, problem-solving, and the development of solutions to complex problems.[15] Higher education's leaders must look deep within themselves to rethink their assumptions about what and who is meritorious and commit deeply to equity, diversity, and inclusion efforts across all educational fields and activities. In putting this principle into effect, higher-education leaders must develop relevant metrics and track progress toward them. Applying new measures of merit and encouraging the kinds of learning outcomes that diversity provides are critical to ensuring that inclusion is more than just a buzzword and to making sure that the educational benefits of diversity accrue across the student population.

4. CHANGE THE NARRATIVE SURROUNDING HIGHER EDUCATION BY COMMUNICATING MORE EFFECTIVELY AND TRANSPARENTLY

At present, higher education is losing in the court of public opinion. Considered elitist, disconnected, and of waning relevance, the higher-education industry needs to change the narrative by changing the way that it operates and communicates. The language of higher education is complex and inaccessible to many, particularly to the populations that are the subject of this set of reforms. One of the lessons learned on campuses while combating enrollment uncertainty during the COVID-19 pandemic was that technology can be adapted to reach into communities where recruiters have infrequently traveled and to speak in a language and languages that can influence previously underserved groups.[16] Simplification, greater transparency, and strategic approaches to enhance equity can yield results.

Indeed, achieving greater transparency in higher education is worthy of a book on its own, but a prime example is that colleges do not publish their net prices. Higher education is often compared to the airline industry, where the same seats are sold for different prices. However, the airline industry openly publishes at any moment in time the exact price for the day, time, class of service, and destination of your choice. Higher education does not offer even this low level of transparency. This opaqueness is a problem for all students, but especially those who come from families with no college experience and few resources. As Phillip Levine, professor of economics at Wellesley College, has argued in a recent book, colleges must make clear and understandable the actual price of attendance that students and families must pay.[17] Much the same can be said about other enrollment policies, including published admission, retention, and graduation rates. Would the Operation Varsity Blues admission scandal, in which a private admissions consultant bribed college athletic coaches and other administrators to guarantee admission slots for the children of his extremely wealthy clients, have occurred, for example, if in each special admission category, the numbers of applications, admissions, and enrolled students were always made public? It is said that the light of day cleanses us from all sin.

Part 3: Reforming Enrollment Management as a Profession and a Practice

Enrollment management, as practiced within institutions and among the corporate and consulting entities that support it, is the third leg of the stool in this equation for equitable enrollment results. The enrollment management office is where the application of federal policy and the goals of higher education play out operationally and practically. Most colleges and universities now employ a senior leader to guide their recruitment, admission, financial aid, and registration processes. Some of these leaders are also responsible for retention and graduation rates and institutional research. In many respects, these officials are in a "can't win" situation. They must resolve, in policy, practice, and results, the trade-offs that arise when attempting to achieve the institutional goals of increasing prestige, net revenue, student diversity, and in many cases, student persistence. As stated earlier, when these goals clash, which they often do, colleges invariably act to preserve their financial and reputational strength first. This is why government resources must come to bear to help keep many of these institutions whole, particularly those that serve the populations that are most disadvantaged.

Quite frankly, I have met precious few enrollment leaders who do not share the goals expressed in this chapter. In my view, many will happily lead the charge toward equity and the new measures of institutional effectiveness included in this plan. Nonetheless, there are many ways that enrollment management, as currently practiced, works against equity, and far too many enrollment conferences focus on tactics and tools at the expense of educational needs, ethics, or connections to public policy. These practices and policies, too, must change.

1. CREATING AN ENROLLMENT MANAGEMENT CODE OF ETHICS

College presidents must insist upon ethical enrollment practices and adopt, alongside enrollment leaders, an enrollment management code of ethics. This joint step is a necessary element of real reform, as presidents set the enrollment goals and objectives that they charge enrollment leaders to achieve. The ethical code would be a set of articulated values that guide institutional policy and practice in meeting enrollment goals. And it would be one in which ethical, transparent, student-oriented, trustworthy, and highly professional service is expected within and across institutions.

The code would also guide institutional decision-making around how business consultants from private enrollment management firms are used in student recruitment and institutional financial aid processes. In 2011, I wrote a paper with my colleague Scott Andrew Schulz that documented the tight relationship between enrollment-related business entities and campus enrollment management leaders. The paper showed that the values and influence of profit-motivated external entities often infiltrate and overcome educationally sound practices of attracting and enrolling students.[18] Indeed, these companies regularly bombard campus presidents and enrollment professional with solicitations, pitching their services almost exclusively on the bases of revenue and prestige enhancement. When revenue and prestige are the driving forces, underserved students remain underserved.

The following is a suggested code of ethics for enrollment management that is adapted from the common ethical and professional principles found in published codes in medicine, law, engineering, and counseling:

- *Enrollment professionals perform with competence, knowledge, skill, thoroughness, and integrity*: Education and training in the field are critical, as greater knowledge can bring about greater equity.
- *Enrollment professionals perform with respect for human dignity and differences and are mindful, understanding and accommodating of individual circumstances*: Education is a humanistic endeavor designed for the betterment of society, and therefore must strive for inclusiveness in all policies and practices.
- *Enrollment professionals place the highest value on the academic and social success of prospective and current students*: Recruitment, admission, selection, and enrollment processes are conducted toward educational and degree attainment.
- *Enrollment professionals uphold student confidentiality*: Legal and ethical responsibilities are honored within institutions and among individuals.
- *Enrollment professionals design and implement policies and practices independent of conflict of interest or any real or implied quid pro quo for themselves or their institutions*: Potential or existing conflicts of interest in policy and practice are disclosed, and appropriate action to recuse enrollment professionals from decision-making is taken if necessary.
- *Enrollment professionals uphold professional standards as set by professional organizations in which enrollment practitioners are members, such as the American Association of Collegiate Registrars and Admissions Officers (AACRAO), the NACAC, and the National Association of Student Financial Aid Administrators*: These national membership organizations can debate, refine, adapt, and adopt these principles.

- *Enrollment professionals uphold responsibility to the community. In doing so, they act to advance educational attainment in the local, regional, and national interest*: Value is placed on educational access for all.
- *Transparency, honesty, and openness in policy, practice, and public information are the foundations of everything that enrollment professionals do*: Enrollment professionals publish in a truthful, objective, and understandable manner, as transparency in policy and practice is critical to informed students and families. They also provide effective information and outreach to historically underserved populations.

2. TRANSPARENCY IN PUBLIC INFORMATION IS NECESSARY FOR ACHIEVING GREATER EQUITY

Nothing that is done in admission and recruitment should be a secret. Colleges and universities should make each admission criterion and each category of admission open, clear, and equity focused.

Every admission space, for example, should be available to all without influence. If admission exceptions are made, they should be reported in the light of day. In addition, the processes for talent-based admission should be openly published, and special admission categories, like those for alumni, donors, and influencers, should be eliminated. Any special categories that persist should be openly reported, as the pressure of transparency will reduce these exceptions. And importantly, there must be an absolute firewall between development (fundraising) and admissions. Finally, published institutional data should be relevant to student decision-making, as well as being clear, accurate, consistent, reliable, and verifiable. Clearly, to make this work, there must be responsibility and accountability for transparency at the highest levels, from the president or chancellor to the entry-level enrollment professional.

3. EXAMINE AND OVERHAUL ADMISSION AND AID PROCESSES THAT ADVANTAGE THE ALREADY ADVANTAGED

College leaders need to reconsider and replace policies and practices that favor students who hail from high-income families and attend well-resourced schools. These policies include the rote use of test scores in admitting students and awarding non-need-based aid, early decision plans, alumni legacy admissions, and any tip in the admission process that is given to prospective students who have the financial wherewithal to demonstrate interest in the campus through campus visits and the like, on the premise that they won't require as much institutional aid to attend because they already appear to be leaning toward enrolling. Further, enrollment managers must overhaul recruitment activities that exclude low- and lower-middle-income students, the areas these students live, and the high schools that they predominantly attend, thereby disadvantaging individuals who already have fewer educational and counseling resources available to them.

4. REFORM INSTITUTIONAL AID PRACTICES

Enrollment managers need to carry out the financial aid reforms highlighted in the previous section, including redirecting merit aid resources to low- and lower-middle-income students, and ending the practice of financial aid leveraging whereby no student pays the same price nor are ultimate prices published. Making these changes will mean redirecting the analytics championed by consultants from private enrollment management firms to goals that meet the basic revenue needs of the institution, while also serving the public interest. Some colleges and universities have made great progress on this, but many have not.

CONCLUSION

This chapter has presented a framework for reform and results. The elements need not take place exactly as they are presented here, but this three-pronged formula will work. Another federal program may be needed to counterbalance the revenue needs of institutions if the two outlined in this discussion prove to be insufficient. Statewide programs can and should be folded into the plan. A new higher-education organization, agency, or arm of the Department of Education may be needed to ensure cooperation and results. A consortium of national higher-education organizations working together toward these ends should be formed, as political pressure and concerted effort may be needed to confront and change antitrust concerns. Nonetheless, the steps here offer new hope for the generations that will soon contribute to the redefinition and future of American society.

Readers of this plan have reason to be skeptical, as it asks for dramatic change and is unapologetically hopeful. However, it takes a much-needed and open-eyed look in the mirror without casting blame. In doing so, it offers a new covenant for higher education built on the needs of the nation and executed with common values and principles.

To conclude, I would like to make three summary points. First, colleges cannot survive without the resources they need. In fact, some institutions admit every student who applies that has a chance to be successful in their quest to meet revenue requirements. Other colleges stretch themselves to the limits to serve financially needy students. Government and institutional partnerships must be built for these reforms to work. If this means that colleges must give up a modest measure of independence to receive new and continuing public subsidies, so be it. The colleges and universities in the United States must demonstrate progress in enrolling and graduating students from low- and lower-middle-income backgrounds, as well as other groups who have been poorly served. The degree of accountability required for measuring progress need not be onerous or result in massive reporting responsibilities.

Next, the goals and methods of enrollment management as an industry, and as a set of policies and practices, will change as the incentives that drive institutions change. Reforms will not be successful if they are directed solely at enrollment managers, who would risk being fired for not doing their institutions' bidding. I sincerely believe that the enrollment leaders themselves, who are often already at the heart of pushing their campuses toward equity, will embrace the changes and lead the effort to develop the new measures of institutional effectiveness that the plan proposes.

Finally, higher education depends upon the society in which it is embedded. Ours is one with great income and other disparities. As the noted scholars and economists Sandy Baum and Michael McPherson demonstrate in their new book *Can College Level the Playing Field?*, children grow up in vastly different circumstances, and our nation's K–12 system needs reform alongside higher education and other social systems.[19] This chapter directs its attention toward the enrollment results of higher education, but the larger social fabric needs to change as well.

Fortunately, we've faced moments like this before as a nation, and we've responded. The Morrill Act, the GI Bill, and the Higher Education Act of 1965 all ushered in new eras of educational vigor and progress when the nation needed it. Perhaps the question of our time is whether our nation has the will to respond to lift up the coming generations, who will hail primarily from populations who currently fare least well in the systems that we have built. The answer to that question will determine whether we are able to achieve what the Princeton sociologist Marta Tienda calls a "demographic dividend"—a stronger nation built on investing in its emerging populations.[20]

CONCLUSION

There is an overriding myth in the higher-education policy-making world. The myth is fostered by politicians in both political parties, journalists, researchers, and policy wonks at think tanks like the one that I work at in Washington, DC.

The myth is that the federal government is in the driver's seat when it comes to setting the incentives by which public and private four-year colleges operate. It goes like this: sure, there are huge problems in higher education related to college access, affordability, and student indebtedness, but the government can solve these problems by doubling down on what it is already doing. All that Congress and the White House need to do is double the maximum Pell Grant; radically simplify the Free Application for Federal Student Aid (FAFSA), the federal student aid application; provide broad-based student loan forgiveness; or make income-based student loan repayment options ever more generous. Some higher-education experts, particularly Ivy League economists, argue that the primary problem that low-income students face is not lack of money, but lack of knowledge. If the government made sure that these students were better informed about their college options and the availability of financial aid, they would make more rational decisions and choose better colleges that would fully support them.[1]

The idea that the federal government, which spends tens of billions of dollars each year on student aid and provides colleges with enormous tax subsidies, is steering higher education in the right direction still had some truth to it when I started reporting on higher education in the early 1990s. While it's a myth now, it didn't used to be. In fact, the government played a predominant role during much of the history of higher education in this country before the emergence of the extremely influential and lucrative enrollment management industry.

After all, it was the federal government, during the Civil War, that incentivized states to establish land-grant colleges. The Morrill Act of 1862 singlehandedly laid the groundwork for the creation of the public college and university sector, which would provide "an uncommon education for the common man," as James Angell, the University of Michigan's longest-serving president, said in 1879.[2]

And it was the government, in 1944, that created the GI Bill of Rights, which provided World War II veterans with funds to attend the college of their choice. Within a few years, the number of undergraduates nearly doubled, with veterans accounting for about half of enrollments.[3] Suddenly selective private colleges were opening their doors to less-advantaged students, and that huge influx of students spurred extraordinary growth in the public higher-education sector.

And it was the government that created the federal student aid programs in 1965 and 1972, with the passage and renewal of the Higher Education Act, which opened the doors of college wider to students of all incomes than ever before. For an all-too brief period, private colleges complemented the government efforts by predominantly using their aid dollars to meet financial need. And public universities kept their prices low enough that they were generally accessible for students, regardless of family income.

The federal government has long played such a significant role in higher education that it is difficult to come to grips with the fact that those days are in the past. Over the past four decades, private and, more recently, public colleges and universities have come under the thrall of for-profit consulting firms that have convinced college presidents and their boards that their schools' fortunes and even their survival depend on using their products and strategies, which all too often disadvantage low-income students and many students of color. As Jerry Lucido states in his chapter, these corporate consultants care little about "the educational and social values that are almost invariably expressed in colleges' mission statements." Instead, they push colleges to focus almost exclusively on increasing their rankings and maximizing their revenues. As a result, many colleges, both public and private, are undermining rather than enhancing the government's efforts to make college more accessible for low- and lower-middle-income students by leveraging their financial aid to get the students they want most—who all too often come from privileged backgrounds. Instead of removing barriers, these colleges are adding hurdles, making it more difficult for low-income students to go to college and earn a degree.

What is truly remarkable is how few people know about this multibillion dollar industry that has reshaped the way colleges recruit students and award financial aid. Those who have heard of enrollment management typically think of the college officials who run enrollment management offices at their institutions. These officials complain that they are often portrayed as "the evil ones" on their campuses.[4] The longtime higher education journalist Eric Hoover echoed these concerns in a *Chronicle of Higher Education* article with the headline "The Enrollment Manager as Bogeyman": "It's also worth remembering that though enrollment managers are prominent players with great sway on many campuses, they have bosses, too. They take orders from presidents, answer to trustees, and explain themselves to faculty members. All of these people have great expectations, for more and better applicants, more super-duper young scholars who can fill all the traditional majors and that brand-new one too."[5]

The critiques in this book are not directed at any individual campus enrollment manager. It is certainly true that many people involved in college admissions are well motivated and genuinely would like to make their campuses more socioeconomically and racially diverse. And it is also true that these officials take their marching orders from those who sign off on their paychecks.

But it is also worth remembering, as Peter Schmidt writes in chapter 7, that "college leaders, boards, and even professors at selective colleges operate in a higher-education environment that has been steeped in an enrollment management mindset for decades, where an institution's success is measured by how well it is ranked by *U.S. News & World Report*." The truth is that the enrollment management industry has been extraordinarily successful in defining the goals that colleges have pursued and providing the products, strategies, and algorithms that colleges need to achieve them. And the industry has done this while operating in the shadows, away from public scrutiny.

This book's aim has been to lift the veil on enrollment management. If policy makers have any hope of solving the problems of college access, affordability, equity, and indebtedness, they are going to have to finally acknowledge the industry behind the curtain.

The book is a good start, but much more work needs to be done by journalists, researchers, and policy makers to understand how the enrollment management industry and its many firms operate. For progress to occur, and for colleges to be refocused away from their incessant drive for greater revenues and prestige, policy makers are going to need to curb the industry's influence, or at least repurpose it, and put representative government rather than private, for-profit consulting companies back in the driver's seat.

NOTES

INTRODUCTION

1. Terry Hartle and Chris Nellum, "Where Have All the Low-Income Students Gone?," *Higher Education Today*, American Council on Education (ACE), November 25, 2015, https://www.higheredtoday.org/2015/11/25/where-have-all-the-low-income-students-gone.
2. Maggie McGrath and Matt Schifrin, "The Invisible Force Behind College Admissions," *Forbes*, July 30, 2014, https://www.forbes.com/sites/maggiemcgrath/2014/07/30/the-invisible-force-behind-college-admissions.
3. Michael S. McPherson and Morton Owen Schapiro, *The Student Aid Game* (Princeton, NJ: Princeton University Press, 1998), 5–9.
4. Elizabeth A. Duffy and Idana Goldberg, *Crafting a Class: College Admissions and Financial Aid, 1955–1994* (Princeton, NJ: Princeton University Press, 1998), 207–209.
5. Max Kutner, "Higher Education Spent a Fortune for Prestige," *Boston Globe*, April 5, 2019, https://www.bostonglobe.com/ideas/2019/04/05/status-for-sale/Q6AVfAtwGZAMLhQz3feAFJ/story.html.
6. Matthew Quirk, "The Best Class Money Can Buy," *The Atlantic*, November 2005, https://www.theatlantic.com/magazine/archive/2005/11/the-best-class-money-can-buy/304307.
7. Stephen Burd, "Crisis Point: How Enrollment Management and the Merit-Aid Arms Race Are Derailing Public Higher Education," New America, February 13, 2020, https://www.newamerica.org/education-policy/reports/crisis-point-how-enrollment-management-and-merit-aid-arms-race-are-destroying-public-higher-education.

CHAPTER 1

* Sophie Brill Weitz provided research assistance to the author for this chapter, with support from the Brandeis Undergraduate Research and Creative Collaborations Office.

1. To get a glimpse of the Osborne Executive 2 "portable" computer and its resemblance to a sewing machine, see "Osborne OCC-2 Executive," last modified December 26, 2002, https://vintagecomputer.com/osborne-occ-2-executive.html.
2. David Kalsbeek, in discussions with the author, March 2021.
3. Ben Birnbaum and Thomas Cooper, "Presences," *Boston College Magazine*, Fall 2012, https://bcm.bc.edu/index.html%3Fp=863.html.
4. Jon Boeckenstedt (vice provost of enrollment management at Oregon State University), in discussions with the author, January 2021.
5. David Kalsbeek, email message to the author, January 8, 2021.

6. Kalsbeek, email message to the author, January 8, 2021.
7. David Elfin, email interview with the author, June 2021.
8. William Triplett, "*U.S. Snooze* Wakes Up," *American Journalism Review*, October 1992, https://ajrarchive.org/Article.asp?id=1683.
9. Chris Smith, "News You Can Abuse," *University of Chicago Magazine*, October 2001, https://magazine.uchicago.edu/0110/features/abuse.html.
10. Deirdre Carmody, "Ranking of 'Best Colleges' Rankles Many Educators," *New York Times*, October 25, 1989, https://www.nytimes.com/1989/10/25/us/education-ranking-of-best-colleges-rankles-many-educators.html.
11. Triplett, "*U.S. Snooze* Wakes Up."
12. Jack Maguire, in discussions with the author, November 2019; Birnbaum and Cooper, "Presences."
13. Jack Dunn and Reid Oslin, "Manager, Innovator, Leader Changed BC," *BC News*, January 20, 2011, https://www.bc.edu/bc-web/bcnews/chronicle/2011-archive/Campanella.html.
14. Maguire, in discussions with the author, November 2019.
15. John Maguire, "To the Organized, Go the Students," *Bridge Magazine*, Fall 1976, https://cdn2.hubspot.net/hubfs/1940013/To%20the%20Organized%20Go%20the%20Students%20-%20Boston%20College.pdf.
16. John Underwood, "It Wasn't a Fluke. It Was a Flutie," *Sports Illustrated Vault*, December 3, 1984, https://vault.si.com/vault/1984/12/03/it-wasnt-a-fluke-it-was-a-flutie.
17. Maguire, in discussions with the author, November 2019.
18. Max Kutner, "Higher Education Spent a Fortune for Prestige," *Boston Globe*, April 5, 2019, https://www.bostonglobe.com/ideas/2019/04/05/status-for-sale/Q6AVfAtwGZAMLhQz3feAFJ/story.html.
19. Isabel Wilkerson, "Heavy Burden of College Debt Raises Anxiety for Young Families' Future," *New York Times*, January 29, 1987, https://www.nytimes.com/1987/01/29/us/heavy-burden-of-college-debt-raises-anxiety-for-young-families-future.html.
20. David H. Autor, "Skills, Education, and the Rise of Earnings Inequality Among the 'Other 99 Percent,'" *Science* 344, no. 6186 (2014): 843–851, https://doi.org/10.1126/science.1251868.
21. Neil Swidey, "Why Do People Earn What They Earn?," *Boston Globe Magazine*, June 2, 2015, https://www.bostonglobe.com/magazine/2014/10/30/why-people-earn-what-they-earn/PAhbjmYnoD1fcfjduUCWjI/story.html.
22. Eric Hoover, "The Uncommon Rise of the Common App," *Chronicle of Higher Education*, November 18, 2013, https://www.chronicle.com/article/the-uncommon-rise-of-the-common-app.
23. *Impact and Trends*, Common App, 2019–2020, https://mcusercontent.com/1436e2ab2417019e4ccbb5ac1/files/bac5ff3a-ebf6-4ab4-96df-f59943b63758/CA_Impact_Report_2019_2020.F.pdf.
24. Andrew R. Goetz and Christopher J. Sutton, "The Geography of Deregulation in the U.S. Airline Industry," *Annals of the Association of American Geographers* 87, no. 2 (1997): 238–263, https://doi.org/10.1111/0004-5608.872052.
25. Alfred E. Khan, "Airline Deregulation," in *The Fortune Encyclopedia of Economics*, ed. David R. Henderson (New York: Warner, 1993), accessed at https://www.econlib.org/library/Enc1/AirlineDeregulation.html.

26. Brooke W. Tunstall, *Disconnecting Parties: Managing the Bell System Breakup: An Inside View* (New York: McGraw Hill, 1985).
27. Richard Morrison, "Price Fixing Among Elite Colleges and Universities," *University of Chicago Law Review* 59, no. 2 (1992): 807–835, https://doi.org/10.2307/1599922.
28. Maggie McGrath and Matt Schifrin, "The Invisible Force Behind College Admissions," *Forbes*, July 30, 2014, https://www.forbes.com/sites/maggiemcgrath/2014/07/30/the-invisible-force-behind-college-admissions/?sh=e8fde2270a55.
29. "Bill Hicks on Presidential Agendas (ENG SUB)," August 5, 2012, https://www.youtube.com/watch?v=NPTJXdBBrcU.
30. James Fallows, in discussions with the author, December 2020.
31. Fallows, in discussions with the author, December 2020.
32. Kendric Charles Babcock, *A Classification of Universities and Colleges with Reference to Bachelor's Degrees* (Washington, DC: Govt. print. off., 1911).
33. Peter Applebome, "Fighting the Rankings of a College Guide," *New York Times*, January 5, 1997, https://www.nytimes.com/1997/01/05/education/fighting-the-rankings-of-a-college-guide.html.
34. Alvin P. Sanoff, "The *U.S. News* College Rankings: A View from the Inside" (draft, Institute for Higher Education Policy, Washington, DC, May 2006).
35. Damon Chetson, "Class of '95 is Least Selective in Ivy League," *The Daily Pennsylvanian*, April 12, 1991, https://www.thedp.com/article/1991/04/class_of_95_is_least_selective_in_ivy_league.
36. Smith, "News You Can Abuse."
37. Leanna Tilitei, "Penn Accepts Record-Low 5.68% of Applicants to the Class of 2025," *The Daily Pennsylvanian*, April 6, 2021, https://www.thedp.com/article/2021/04/penn-admissions-class-of-2025-acceptance-rate; "University of Chicago Acceptance Rate and Admission Statistics," Ivy League Prep, https://ivyleagueprep.com/university-of-chicago/.
38. Robert Daly, Anne Muchung, and Gina Roque, "Running to Stay in Place: The Stability of *U.S. News*' Ranking System" (paper presented at the annual forum of the Association for Institutional Research, Chicago, Illinois, May 14–18, 2006), https://files.eric.ed.gov/fulltext/ED493830.pdf.
39. Steve Stecklow, "Educators Aim to Standardize Date Used to Rate Colleges," *Wall Street Journal*, September 24, 1996, https://www.wsj.com/articles/SB843522447136035000.
40. Smith, "News You Can Abuse."
41. Smith, "News You Can Abuse."
42. Alvin Sanoff, "The Consulting Game," *SPAN Magazine*, December 1995, https://issuu.com/spanmagazine/docs/1995-12-cr.
43. Thompson is now chief executive officer (CEO) of *The Atlantic*.
44. Gerhard Casper, "Criticism of College Rankings," Stanford University, Office of the President, September 23, 1996, https://web.stanford.edu/dept/pres-provost/president/speeches/961206gcfallow.html.
45. Fallows, in discussions with the author, December 2020.
46. Fallows, in discussions with the author, December 2020.
47. In 1996, to address the criticism that the rankings were merely measuring inputs, *U.S. News* added a "value added" measure, aiming to track how the colleges' graduation rates underperformed or overperformed expectations based on the credentials of their incoming students.

48. In 2004, the editors removed "yield" as a factor in their algorithm over concerns that the metric had pushed selective colleges to substantially increase their reliance on early-decision admissions, which significantly disadvantages low-income students.
49. Nicholas Thompson, "Playing with Numbers," *Washington Monthly*, September 1, 2002, https://washingtonmonthly.com/2000/09/01/playing-with-numbers/.
50. Smith, "News You Can Abuse."
51. Thompson, "Playing with Numbers."
52. Scott Heller and Ben Gose, "Renowned Anthropologists Protest Firing of Allegheny College Scholar; 'U.S. News' College-Rankings Editor Becomes a Consultant," *Chronicle of Higher Education*, March 6, 1998, https://www.chronicle.com/article/renowned-anthropologists-protest-firing-of-allegheny-college-scholar-u-s-news-college-rankings-editor-becomes-a-consultant/?sra=true.
53. Thompson, "Playing with Numbers."
54. Howard Kurtz, "James Fallows Fired After Stormy Tenure at *U.S. News*," *Washington Post*, June 30, 1998, https://www.washingtonpost.com/wp-srv/style/features/fallows.htm.
55. Don Hossler, in discussions with the author, March 2021.
56. "Fire Safety Honor Roll," *Princeton Review*, https://www.princetonreview.com/college-rankings/fire-safety-honor-roll.
57. James Fallows, "The Early-Decision Racket," *The Atlantic*, September 2001, https://www.theatlantic.com/magazine/archive/2001/09/the-early-decision-racket/302280/.
58. Philomena Mantella, in discussions with the author, May 2021.
59. Now president of Grand Valley State University (and its first female president), Mantella stresses that she and her Northeastern colleagues focused on improving the school's ranking by concentrating on the metrics that also fit Northeastern's mission, such as boosting the graduation rate.
60. Max Kutner, "How Northeastern University Gamed the College Rankings," *Boston Magazine*, August 26, 2014, https://www.bostonmagazine.com/news/2014/08/26/how-northeastern-gamed-the-college-rankings/.
61. "Private College Tuition Discontinuing Upward Trend During COVID-19 Pandemic," National Association of College and University Business Officers (NACUBO), May 19, 2021, https://www.nacubo.org/Press-Releases/2021/Private-College-Tuition-Discounting-Continued-Upward-Trend-During-COVID19-Pandemic.
62. Hossler, in discussions with the author, March 2021.
63. Matthew Quirk, "The Best Class Money Can Buy," *The Atlantic*, November 2005, https://www.theatlantic.com/magazine/archive/2005/11/the-best-class-money-can-buy/304307/.
64. Quirk, "The Best Class Money Can Buy."
65. Quirk, "The Best Class Money Can Buy."
66. Quirk, "The Best Class Money Can Buy."
67. Don Hossler and David Kalsbeek, "Enrollment Management and Managing Enrollments: Revisiting the Context for Institutional Strategy," *Strategic Enrollment Management Quarterly* 1 (2013): 5–25, https://doi.org/10.1002/sem3.20002.
68. Kalsbeek, in discussions with the author, March 2021.
69. Kalsbeek, in discussions with the author, March 2021.
70. Susan Paterno, *Game On: Why College Admission Is Rigged and How to Beat the System* (New York: St. Martin's, 2021).

71. "Carnegie Announces the Acquisition of Maguire Associates," Carnegie Higher Ed, July 11, 2022, https://www.carnegiehighered.com/blog/carnegie-announces-the-acquisition-of-maguire-associates/.
72. Kalsbeek, in discussions with the author, March 2021.

CHAPTER 2

1. Jennifer Winn (EAB's senior vice president of marketing and enrollment services), in discussions with the author, June 2020.
2. John Reid Blackwell, "Henrico-Based Royall & Co. Acquired for $850 Million," *Richmond Times-Dispatch*, December 11, 2014, https://www.richmond.com/business/henrico-based-royall-co-acquired-for-850-million/article_27ab7f14-ed33-5f52-a7fd-df71e1a1193f.html.
3. Drew Hansen, "Advisory Board Closes Sale of Its Education Division," *Washington Business Journal*, November 20, 2017, https://www.bizjournals.com/washington/news/2017/11/20/advisory-board-completes-spinoff-sale-of-its.html.
4. Winn, in discussions with the author, June 2020.
5. Jessica Ronky Haddad, "Collecting for the Love of It," *Richmond Magazine*, March 13, 2016, https://richmondmagazine.com/arts-entertainment/collecting-for-the-love-of-it/.
6. Winn, in discussions with the author, June 2020.
7. Blackwell, "Henrico-Based Royall & Co. Acquired for $850 Million."
8. "RuffaloCODY Announces Merger with Noel-Levitz," RuffaloCODY, August 21, 2014, https://www.ruffalonl.com/about-ruffalo-noel-levitz/press-releases/ruffalocody-announces-merger-with-noel-levitz/.
9. Veronica Garabelli, "The Advisory Board to Acquire Royall & Co. for $850 Million," *Virginia Business*, December 10, 2014, https://www.virginiabusiness.com/article/the-advisory-board-to-acquire-royall-co-for-850-million/.
10. Maggie McGrath and Matt Schifrin, "The Invisible Force Behind College Admissions," *Forbes*, July 30, 2014, https://www.forbes.com/sites/maggiemcgrath/2014/07/30/the-invisible-force-behind-college-admissions/#3667d4470a55.
11. EAB, "Strategic Use of Grant Aid, 101: Understanding the Mechanics of Aid Optimization," September 20, 2019, https://eab.com/insights/blogs/enrollment/how-to-create-a-financial-aid-policy.
12. IRS Form 990s for Bryant University in 2017 and Linfield University in 2019, which can be accessed at ProPublica's Nonprofit Explorer, https://projects.propublica.org/nonprofits/. For Bryant University, see Part VII Section B, "Independent Contractors," https://projects.propublica.org/nonprofits/organizations/50258810/201901359349312125/full; for Linfield University, see Attachment 3: Part VII Section B, "Independent Contractors," https://projects.propublica.org/nonprofits/display_990/930391586/download990pdf_03_2022_prefixes_86-95%2F930391586_202006_990_2022032219802521.
13. Ozan Jaquette and Crystal Han, "Follow the Money: Recruiting and the Enrollment Priorities of Public Research Universities" (Washington, DC: Third Way, March 2, 2020), https://www.thirdway.org/report/follow-the-money-recruiting-and-the-enrollment-priorities-of-public-research-universities.
14. Jim Jump (academic dean and director of college counseling, St. Christopher's School in Richmond, Virginia), in discussions with the author, September 2020.
15. Adam Davidson, "Is College Tuition Really Too High?," *New York Times*, September 8, 2015, https://www.nytimes.com/2015/09/13/magazine/is-college-tuition-too-high.html.

16. College Board, *Trends in Student Aid 2019*, November 2019, https://research.collegeboard.org/pdf/trends-student-aid-2019-full-report.pdf.
17. Lloyd Thacker (founder and executive director, the Education Conservancy), in discussions with the author, September 2020.
18. National Association of College and University Business Officers, "Before COVID-19, Private College Tuition Discount Rates Reached Record Highs," May 20, 2020, https://www.nacubo.org/Press-Releases/2020/Before-COVID-19-Private-College-Tuition-Discount-Rates-Reached-Record-Highs.
19. Kenneth E. Redd, "No End in Sight," *Business Officer Magazine*, May/June 2020, https://www.businessofficermagazine.org/features/no-end-in-sight/.
20. S. Georgia Nugent (president, Illinois Wesleyan University), in discussions with the author, September 2020.
21. Abril Castro, "Early Decision Harms Students of Color and Low-Income Students," Center for American Progress, November 4, 2019, https://www.americanprogress.org/issues/race/news/2019/11/04/476789/early-decision-harms-students-color-low-income-students/.
22. Jump, in discussions with the author, September 2020.
23. Jack Maguire (founder, Maguire Associates), in discussions with the author, May 2020.
24. Tom Williams (former principal, Noel-Levitz), in discussions with the author, June 2020.
25. Richard Freeland (former president, Northeastern University), in discussions with the author, June 2020.
26. Marten Roorda, "Sixty Years, and Counting, of Serving Students' Needs," ACT, November 7, 2019, https://leadershipblog.act.org/2019/11/sixty-years-and-counting-of-serving.html.
27. ACT's IRS Form 990 for 2017, which can be accessed at ProPublica's Nonprofit Explorer, see Part 1 Line 12, "Total Revenue," https://projects.propublica.org/nonprofits/organizations/420841485/201941929349300714/full.
28. Ruffalo Noel Levitz (RNL), "History of RNL," https://www.ruffalonl.com/about-ruffalo-noel-levitz/the-history-of-ruffalo-noel-levitz/.
29. Al Ruffalo (cofounder, RuffaloCODY), in discussions with the author, June 2020.
30. Stamats, "About Us," https://www.stamats.com/about/.
31. Williams, in discussions with the author, June 2020.
32. Kevin Crockett (president, RNL), in discussions with the author, June 2020.
33. Williams, in discussions with the author, June 2020.
34. RNL, "History of RNL."
35. Crockett, in discussions with the author, June 2020.
36. Maguire, in discussions with the author, May 2020.
37. Jacques Steinberg, "Colleges Market Easy, No-Fee Sell to Applicants," *New York Times*, January 25, 2010.
38. Williams, in discussions with the author, June 2020.
39. Steinberg, "Colleges Market Easy, No-Fee Sell to Applicants."
40. Crockett, in discussions with the author, June 2020.
41. Jon Marcus, "The M Word," *National Crosstalk* (San Jose, CA: National Center for Public Policy and Higher Education, 2006), https://www.highereducation.org/crosstalk/ct0306/news0306-the_m_word.shtml.
42. Meghan Dalessandro (chief operating officer, Carnegie Dartlet), in discussions with the author, June 2020.

43. Elizabeth Scarborough Johnson (chair, Simpson Scarborough), in discussions with the author, June 2020.
44. Jon Marcus, "Strapped for Students, Nonprofit Colleges Borrow Recruiting Tactic from For-Profits," *Hechinger Report*, August 3, 2016, https://hechingerreport.org/strapped-for-students-nonprofit-colleges-borrow-recruiting-tactic-from-for-profits/.
45. Robert Massa (former enrollment and admissions officer), in discussions with the author, June 2020.
46. Nathalie Mainland (senior vice president and general manager of Education Cloud, Salesforce), in discussions with the author, June 2020.
47. Crockett, in discussions with the author, June 2020.
48. Eric Hoover, "A Tech Whiz Is Conquering College Admissions. It Takes Charm, Innovation, and Dancing Sharks," *Chronicle of Higher Education*, August 20, 2018, https://www.chronicle.com/article/a-tech-whiz-is-conquering-college-admissions-it-takes-charm-innovation-and-dancing-sharks/.
49. Douglas MacMillan and Nick Anderson, "Student Tracking, Secret Scores: How College Admissions Offices Rank Prospects Before They Apply," *Washington Post*, October 19, 2019, https://www.washingtonpost.com/business/2019/10/14/colleges-quietly-rank-prospective-students-based-their-personal-data/.
50. Tom Green (associate executive director for consulting and strategic enrollment management, AACRAO; editor-in-chief, *Enrollment Management Quarterly*), in discussions with the author, June 2020.
51. ACT, "ACT Acquires NRCCUA," July 24, 2018, https://leadershipblog.act.org/2018/07/act-acquires-nrccua.html.
52. Carl Staumsheim, "NRCCUA Acquires Research Firm Eduventures," *Inside Higher Ed*, September 16, 2016, https://www.insidehighered.com/quicktakes/2016/09/16/nrccua-acquires-research-firm-eduventures.
53. Hobsons, "Hobsons U.S. Acquires Naviance," June 25, 2007, https://www.crunchbase.com/acquisition/hobsons-acquires-naviance--94069b51.
54. Dian Schaffhause, "Hobsons Acquires High School Counselor-College Admissions App," *The Journal*, February 14, 2017, https://thejournal.com/articles/2017/02/14/hobsons-acquires-high-school-counselor-college-admissions-app.aspx.
55. Hobsons, "Hobsons Acquires College Confidential," June 4, 2008, https://www.businesswire.com/news/home/20080604005246/en/Hobsons-Acquires-College-Confidential.
56. Hobsons, "Hobsons Acquires Intelliworks: Powerful Combination Shaping the Future of Enrollment Management Technology," December 13, 2011, https://www.prnewswire.com/news-releases/hobsons-acquires-intelliworks-powerful-combination-shaping-the-future-of-enrollment-management-technology-135494808.html.
57. Starfish, "About Us," https://www.starfishsolutions.com/about-us/.
58. Civitas Learning, "Civitas Learning Acquires College Scheduler, Leader in Schedule Planning Solutions," January 20, 2016, https://www.civitaslearning.com/press/civitas-learning-acquires-college-scheduler-leader-schedule-planning-solutions/.
59. Michael Stoner (cofounder and co-owner, mStoner), in discussions with the author, June 2020.
60. Alloy, "Alloy Acquires Carnegie Communications to Build on Its Leadership Position in Higher Education Marketing, Media and Consulting," April 22, 2010, https://www.prnewswire.com/news-releases/alloy-acquires-carnegie-communications-to-build-on

-its-leadership-position-in-higher-education-marketing-media-and-consulting-91832849.html.

61. Dalessandro, in discussions with the author, June 2020.
62. Blackwell, "Henrico-Based Royall & Co. Acquired for $850 Million."
63. EAB, "EAB Extends Student Success Collaborative with GradesFirst Acquisition," February 12, 2015, https://www.prnewswire.com/news-releases/eab-extends-student-success-collaborative-with-gradesfirst-acquisition-300035432.html.
64. EAB, "EAB Acquires Leading Interactive Content Provider YouVisit," December 4, 2019, https://eab.com/about/newsroom/press/youvisit/#:~:text=EAB%20Acquires%20Leading%20Interactive%20Content%20Provider%20YouVisit%20Acquisition,tour%20and%20interactive%20web%20content%20for%20higher%20education.
65. EAB, "EAB Acquires Cappex, a Leading College Research and Decision Platform," news release, September 9, 2020, https://eab.com/insights/press-release/enrollment/cappex-acquisition/#:~:text=Education%20firm%20EAB%20has%20acquired%20Cappex%2C%20a%20market,despite%20major%20shifts%20in%20the%20college%20search%20process.
66. Kate Lucariello, "EAB Acquires Concourse to Help Colleges and Universities Recruit Students," *Campus Technology*, September 30, 2022, https://campustechnology.com/articles/2022/09/30/eab-acquires-concourse-to-help-colleges-and-universities-recruit-students.aspx.
67. RNL, "History of RNL."
68. RNL, "RNL Strategically Acquires Higher Education Digital Marketing Agency Converge," May 2, 2019, https://convergeconsulting.org/2019/05/02/rnl-acquires-converge/.
69. RNL, "History of RNL."
70. Ruffalo, in discussions with the author, June 2020.
71. Elissa Nadworny, "Fewer Students Are Going to College. Here's Why That Matters," *Morning Edition*, National Public Radio, December 16, 2019, https://www.npr.org/2019/12/16/787909495/fewer-students-are-going-to-college-heres-why-that-matters.
72. Blackwell, "Henrico-Based Royall & Co. Acquired for $850 Million."
73. Summit Partners, "Growth & Ventures Companies," https://www.summitpartners.com/companies/ruffalo-noel-levitz.
74. Civitas Learning, "Civitas Learning Acquires College Scheduler."
75. Laura Yeager (managing director, Huron), in discussions with the author, June 2020.
76. 160over90, "Recent Work," https://160over90.com/work.
77. Stoner, in discussions with the author, June 2020.
78. LeadsCouncil, "FAQ," https://www.leadscouncil.org/faq/.
79. Scott Brinker, "Marketing Technology Landscape," ChiefMarTec blog, April 22, 2020, https://chiefmartec.com/2020/04/marketing-technology-landscape-2020-martech-5000/.
80. National Association for College Admissions Counseling, "Exhibit Hall Map," 2019 National Conference, https://fp37.a2zinc.net/clients/nacac/nc19/Public/EventMap.aspx.
81. Andrew Delbanco, "Do We Do What We Say We Do in Our Colleges and Universities?" (keynote address presented at the College Board Colloquium, Laguna Beach, CA, January 2002).
82. Nugent, in discussions with the author, September 2020.
83. Education Conservancy, "Financial Aid: Examining the Thinking Behind the Policy," June 2015, https://educationconservancy.org/PresidentialThinking.pdf.

84. Thacker, in discussions with the author, September 2020.
85. National Association of College and University Business Officers, "2021 NACUBO Discounting Study," May 19, 2022, https://www.nacubo.org/Research/2021/NACUBO-Tuition-Discounting-Study.
86. Williams, in discussions with the author, June 2020.
87. National Student Clearinghouse Research Center, "Persistence & Retention 2019," July 10, 2019, https://nscresearchcenter.org/snapshotreport35-first-year-persistence-and-retention/?highlight=retention&hilite=%27retention%27.
88. Peace Bransberger, Colleen Falkenstern, and Patrick Lane, "Knocking at the College Door: Projections of High School Graduates," Western Interstate Commission for Higher Education, December 2020, https://www.wiche.edu/wp-content/uploads/2020/12/Knocking-pdf-for-website.pdf.
89. Brady E. Hamilton, Joyce A. Martin, and Michelle J. K. Osterman, "Births: Provisional Data for 2020," Centers for Disease Control and Prevention, May 2021, https://www.cdc.gov/nchs/data/vsrr/vsrr012-508.pdf.
90. Kristin Tichenor (senior advisor to the president and former senior vice president for enrollment and institutional strategy, Worcester Polytechnic Institute), in discussions with the author, June 2020.

CHAPTER 3

1. Francie Diep and Nell Gluckman, "Colleges Still Obsess over National Rankings. For Proof, Look at Their Strategic Plans," *Chronicle of Higher Education*, September 13, 2021, https://www.chronicle.com/article/colleges-still-obsess-over-national-rankings-for-proof-look-at-their-strategic-plans.
2. Colin S. Diver, *Breaking Ranks: How the Rankings Industry Rules Higher Education and What to Do about It* (Baltimore, MD: Johns Hopkins University Press, 2022); Scott Jaschik, "Suit Charges Rutgers Rigged M.B.A. Rankings," *Inside Higher Ed*, April 11, 2022, https://www.insidehighered.com/quicktakes/2022/04/11/suit-charges-rutgers-rigged-mba-rankings#:~:text=A%20lawsuit%20filed%20Friday%20charged,business%20school's%20human%20resources%20manager; Alyssa Lupkat, "Former Temple U. Dean Found Guilty of Faking Data for National Rankings," *New York Times*, November 29, 2021, https://www.nytimes.com/2021/11/29/us/temple-university-moshe-porat-fraud.html.
3. Stephen Burd, "Merit vs. Need-Based Aid: What the Research Says," New America's *Ed Central* (blog), May 27, 2013, https://www.newamerica.org/education-policy/higher-education/higher-ed-watch/merit-vs-need-based-aid-what-the-research-says-2/.
4. Crystal Han, Ozan Jaquette, and Karen Salazar, "Recruiting the Out-of-State University," Joyce Foundation, March 2019, https://emraresearch.org/sites/default/files/2019-03/joyce_report.pdf.
5. Douglas MacMillan and Nick Anderson, "Student Tracking, Secret Scores: How College Admissions Offices Rank Prospects Before They Apply," *Washington Post*, October 19, 2019, https://www.washingtonpost.com/business/2019/10/14/colleges-quietly-rank-prospective-students-based-their-personal-data/.
6. MacMillan and Anderson, "Student Tracking, Secret Scores."
7. Laura W. Perna, Jeremy Wright-Kim, and Nathan Jiang, "Money Matters: Understanding How Colleges and Universities Use Their Websites to Communicate Information about How to Pay College Costs," *Educational Policy* 35, no. 7 (2021): 1311–1348.

8. Stephen Burd, Laura Keane, Rachel Fishman, and Julie Habbert, "Decoding the Cost of College: The Case for Transparent Financial Aid Award Letters," New America and uAspire, June 2018, https://files.eric.ed.gov/fulltext/ED612526.pdf.
9. Burd et al., "Decoding the Cost of College."
10. US Department of Education, Federal Student Aid Office, "(General-21-70) Issuing Financial Aid Offers—What Institutions Should Include and Avoid," accessed May 28, 2022, https://fsapartners.ed.gov/knowledge-center/library/electronic-announcements/2021-10-28/issuing-financial-aid-offers-what-institutions-should-include-and-avoid; National Association of Student Financial Aid Administrators, "Improving Financial Aid Offers," May 28, 2022, https://www.nasfaa.org/Improving_Aid_Offers.
11. Monikah Schuschu, "What Is Financial Aid Gapping?," *CollegeVine* (blog), September 28, 2018, https://blog.collegevine.com/what-is-financial-aid-gapping/.
12. Dave Byrnes, "Elite Universities Accused of Conspiring to Exclude Low-Income Students," Courthouse News Service, January 10, 2022, https://www.courthousenews.com/elite-universities-accused-of-conspiring-to-exclude-low-income-students/.
13. Tucker Sechrest, "The DOJ vs. NACAC: Autonomy and Paternalism in Higher Ed," *Prindle Post*, November 13, 2019, https://www.prindlepost.org/2019/10/the-doj-vs-nacac-autonomy-and-paternalism-in-higher-ed/.

CHAPTER 4

1. The Campus-Based Aid programs in the HEA included Education Opportunity Grants, later known as Supplemental Educational Opportunity Grants (SEOGs); College Work-Study; and National Defense Student Loans, which were created in 1958 and later were renamed Perkins Loans.
2. Ronald M. Brown, "Equity Packaging of Student Financial Aid," College Scholarship Service, 1976, https://files.eric.ed.gov/fulltext/ED129176.pdf.
3. Jon H. Oberg, "Testing Federal Student-Aid Fungibility in Two Competing Versions of Federalism," *Publius: The Journal of Federalism* 27, no. 1 (Winter 1997), 115–134, https://doi.org/10.1093/oxfordjournals.pubjof.a029888.
4. Jon H. Oberg, "A Natural Experiment of the 1990s: Responses to Changes in Pell Grants and Stafford Loans," working paper at the US Department of Education's Institute of Education Sciences, 2003.
5. Ben Miller, "The Continued Student Loan Crisis for Black Borrowers," Center for American Progress, December 2, 2019, https://www.americanprogress.org/issues/education-postsecondary/reports/2019/12/02/477929/continued-student-loan-crisis-black-borrowers/.
6. Sarah Turner, "Does Federal Aid Affect the Price Students Pay for College? Evidence from the Pell Program," mimeo, 1997.
7. Lesley J. Turner, "The Incidence of Student Financial Aid: Evidence from the Pell Grant Program," PhD diss., Columbia University, New York, 2012.
8. Matthew Quick, "The Best Class Money Can Buy," *The Atlantic*, November 2005, https://www.theatlantic.com/magazine/archive/2005/11/the-best-class-money-can-buy/304307/.
9. Doug Lederman, "Enrollment Managers Struggle with Image," *Inside Higher Ed*, March 27, 2008, https://www.insidehighered.com/news/2008/03/27/enrollment-managers-struggle-image.

CHAPTER 5

1. The US Department of Education's FY 2020 Justifications of Appropriation Estimates to Congress: Student Financial Assistance, US Department of Education, March 2019, 9–22, https://www2.ed.gov/about/overview/budget/budget21/justifications/p-sfa.pdf.
2. Rupert Wilkinson, *Aiding Students, Buying Students: Financial Aid in America* (Nashville, TN: Vanderbilt University, 2005), 131–132.
3. Deborah Jones Merritt and Andrew Lloyd Merritt, "Agreements to Improve Student Aid: An Anti-Trust Perspective," *Journal of Legal Education* 67, no. 1 (Autumn 2017): 22, https://jle.aals.org/cgi/viewcontent.cgi?article=1529&context=home.
4. Dennis W. Carlton, Gustavo E. Bamberger, and Roy J. Epstein, "Antitrust and Higher Education: Was There a Conspiracy to Restrict Financial Aid?," *RAND Journal of Economics* 26, no. 1 (Spring 1995): 131–147.
5. Kenneth D. Campbell, "MIT Summation Labels Antitrust Suit 'Myopic . . . ,'" MIT News, July 15, 1992, https://news.mit.edu/1992/myopic-0715.
6. Campbell, "MIT Summation Labels Antitrust Suit 'Myopic . . . .'"
7. Wayne D. Collins and Vittorio E. Cottafavi, "Antitrust and Financial Aid in Higher Education," in *Time to Reexamine Institutional Cooperation on Financial Aid*, Institute for College Access and Success, June 2008, 19.
8. Gustavo E. Bamberger and Dennis W. Carlton, "Antitrust and Higher Education: MIT Financial Aid," in *The Antitrust Revolution: Economics, Competition, and Policy*, ed. J. E. Kwoka Jr. and L. J. White (Oxford: Oxford University Press, 1999), 202, https://global.oup.com/us/companion.websites/fdscontent/uscompanion/us/pdf/kwoka/9780195322972_07.pdf.
9. See www.568group.org for a discussion of the agreement and section 568 of the Improving America's Schools Act (IASA) of 1994, which set forth the various aspects of the agreement. This provision has been extended by Congress several times, including in 2015 until September 30, 2022.
10. "Antitrust Case Settled," MIT News Office, December 22, 1993, http://tech.mit.edu/Bulletins/ovrlp-pr.html.
11. See www.568group.org. Current members include Amherst College, Boston College, California Institute of Technology, Claremont McKenna College, Columbia University, Cornell University, Dartmouth College, Davidson College, Duke University, Georgetown University, Grinnell College, MIT, Middlebury College, Northwestern University, Pomona College, Rice University, Swarthmore College, University of Notre Dame, Wellesley College, Williams College, and Yale University.
12. Stephen Burd, "Merit Aid Madness," *Washington Monthly*, September/October 2013, https://washingtonmonthly.com/magazine/septoct-2013/merit-aid-madness/.
13. Eric Hoover, "U.S. Opens Antitrust Investigation into Colleges' Talk of Student-Aid Reform," *Chronicle of Higher Education*, June 17, 2013, https://www.chronicle.com/article/u-s-opens-antitrust-investigation-into-colleges-talk-of-student-aid-reform/.
14. Eric Hoover, "'Welcome to the Wild West': The Competition for College Applicants Just Intensified," *Chronicle of Higher Education*, September 29, 2019, https://www.chronicle.com/article/welcome-to-the-wild-west-the-competition-for-college-applicants-just-intensified/.
15. The settlement between NACAC and the Justice Department can be found at https://www.justice.gov/atr/case/us-v-national-association-college-admission-counseling/.

16. Eric Hoover, "Some Colleges Share Lists of Early-Decision Admits. Now the Justice Department Is Investigating," *Chronicle of Higher Education*, April 8, 2018, https://www.chronicle.com/article/some-colleges-share-lists-of-early-decision-admits-now-the-justice-department-is-investigating/.
17. Gordon C. Winston, Jared C. Carbone, and Laurie C. Hurshman, "Saving, Wealth, Performance, and Revenues in US Colleges and Universities," Williams Project on the Economics of Higher Education, DP 59 (May 2001), https://www.econstor.eu/bitstream/10419/23506/1/DP-59.pdf.
18. Henry Hansmann, "The Role of Nonprofit Enterprise," *Yale Law Journal* 89, no. 5 (1980): 835.
19. Henry Hansmann, "The Evolving Structure of Higher Education," *University of Chicago Law Review* 79, no. 1 (2012): 159.
20. Steven C. Salop and Lawrence J. White, "Antitrust Goes to College," *Journal of Economic Perspectives* 5, no. 3 (Summer 1991) and Carlton, Bamberger, and Epstein, "Antitrust and Higher Education," both discuss these issues.
21. Hansmann, "The Evolving Structure of Higher Education."
22. Gordon C. Winston and David J. Zimmerman, "Peer Effects in Higher Education," Williams Project on the Economics of Higher Education, DP 64 (January 2003), https://sites.williams.edu/wpehe/files/2011/06/DP-64.pdf.
23. *Regents of the University of California v. Bakke* 438 US 265 (1978), was a decision by the Supreme Court that upheld the use of affirmative action in college admission policy, so long as race was only one of several factors taken into account. The Court ruled that racial quotas were not permissible. The decision, written by Justice Lewis F. Powell Jr., argued that diversity in the classroom was a compelling state interest. The decision was upheld in 2003 in *Grutter v. Bollinger* 539 US 306 (2003).
24. Ruby Z. Afram, "Civil Rights, Antitrust, and Early Decision Programs," *Yale Law Journal* 115, no. 4 (2006): 880–920, https://www.yalelawjournal.org/pdf/340_omwvk2gt.pdf.
25. Hansmann, "The Evolving Structure of Higher Education."
26. Alternative solutions to this problem include government financing, which does exist, and private market income share agreements, which are increasingly being experimented with. Neither of these solutions have worked perfectly for a variety of reasons, including adverse selection and moral hazard.
27. Arthur M. Okun, *Equality and Efficiency: The Big Tradeoff* (Washington, DC: Brookings Institution, 1975).
28. In "Antitrust Goes to College," Salop and White discussed a possible defense in the Overlap case based on the efficiency gains of increasing student diversity. In the end, they recommended that colleges try to persuade the Department of Justice to use its "prosecutorial discretion" and not bring the case to court.
29. Catharine B. Hill, "American Higher Education and Income Inequality," *Education Finance and Policy* 11, no. 5 (Summer 2016): 325–339.

CHAPTER 6

* This chapter has been adapted from three reports that the Institute for College Access and Success (TICAS) published in September 2022: "Geodemographics of Student List Purchases: A First Look," "The Student List Business: Primer and Market Dynamics," and "Student List Policy: Problems, Regulations, and a Solution," https://ticas.org/

student-success/series-of-reports-find-common-recruiting-practice-perpetuate-bias-but-crucial-for-college-access-of-underrepresented-students-2.

1. College Board, "Segment Analysis Service: An Educationally Relevant Geodemographic Tagging Service," 2011, http://secure-media.collegeboard.org/mSSS/media/pdf/segment-analysis-service-overview.pdf.
2. College Board, "Enrollment Planning Service: Best Practices and Getting Started," 2022, https://cbsearch.collegeboard.org/media/pdf/eps-whitepaper.pdf.
3. Stephen Burd, "The Faux Righteousness of Test-Optional Admissions," *Chronicle of Higher Education*, November 12, 2020, https://www.chronicle.com/article/the-faux-righteousness-of-test-optional-admissions.
4. FairTest, "Record 1835+ Schools Are Test Optional or Test Free for Admissions," November 14, 2022, https://fairtest.org/record-1835-schools-are-test-optional-or-test-free-for-admissions.
5. Kevin Corr, "Diversifying Your Prospective Student Name Sources to Strengthen Your Enrollment Outcomes," Ruffalo Noel Levitz (RNL), May 12, 2022, https://www.ruffalonl.com/blog/enrollment/diversifying-your-prospective-student-sources-to-strengthen-your-enrollment-outcomes.
6. Ozan Jaquette and Crystal Han, "Follow the Money: Recruiting and the Enrollment Priorities of Public Research Universities," Third Way, March 2, 2020, https://www.thirdway.org/report/follow-the-money-recruiting-and-the-enrollment-priorities-of-public-research-universities.
7. Crystal Han, Ozan Jaquette, and Karina Salazar, "Recruiting the Out-of-State University: Off-Campus Recruiting by Public Research Universities," Joyce Foundation, March 2019, https://emraresearch.org/sites/default/files/2019-03/joyce_report.pdf.
8. Jeffrey Pfeffer and Gerald R. Salancik, *The External Control of Organizations: A Resource Dependence Perspective* (New York: Harper & Row, 1978).
9. Richard Marc Emerson, "Power-Dependence Relations," *American Sociological Review* 27, no. 1 (1962): 31–41, https://web.mit.edu/curhan/www/docs/Articles/15341_Readings/Power/Emerson_1962_Power-dependence_relations.pdf.
10. Pfeffer and Salancik, *The External Control of Organizations.*
11. Gerald F. Davis and J. Adam Cobb, "Resource Dependence Theory: Past and Future," *Research in the Sociology of Organizations* 28, no. 6 (2010), https://repository.upenn.edu/cgi/viewcontent.cgi?article=1170&context=mgmt_papers.
12. W. Richard Scott and Gerald F. Davis, "The Dyadic Environment of the Organization," in *Organizations and Organizing: Rational, Natural, and Open Systems Perspectives*, ed. W. Richard Scott and Gerald F. Davis (Upper Saddle River, NJ: Pearson Prentice Hall, 2007), 237.
13. Scott and Davis, "The Dyadic Environment of the Organization."
14. Scott and Davis, "The Dyadic Environment of the Organization," 236–237.
15. Pfeffer and Salancik, *The External Control of Organizations.*
16. John W. Meyer and Brian Rowan, "Institutionalized Organizations: Formal Structure as Myth and Ceremony," *American Journal of Sociology* 83, no. 2 (1977): 340–363.
17. Meyer and Rowan, "Institutionalized Organizations," 341.
18. Paul J. DiMaggio and Walter W. Powell, "The Iron Cage Revisited: Institutional Isomorphism and Collective Rationality in Organizational Fields," *American Sociological Review* 48, no. 2 (1983): 147–160, https://www.uio.no/studier/emner/matnat/ifi/INF9200/v10/readings/papers/DeMaggio.pdf.

19. Pamela S. Tolbert and Lynne G. Zucker, "Institutional Sources of Change in the Formal Structure of Organizations: The Diffusion of Civil-Service Reform, 1880–1935," *Administrative Science Quarterly* 28, no. 1 (1983): 22–39, https://ecommons.cornell.edu/bitstream/handle/1813/75701/Tolbert3_Institutional_sources_of_change.pdf.
20. Gerald F. Davis, Kristina Diekmann, and Catherine H. Tinsley, "The Decline and Fall of the Conglomerate Firm in the 1980s: The Deinstitutionalization of an Organization Form," *American Sociological Review* 59, no. 4 (1994): 547–570; Christina L. Ahmadjian and Patricia Robinson, "Safety in Numbers: Downsizing and the Deinstitutionalization of Permanent Employment in Japan," *Administrative Science Quarterly* 46, no. 4 (2001): 622–654.
21. Alfred D. Chandler, *The Visible Hand: The Managerial Revolution in American Business* (New York: Belknap, 1977); Joseph Schumpeter, *Capitalism, Socialism, and Democracy*, 3rd ed. (New York: Harper Perennial, 1942); Doug McAdam, Sidney Tarrow, and Charles Tilley, *Dynamics of Contention* (Cambridge: Cambridge University Press, 2001).
22. Gerald F. Davis, "Firms and Environments," in *The Handbook of Economic Sociology*, ed. Neil J. Smelser and Richard Swedberg (New York: Russell Sage Foundation, 2005), 478–502.
23. David Karen, "The Politics of Class, Race, and Gender: Access to Higher Education in the United States, 1960–1986," *American Journal of Education* 99, no. 2 (1991): 224, https://repository.brynmawr.edu/cgi/viewcontent.cgi?article=1004&context=soc_pubs.
24. Students may also be included in the College Board Student Search service by participating in the Big Future college search engine. Similarly, students may participate in ACT student list products by completing the myOptions survey. However, several of the most commonly utilized filters on College Board and ACT student list products are based on standardized test scores.
25. Roy Freedle, "Correcting the SAT's Ethnic and Social Class Bias: A Method for Reestimating SAT Scores," *Harvard Educational Review* 73, no. 1 (2003): 1–43; Maria Veronica Santelices and Mark Wilson, "Unfair Treatment? The Case of Freedle, the SAT, and the Standardization Approach to Differential Item Functioning," *Harvard Educational Review* 80, no. 1 (2010): 106–133.
26. Kayla Patrick, Allison Socol, and Ivy Morgan, "Inequities in Advanced Coursework: What's Driving Them and What Leaders Can Do," *Education Trust*, January 9, 2020, https://edtrust.org/wp-content/uploads/2014/09/Inequities-in-Advanced-Coursework-Whats-Driving-Them-and-What-Leaders-Can-Do-January-2019.pdf; Douglas J. Gagnon and Marybeth J. Mattingly, "Advanced Placement and Rural Schools: Access, Success, and Exploring Alternatives," *Journal of Advanced Academics* 27, no. 4 (2016): 266–284, https://journals.sagepub.com/doi/abs/10.1177/1932202X16656390.
27. Craig M. Dalton and Jim Thatcher, "Inflated Granularity: Spatial 'Big Data' and Geodemographics," *Big Data & Society* 2, no. 2 (2015), https://doi.org/10.1177/2053951715601144.
28. College Board, "Segment Analysis Service," 1.
29. Cheryl I. Harris, "Whiteness as Property," *Harvard Law Review* 106, no. 8 (1993): 1707–1791, https://harvardlawreview.org/1993/06/whiteness-as-property/.
30. College Board, "Segment Analysis Service," 3–4.
31. College Board, "Segment Analysis Service," 26.
32. Karina Salazar, Ozan Jaquette, and Crystal Han, "Geodemographics of Student List Purchases by Public Universities: A First Look," Institute for College Access and

Success, September 2022, 28–31, https://ticas.org/wp-content/uploads/2022/09/Geodemographics-of-Student-List-Purchases_A-First-Look.pdf.

33. Salazar, Jaquette, and Han, "Geodemographics of Student List Purchases by Public Universities," 30–31.
34. National Research Center for College and University Admissions, "NRCCUA Acquires Leading Higher Education Research Firm Eduventures," September 15, 2016, https://www.bloomberg.com/press-releases/2016-09-15/nrccua-acquires-leading-higher-education-research-firm-eduventures.
35. ACT, "ACT Acquires NRCCUA," July 24, 2018, https://leadershipblog.act.org/2018/07/act-acquires-nrccua.html.
36. Encoura, "Encoura Eduventures Research: Research and Advisory Services," n.d., https://encoura.org/products-services/eduventures-research-and-advisory-services/.
37. EAB, "EAB Acquires Leading Interactive Content Provider YouVisit," December 4, 2019, https://eab.com/about/newsroom/press/youvisit.
38. EAB, "EAB Acquires Cappex, a Leading College Research and Decision Platform," September 9, 2020, https://eab.com/insights/press-release/enrollment/cappex-acquisition.
39. EAB, "EAB Acquires Cappex."
40. Tony Wan, "Hobsons' Higher Ed Business Split and Sold in Separate Deals Totaling $410m," *EdSurge*, February 20, 2021, https://www.edsurge.com/news/2021-02-20-hobsons-higher-ed-business-split-and-sold-in-separate-deals-totaling-410m.
41. Todd Feathers, "College Prep Software Naviance Is Selling Advertising Access to Millions of Students," *The Markup*, January 13, 2022, https://graphics.reuters.com/USA-ELECTION/ DATA-VISUAL/yxmvjjgojvr/ https://themarkup.org/machine-learning/2022/01/13/ college-prep-software-naviance-is-selling-advertising-access-to millions of students.
42. PowerSchool, Naviance by PowerSchool, 2021, https://www.powerschool.com/solutions/naviance-by-powerschool/.
43. Feathers, "College Prep Software Naviance Is Selling Advertising Access."
44. Sole Source, "Intersect Connection—1 Year Subscription Renewal, University of Utah Purchasing Department—Sole Source Procurement," 2022, https://fbs.admin.utah.edu/uofubid/2022/01/07/intersect-connection-1-year-subscription-renewal.
45. Michael Koppenheffer, "Introducing Enroll360: Unlock the Power of a Thriving Recruitment Ecosystem," EAB, 2021, https://eab.com/insights/blogs/enrollment/introducing-enroll360-recruitment-ecosystem (emphasis in original).
46. Koppenheffer, "Introducing Enroll360" (emphasis in original).
47. EAB, "EAB Is Now Exclusive Provider of Intersect Student Recruitment Technology," 2021, https://eab.com/intersect.
48. Koppenheffer, "Introducing Enroll360."
49. There have long been at least two exceptions: Bates and Bowdoin, two highly selective private colleges in Maine. In 1969, Bowdoin stopped requiring prospective students to submit standardized test scores. Bates followed suit in 1984.
50. Freedle, "Correcting the SAT's Ethnic and Social-Class Bias"; Santelices and Wilson, "Unfair Treatment?"; Elaine M. Allensworth and Kallie Clark, "High School GPAs and ACT Scores as Predictors of College Completion: Examining Assumptions about Consistency Across High Schools," *Educational Researcher* 49, no. 3 (2020): 198–211, https://doi.org/10.3102/0013189X20902110.

51. FairTest, "Record 1835+ Schools Are Test Optional."
52. Scott Jaschik, "Will Test Optional Become the 'New Normal'?," *Inside Higher Ed*, January 24, 2022, https://www.insidehighered.com/admissions/article/2022/01/24/will-test-optional-become-new-normal-admissions.
53. Ashley Clark and Stephen Burd, "How College Board's Aggressive Campaign to Save the SAT May Kill It," Ed Central (Washington, DC: New America, May 16, 2019), https://www.newamerica.org/education-policy/edcentral/how-college-boards-aggressive-campaign-to-save-the-sat-may-kill-it/.
54. Elizabeth Culliford, "How Political Campaigns Use Your Data," Reuters, October 12, 2020, https://www.reuters.com/graphics/USA-ELECTION/DATA-VISUAL/yxmvjjgojvr/.
55. College Board Communications, "Pricing and Program Updates Coming to Search This Fall," April 2021, https://allaccess.collegeboard.org/pricing-and-program-updates-coming-search-fall.
56. Megan M. Holland, *Divergent Paths to College: Race, Class, and Inequality in High Schools* (New Brunswick, NJ: Rutgers University Press, 2019).

CHAPTER 7

1. Peter Schmidt, "Cold Reality Intrudes on Diversity Conference in Disney World," *Chronicle of Higher Education*, May 30, 2008, https://www.chronicle.com/article/cold-reality-intrudes-on-diversity-conference-in-disney-world-849.
2. Lorelle L. Espinosa, Matthew N. Gaertner, and Gary Orfield, "Race, Class, and College Access: Achieving Diversity in a Shifting Legal Landscape," American Council on Education, 2015, www.acenet.edu/Documents/Race-Class-and-College-Access-Achieving-Diversity-in-a-Shifting-Legal-Landscape.pdf.
3. Jerome A. Lucido (then executive director of the University of Southern California's Center for Enrollment Research, Policy, and Practice), in discussions with the author, September 2020.
4. Anthony P. Carnevale, Peter Schmidt, and Jeff Strohl, *The Merit Myth: How Our Colleges Favor the Rich and Divide America* (New York: New Press, 2020).
5. Lucido, in discussions with the author, September 2020.
6. Doug Lederman, "Enrollment Managers Struggle with Image," *Inside Higher Ed*, March 27, 2008, https://www.insidehighered.com/news/2008/03/27/enrollment-managers-struggle-image.
7. Paul Tough, *The Years That Matter Most: How College Makes or Breaks Us* (New York: Houghton Mifflin Harcourt, 2019), 168.
8. Jerome Karabel, *The Chosen: The Hidden History of Admission and Exclusion at Harvard, Yale, and Princeton* (New York: Houghton Mifflin, 2005), 2.
9. For example, see Bradley R. Curs, Ozan Jaquette, and Julie R. Posselt, "Tuition Rich, Mission Poor: Nonresident Enrollment and the Changing Proportions of Low-Income and Underrepresented Minority Students at Public Research Universities," *Journal of Higher Education* 87, no. 5 (September 2016): 635–673, https://doi.org/10.1353/jhe.2016.0025.
10. Karabel, *The Chosen*, 397–409, 483–484.
11. John Aubrey Douglass, "Anatomy of Conflict: The Making and Unmaking of Affirmative Action at the University of California," in *Color Lines: Affirmative Action, Immigration, and Civil Rights Options for America*, ed. John D. Skrentny (Chicago: University of Chicago Press, 2001), 118–144.

12. Carnevale, Schmidt, and Strohl, *The Merit Myth*, 137–165; Peter Schmidt, *Color and Money: How Rich White Kids Are Winning the War over College Affirmative Action* (New York: Palgrave Macmillan, 2007), 111–130, 173–220.
13. Schmidt, *Color and Money*, 163–165.
14. Peter Schmidt, "'Bakke' Set a New Path to Diversity for Colleges," *Chronicle of Higher Education*, June 20, 2008, https://www.chronicle.com/article/bakke-set-a-new-path-to-diversity-for-colleges.
15. Schmidt, "'Bakke' Set a New Path to Diversity for Colleges."
16. Schmidt, *Color and Money*, 65–86, 97–110.
17. Schmidt, *Color and Money*.
18. Espinosa, Gaertner, and Orfield, "Race, Class, and College Access."
19. Douglas S. Massey, Margarita Mooney, Kimberly C. Torres, and Camille Z. Charles, "Immigrants and Black Natives Attending Selective Colleges and Universities in the United States," *American Journal of Education* 113, no. 2 (February 2007), 243–271.
20. Sara Rimer and Karen W. Arenson, "Top Colleges Take More Blacks, But Which Ones?," *New York Times*, June 24, 2004, https://www.nytimes.com/2004/06/24/us/top-colleges-take-more-blacks-but-which-ones.html; Nathan Heller, "People Who Look Like You," *Harvard Magazine*, January 2004, https://www.harvardmagazine.com/2004/01/people-who-look-like-you-html.
21. Scott Jaschik, "Cornell Students Revive Debate on Whom Colleges Should Count as a Black Student," *Inside Higher Ed*, October 9, 2017, https://www.insidehighered.com/admissions/article/2017/10/09/cornell-students-revive-debate-whom-colleges-should-count-black.
22. Don Hossler and David Kalsbeek, "Enrollment Management and Managing Enrollments: Revisiting the Context for Institutional Strategy," *Strategic Enrollment Management Quarterly* 1 (2013): 5 25, https://doi.org/10.1002/sem3.20002.
23. Carnevale, Schmidt, and Strohl, *The Merit Myth*.
24. Hossler and Kalsbeek, "Enrollment Management and Managing Enrollments."
25. Schmidt, *Color and Money*, 65–86; Carnevale, Schmidt, and Strohl, *The Merit Myth*, 137–165.
26. Robert J. Massa (former vice president for enrollment at Dickinson College), in discussions with the author, September 2020. Also, Don Hossler, in discussions with the author, September 2020, and Lucido, in discussions with the author, September 2020.
27. Hossler and Massa, in discussions with the author, September 2020.
28. Massa, in discussions with the author, September 2020.
29. Crystal Han, Ozan Jaquette, and Karina Salazar, "Recruiting the Out-of-State University: Off-Campus Recruiting by Public Research Universities," Joyce Foundation, March 2019, https://emraresearch.org/sites/default/files/2019-03/joyce_report.pdf.
30. Andrew H. Nichols, "Segregation Forever? The Continued Underrepresentation of Black and Latino Undergraduates at the Nation's 101 Most Selective Public Colleges," Education Trust, 2020, https://edtrust.org/resource/segregation-forever.
31. Nichols, "Segregation Forever?"
32. Nichols, "Segregation Forever?"
33. Anthony P. Carnevale and Jeff Strohl, "Separate and Unequal: How Higher Education Reinforces the Intergenerational Reproduction of White Racial Privilege," Georgetown University's Center on Education and the Workforce, 2013, https://cew.georgetown.edu/cew-reports/separate-unequal.

34. Anthony P. Carnevale et al., "Our Separate & Unequal Public Colleges: How Public Colleges Reinforce White Racial Privilege and Marginalize Black and Latino Students," Georgetown University's Center on Education and the Workforce, 2018, https://cew.georgetown.edu/cew-reports/sustates/#resources.
35. Carnevale et al., "Our Separate & Unequal Public Colleges"; Doug Shapiro et al., "Signature 12 Supplement: Completing College: A National View of Student Attainment Rates by Race and Ethnicity—Fall 2010 Cohort," National Student Clearinghouse Research Center, April 26, 2017, https://nscresearchcenter.org/wp-content/uploads/Signature12-RaceEthnicity.pdf.
36. A group of forty-nine college groups, including the American Council on Education and the National Association for College Admission Counseling, acknowledged that political pressure from these and other constituencies influence admissions policies and practices in briefs filed in support of a lawsuit seeking to overturn Michigan's 2006 ban on race-conscious admissions at public colleges. The briefs said that the ban violated minority students' constitutional right to equal protection by precluding them alone from lobbying public colleges for the same preferential admissions treatment sought by alumni, wealthy donors, and powerful politicians. See *Bill Schuette v. Coalition to Defend Affirmative Action, Integration and Immigrant Rights and Fight for Equality by Any Means Necessary (BAMN), et al.*, filed before the US Supreme Court on August 30, 2013.
37. Carnevale, Schmidt, and Strohl, *The Merit Myth*.
38. Carnevale, Schmidt, and Strohl, *The Merit Myth*, 87–114; Schmidt, *Color and Money*, 13–38; Anthony P. Carnevale and Stephen J. Rose, "Socioeconomic Status, Race/Ethnicity, and Selective Colleges Admissions," in *America's Untapped Resource: Low-Income Students in Higher Education*, ed. Richard D. Kahlenberg (New York: Century Foundation, 2003), 11.
39. Peter Arcidiacono, Josh Kinsler, and Tyler Ransom, "Legacy and Athlete Preferences at Harvard," *Journal of Labor Economics* 40, no. 1 (2022): 133–156.
40. Cameron Howell and Sarah E. Turner, "Legacies in Black and White: The Racial Composition of the Legacy Pool," *Research in Higher Education* 45, no. 4 (June 2004): 325–351.
41. Michael Hurwitz, "The Impact of Legacy Status on Undergraduate Admissions at Elite Colleges and Universities," *Economics of Education Review* 30 (2011): 480–492.
42. Stephanie Saul, "Elite Colleges' Quiet Fight to Favor Alumni Children," *New York Times*, July 13, 2022, https://www.nytimes.com/2022/07/13/us/legacy-admissions-colleges-universities.html.
43. "Editorial: First-Year Legacy Reception Highlights Tufts' Elitism," *Tufts Daily*, September 9, 2019, https://tuftsdaily.com/opinion/editorial/2019/09/09/editorial-first-year-legacy-reception-highlights-tufts-elitism.
44. Jacques Steinberg, "Of Sheepskin and Greenbacks," *New York Times*, February 13, 2003, https://www.nytimes.com/2003/02/13/us/of-sheepskins-and-greenbacks.html.
45. Jack Stripling and Eric Hoover, "In Admissions, the Powerful Weigh In," *Chronicle of Higher Education*, November 29, 2015, https://www.chronicle.com/article/in-admissions-the-powerful-weigh-in.
46. Stripling and Hoover, "In Admissions, the Powerful Weigh In"; Carnevale, Schmidt, and Strohl, *The Merit Myth*, 95–97.
47. Stripling and Hoover, "In Admissions, the Powerful Weigh In."
48. Stripling and Hoover, "In Admissions, the Powerful Weigh In."

49. Schmidt, *Color and Money.*
50. Schmidt, *Color and Money*, 141–160, 173–180.
51. Schmidt, *Color and Money*, 141–160.
52. Tough, *The Years That Matter Most*, 208–211.
53. Tough, *The Years That Matter Most*, 222–223.
54. Espinosa, Gaertner, and Orfield, "Race, Class, and College Access."

CHAPTER 8

1. Doug Lederman, " 'Manipulating,' er, Influencing 'U.S. News,' " *Inside Higher Ed*, June 3, 2009, https://www.insidehighered.com/news/2009/06/03/manipulating-er-influencing-us-news; Clemson University, "Budget and Control Board Accountability Report: 2006–2007," November 1, 2007, 4, 7, 25–39, www.clemson.edu/institutional-effectiveness/media/accountabilityreports/AccountabilityReport2007.pdf.
2. Lederman, " 'Manipulating,' er, Influencing 'U.S. News.' "
3. Lederman, " 'Manipulating,' er, Influencing 'U.S. News.' "
4. Huron Education Consulting, "Case Study: Improving Clemson's Enrollment Management Strategy to Align with University Goals," 2012, https://cdn.featuredcustomers.com/CustomerCaseStudy.document/Clemsoncasestudyv14.pdf.
5. Huron Education Consulting, "Case Study," 3.
6. Data on Clemson's yearly spending on non-need-based aid and on the share of freshmen receiving these awards comes from an annual survey that the college guidebook publisher Peterson's conducts of colleges and universities. New America licensed data from Peterson's "Undergraduate Financial Aid and Undergraduate Databases," copyright 2023 Peterson's LLC.
7. According to data that Clemson submitted to the US Department of Education's Integrated Postsecondary Education Data System (IPEDS), its acceptance rate dropped from 63 percent in 2011 to 47 percent in 2019; and its incoming students' average SAT scores rose from 1235 to 1315 during that period.
8. Clemson News, "Clemson Remains Top University in South Carolina in *U.S. News* Rankings," September 12, 2022, https://news.clemson.edu/clemson-remains-top-university-in-south-carolina-in-u-s-news-rankings.
9. Data on the average amount of financial need that Clemson meets each year of its freshmen financial aid recipients comes from Peterson's "Undergraduate Financial Aid and Undergraduate Databases."
10. Colleges report the average net-price-by-income data annually to the US Department of Education's Integrated Postsecondary Education Data System (IPEDS), which displays the school-by-school data on its College Navigator site. Clemson's data can be found at https://nces.ed.gov/collegenavigator/?q=clemson&s=all&id=217882#netprc.
11. Rachel Fishman, "The Wealth Gap PLUS Debt: How Federal Loans Exacerbate Inequality for Black Families," New America, May 2018, 6, https://d1y8sb8igg2f8e.cloudfront.net/documents/Wealth_Gap_Plus_Debt_FINAL.pdf.
12. "Parent Loans," in "H1: Aid Awarded to Enrolled Undergraduates," Clemson University's Common Data Set 2019–2020, 46, https://www.clemson.edu/institutional-effectiveness/documents/2020/CDSClemsonUniversityallcompleted20200310.pdf.
13. The PLUS Loan borrowing data "are produced for rolling two-year pooled cohorts" for the College Scorecard. In this case, the cohort consists of PLUS Loan borrowers who are in the families of Pell Grant recipients who graduated in 2018–2019 and 2019–2020. See US Department of Education, "Technical Documentation: College Scorecard

Institution-Level Data," May 2022, 20–21, https://collegescorecard.ed.gov/assets/InstitutionDataDocumentation.pdf.

14. Gal Wettstein and Siyan Liu, "How Do Unpaid Student Loans Impact Social Security Benefits?," Boston College's Center for Retirement Research 23-1, January 2023, https://crr.bc.edu/wp-content/uploads/2023/01/IB_23-1.pdf.
15. Anthony P. Carnevale, Peter Schmidt, and Jeff Strohl, *The Merit Myth: How Our Colleges Favor the Rich and Divide America* (New York: New Press, 2020), 49–50.
16. The New America analysis examined how 575 selective public and private colleges spent their institutional aid dollars from 2000–2020. The institutions include 307 private colleges and 268 public universities with an undergraduate enrollment of at least 500 students and an acceptance rate of 85 percent or less. These institutions include the country's most elite colleges, as well as those considered at least minimally selective. Data on institutional financial aid and "average financial need met" come from Peterson's "Undergraduate Financial Aid and Undergraduate Databases."
17. Matthew Quirk, "The Best Class Money Can Buy," *The Atlantic*, November 2005, https://www.theatlantic.com/magazine/archive/2005/11/the-best-class-money-can-buy/304307.
18. Donald Hossler, "The Role of Financial Aid in Enrollment Management," in *The Role Student Aid Plays in Enrollment Management*, ed. Michael D. Coomes (San Francisco: Jossey-Bass, 2000), 83.
19. Elizabeth A. Duffy and Idana Goldberg, *Crafting a Class: College Admissions and Financial Aid, 1955–1994* (Princeton, NJ: Princeton University Press, 1998), 208.
20. Maggie McGrath and Matt Schifrin, "The Invisible Force Behind College Admissions," *Forbes*, July 30, 2014, https:// www.forbes.com/sites/maggiemcgrath/2014/07/30/ the-invisible-force-behind-college-admissions.
21. EAB, "Financial Aid Optimization," https://eab.com/products/financial-aid-optimization.
22. Stephen Burd, "Crisis Point: How Enrollment Management and the Merit Aid Arms Race Are Derailing Public Higher Education," New America, February 2020, 25–32, https://www.newamerica.org/education-policy/reports/crisis-point-how-enrollment-management-and-merit-aid-arms-race-are-destroying-public-higher-education.
23. John Reid Blackwell, "Henrico-Based Royall & Co. Acquired for $850 Million," *Richmond Times-Dispatch*, December 11, 2014, https://www.richmond.com/business/henrico-based-royall-co-acquired-for-850-million/article_27ab7f14-ed33-5f52-a7fd-df71e1a1193f.html.
24. EAB, "EAB Helps You Find and Enroll the Right Students," https://eab.com/colleges-and-universities/enrollment.
25. Josh Mitchell, *The Debt Trap: How Student Loans Became a National Catastrophe* (New York: Simon and Schuster, 2021), 179.
26. The Education Department's College Scorecard had Parent PLUS Loan data for Pell Grant recipients at 151 of the 307 selective private colleges included in the analysis.
27. The Education Department's College Scorecard had Parent PLUS Loan data for Pell Grant recipients at 236 of the 268 selective public universities included in the analysis.
28. Fishman, "The Wealth Gap PLUS Debt," 8.
29. Sandy Baum, Kristin Blagg, and Rachel Fishman, "Reshaping Parent PLUS Loans: Recommendations for Reforming the Parent PLUS Program," Urban Institute,

April 2019, 4, https://www.urban.org/sites/default/files/publication/100106/2019_04_30_reshaping_parent_plus_loans_finalizedv2.pdf.

30. US Government Accountability Office, *Financial Aid Offers: Action Needed to Improve Information on College Costs and Financial Aid*, GAO-23-104708, Washington, DC, 2022, 23, https://www.gao.gov/assets/gao-23-104708.pdf.
31. Jerome Karabel, *The Chosen: The Hidden History of Admission and Exclusion at Harvard, Yale, and Princeton* (New York: Clarion & Mariner, 2005), 1–2.
32. Milton Greenberg, "How the GI Bill Changed Higher Education," *Chronicle of Higher Education*, June 18, 2004, https://www.chronicle.com/article/how-the-gi-bill-changed-higher-education.
33. Michael S. McPherson and Morton Owen Schapiro, *The Student Aid Game* (Princeton, NJ: Princeton University Press, 1998), 7.
34. McPherson and Schapiro, *The Student Aid Game*, 7.
35. Duffy and Goldberg, *Crafting a Class*, 203–204.
36. Juan Olavarria, "A Focus on Cost-Cutting Saved BC from Bankruptcy, Financial Woes in the 1970s," *The Heights*, November 2, 2014, https://www.bcheights.com/2014/11/02/focus-cost-cutting-saved-bc-bankruptcy-financial-woes-1970s.
37. John Maguire, "To the Organized, Go the Students," Boston College, *Bridge Magazine*, Fall 1976, https://archive.org/stream/bridgemagazinefof1976bost/bridgemagazinefof1976bost_djvu.txt.
38. Maguire, "To the Organized, Go the Students."
39. McGrath and Schifrin, "The Invisible Force Behind College Admissions."
40. Scott Jaschik, "Justice Dept. Documents Raise New Questions about Workings of College 'Overlap' Group," *Chronicle of Higher Education*, May 13, 1992, https://www.chronicle.com/article/justice-dept-documents-raise-new-questions-about-workings-of-college-overlap-group.
41. "*The New York Times* Spotlights WUSTL's Rapid Ascent to National Elite," *The Source*, Washington University in St. Louis, December 22, 2003, https://source.wustl.edu/2003/12/the-new-york-times-spotlights-wustl-rapid-ascent-to-national-elite/.
42. Greg Winter, "A Mighty Fund-Raising Effort Helps Lift a College's Ranking," *New York Times*, December 22, 2003, https://www.nytimes.com/2003/12/22/us/a-mighty-fund-raising-effort-helps-lift-a-college-s-ranking.html.
43. Nick Anderson, "Princeton to Cover All College Bills for Families Making up to $100,000," *Washington Post*, September 8, 2022, https://www.washingtonpost.com/education/2022/09/08/princeton-student-tuition-financial-aid.
44. Quirk, "The Best Class Money Can Buy."
45. John Roush, "Control the Aid Arms Race," *Inside Higher Ed*, January 5, 2010, https://www.insidehighered.com/views/2010/01/05/control-aid-arms-race.
46. McGrath and Schifrin, "The Invisible Force Behind College Admissions."
47. Adam Davidson, "Is College Tuition Really Too High?," *New York Times Magazine*, September 8, 2015, https://www.nytimes.com/2015/09/13/magazine/is-college-tuition-too-high.html.
48. New America analysis, conducted for this chapter, of 2020–2021 average net-price-by-income IPEDS data for the 307 private colleges that we examined.
49. Tawnell D. Hobbs and Andrea Fuller, "How Baylor Steered Lower-Income Parents to Debt They Couldn't Afford," *Wall Street Journal*, October 13, 2021, https://www.wsj.com/articles/baylor-university-college-debt-parent-plus-loans-11634138239.

50. Burd, "Crisis Point."
51. In 1862, Congress approved the Morrill Land-Grant College Act, which provided federal land to states to create land-grant universities that would "promote the liberal and practical education of the industrial classes."
52. Donald E. Heller, "Merit Aid and College Access," presentation for the Wisconsin Center for the Advancement of Postsecondary Education's Symposium on the Consequences of Merit-Based Student Aid, University of Wisconsin at Madison, March 2006.
53. Victoria Jackson and Matt Saenz, "States Can Choose Better Path for Higher Education Funding in COVID-19 Recession," Center on Budget and Policy Priorities, February 17, 2021, 1–2, www.cbpp.org/sites/default/files/2-17-21sfp.pdf.
54. Eric Kelderman and Lee Gardner, "The Looming Enrollment Crisis," *Chronicle of Higher Education*, November 2019, 11, https://www.siena.edu/files/resources/the-looming-enrollment-crisis.pdf.
55. Laura Pappano, "How the University of Alabama Became a National Player," *New York Times*, November 6, 2016, https://www.nytimes.com/2016/11/06/education/edlife/survival-strategies-for-public-universities.html.
56. Stephen Burd, "Undermining Pell Vol. 4: How Enrollment Management and the Merit Aid Arms Race Are Derailing Public Higher Education," New America, February 2020, 13–14, https://www.newamerica.org/education-policy/reports/undermining-pell-iv.
57. The 2008–2009 academic year was the first for which the US Department of Education published average net price data for colleges broken down by income.
58. New America analysis, conducted for this chapter, of 2020–2021 average net-price-by-income IPEDS data for the 268 public universities that we examined.
59. Peter Granville, "Parent PLUS Borrowers: The Hidden Casualties of the Student Debt Crisis," Century Foundation, 4 and figure 1, https://tcf.org/content/report/parent-plus-borrowers-the-hidden-casualties-of-the-student-debt-crisis.
60. Granville, "Parent PLUS Borrowers," 4 and note 13.
61. Fishman, "The Wealth Gap PLUS Debt," 7.
62. Casey Goldvale et al., "Unrepayable Debt: How Economic, Racial, and Geographic Inequality Shape the Distribution of Parent PLUS Loans," Georgetown University Law School's Center on Poverty and Inequality, September 15, 2022, 6–9, https://www.georgetownpoverty.org/wp-content/uploads/2022/09/UnrepayableDebt-September2022.pdf.
63. Granville, "Parent PLUS Borrowers," 3.
64. Alex Engler, "Enrollment Algorithms Are Contributing to the Crises of Higher Education," Brookings Institution, September 14, 2021, https://www.brookings.edu/research/enrollment-algorithms-are-contributing-to-the-crises-of-higher-education.
65. Fishman, "The Wealth Gap PLUS Debt," 31–36; Baum, Blagg, and Fishman, "Reshaping Parent PLUS Loans," 20–22.
66. Dianne Hayes, "Obama Plans Changes to Parent PLUS Loans," *Diverse Issues in Higher Education*, August 15, 2013, https://www.diverseeducation.com/demographics/african-american/article/15093542/obama-administration-plans-changes-to-parent-plus-loans.

CHAPTER 9

1. Jeffrey Selingo, "So You Got Financial Aid for College. But How Do You Pay for the Rest of It?," *New York Times*, February 20, 2020, https://www.nytimes.com/2020/02/20/education/learning/financial-aid-gap-college.html.

2. Mamie Lynch, Jennifer Engle, and José L. Cruz, "Priced Out: How the Wrong Financial Aid Policies Hurt Low-Income Students," Education Trust, June 2011, 2, https://edtrust.org/wp-content/uploads/2013/10/PricedOutFINAL_2.pdf.
3. Stephen Burd, "Crisis Point: How Enrollment Management and the Merit-Aid Arms Race Are Derailing Public Higher Education," New America, February 2020, 5, https://www.newamerica.org/education-policy/reports/crisis-point-how-enrollment-management-and-merit-aid-arms-race-are-destroying-public-higher-education.
4. Lynn O'Shaughnessy, *The College Solutions: A Guide for Everyone Looking for the Right School at the Right Price* (Upper Saddle River, NJ: FT Press, 2012), 3.
5. "Red Hook Initiative," Heckscher Foundation for Children, https://heckscherfoundation.org/grantee/red-hook-initiative/.
6. "Brooklyn Queens Expressway and How It Has Gone Through Red Hook," *Red Hook Water Stories*, May 11, 2016, https://redhookwaterstories.org/items/show/149.
7. "Well-Being in Red Hook, Brooklyn," Measure of America, Social Science Research Center, 2014–2015, http://www.measureofamerica.org/wp-content/uploads/2014/10/RedHook-Fact-Sheet-2014-15.pdf.
8. Stephen Burd, Laura Keane, Rachel Fishman, and Julie Habbert, "Decoding the Cost of College: The Case for Transparent Financial Aid Award Letters," New America and uAspire, June 2018, 2, https://www.newamerica.org/education-policy/policy-papers/decoding-cost-college.
9. Burd et al., "Decoding the Cost of College," 16.
10. Burd et al., "Decoding the Cost of College," 19.
11. Burd et al., "Decoding the Cost of College."
12. Lynch, Engel, and Cruz, "Priced Out," 2.
13. *U.S. News & World Report*, "Ithaca College Tuition and Financial Aid," https://www.usnews.com/best-colleges/ithaca-college-2739/paying.
14. Raj Chetty et al., "Mobility Report Cards: The Role of Colleges in Intergenerational Mobility," Equality of Opportunity Project, July 2017, http://www.equality-of-opportunity.org/papers/coll_mrc_paper.pdf.
15. Rachel Fishman, "The Wealth Gap PLUS Debt: How Federal Loans Exacerbate Inequality for Black Families," New America, May 2018, 6–7, https://d1y8sb8igg2f8e.cloudfront.net/documents/Wealth_Gap_Plus_Debt_FINAL.pdf.
16. Fishman, "The Wealth Gap PLUS Debt," 7.
17. New York City Department of Consumer and Worker Protection, "Unequal Burden: Black Borrowers and the Student Loan Debt Crisis," July 2020, 5, https://www1.nyc.gov/assets/dca/downloads/pdf/partners/SLDBlackBorrowers_Report.pdf.
18. Mark Huelsman, "Debt to Society: The Case for Bold, Equitable Student Loan Cancellation and Reform," Demos, June 2019, 2, https://www.demos.org/sites/default/files/2019-06/Debt%20to%20Society.pdf.
19. Fishman, "The Wealth Gap PLUS Debt," 7.
20. *New York Times*, "Economic Diversity and Student Outcomes at Ithaca College," Upshot column, January 18, 2017, https://www.nytimes.com/interactive/projects/college-mobility/ithaca-college.
21. "H2A: Number of Enrolled Students Awarded Non-Need-Based Scholarships and Grants," Ithaca College's Common Data Set 2019–2020, 31, https://ithacaedu.sharepoint.com/sites/AIRPublicDocuments/Shared%20Documents/Common%20Data%20Set/Ithaca_College_CDS_2019-20.pdf.
22. Burd, "Crisis Point," 6.

23. Susan Kelley, "Endowment Holds Steady in FY 2020 Despite Pandemic," *Cornell Chronicle*, October 12, 2020, https://news.cornell.edu/stories/2020/10/endowment-holds-steady-fy-2020-despite-pandemic.
24. "H2: Number of Enrolled Students Awarded Aid" and "H2A: Number of Enrolled Students Awarded Non-Need-Based Scholarships and Grants," Cornell University's Common Data Set 2019–2020, 20, http://irp.dpb.cornell.edu/wp-content/uploads/2020/05/CDS_2019-2020_FINAL.pdf.
25. *New York Times*, "Economic Diversity and Student Outcomes at Cornell University," Upshot column, January 18, 2017, https://www.nytimes.com/interactive/projects/college-mobility/cornell-university.
26. Colleen Flaherty, "Ithaca Announces Sweeping Faculty Cuts," *Inside Higher Ed*, October 15, 2020, https://www.insidehighered.com/news/2020/10/15/ithaca-announces-sweeping-faculty-cuts.
27. "H1: Aid Awarded to Enrolled Undergraduates" and "H2: Number of Enrolled Students Awarded Aid," Pitzer College's 2019–2020 Common Data Set, 20–21, https://www.pitzer.edu/institutional-research/wp-content/uploads/sites/33/2020/10/CDS_2019-2020.pdf.
28. Colleges report the average net-price-by-income data annually to the US Department of Education's Integrated Postsecondary Education Data System (IPEDS), which displays the school-by-school data on its College Navigator site. Pitzer's data can be found at https://nces.ed.gov/collegenavigator/?q=pitzer&s=all&id=121257#netprc and Ithaca's can be found at https://nces.ed.gov/collegenavigator/?q=ithaca&s=all&id=191968#netprc.
29. "H2A: Number of Enrolled Students Awarded Non-Need-Based Scholarships and Grants," Pitzer College's 2019–2020 Common Data Set, 21; "H2A: Number of Enrolled Students Awarded Non-Need-Based Scholarships and Grants," Ithaca's 2019–2020 Common Data Set, 31.
30. Colleges report the share of freshman Pell Grant recipients whom they enroll to IPEDS, which displays them on the Education Department's College Navigator site. Ithaca's data can be found at https://nces.ed.gov/collegenavigator/?q=Ithaca+college&s=all&id=191968#finaid and Pitzer's can be found at https://nces.ed.gov/collegenavigator/?q=pitzer&s=all&id=121257#finaid.

CHAPTER 10

1. Sarah Pingel and Shanique Broom, "50 State Comparison: State Policy on Postsecondary Tuition, Capping and Freezing," Education Commission of the States, May 20, 2020, https://reports.ecs.org/comparisons/postsecondary-tuition-setting-01.
2. "State Higher Education Finance (SHEF): State Profile: Alabama," State Higher Education Executive Officers Association, 2021, https://shef.sheeo.org/state-profile/alabama.
3. "State Higher Education Finance (SHEF): State Profile: Florida," State Higher Education Executive Officers Association, 2021, https://shef.sheeo.org/state-profile/florida.
4. "State Higher Education Finance (SHEF): State Profile: New York," State Higher Education Executive Officers Association, 2021, https://shef.sheeo.org/state-profile/new-york/.
5. "State Higher Education Finance (SHEF): State Profile: Michigan," State Higher Education Executive Officers Association, 2021, https://shef.sheeo.org/state-profile/michigan.

6. "State Higher Education Finance (SHEF): State Profile: Arizona," State Higher Education Executive Officers Association, 2021, https://shef.sheeo.org/state-profile/arizona.
7. Denisa Gándara and Amy Li, "Promise for Whom? 'Free-College' Programs and Enrollments by Race and Gender Classifications at Public, 2-Year Colleges," *Educational Evaluation and Policy Analysis* 42, no. 4 (2020): 603–627, https://doi.org/10.3102/0162373720962472.

CHAPTER 11

1. Philip Oreopoulos and Kjell G. Salvanes, "Priceless: The Nonpecuniary Benefits of Schooling," *Journal of Economic Perspectives* 25, no. 1 (2011): 159–184; Michael Hout, "Social and Economic Returns to College Education in the United States," *Annual Review of Sociology* 38, no. 1 (2012): 379–400; Roy Y. Chan, "Understanding the Purpose of Higher Education: An Analysis of the Economic and Social Benefits for Completing a College Degree," *Journal of Education Policy, Planning and Administration* 6, no. 5 (2016): 1–40.
2. Juliana Menasce Horowitz, Ruth Igielnik, and Rakesh Kochar, "Trends in Income and Wealth Inequality," Pew Research Center, January 2020, https://www.pewresearch.org/social-trends/2020/01/09/trends-in-income-and-wealth-inequality.
3. John W. Meyer and Brian Rowan, "Institutionalized Organizations: Formal Structure as Myth and Ceremony," *American Journal of Sociology* 83, no. 2 (1977): 340–363; Jeffrey Pfeffer and Gerald R. Salancik, *The External Control of Organizations: A Resource Dependence Perspective* (New York: Harper & Row, 1978); Paul J. DiMaggio and Walter W. Powell, "The Iron Cage Revisited: Institutional Isomorphism and Collective Rationality in Organizational Fields," *American Sociological Review* 48, no. 2 (1983): 147–160.
4. Sheila Slaughter and Larry L. Leslie, *Academic Capitalism: Politics, Policies, and the Entrepreneurial University* (Baltimore, MD: Johns Hopkins University Press, 1997); Sheila Slaughter and Gary Rhoades, *Academic Capitalism and the New Economy: Markets, State, and Higher Education* (Baltimore, MD: Johns Hopkins University Press, 2004).
5. Burton A. Weisbrod, Jeffrey P. Ballou, and Evelyn D. Asch, *Mission and Money: Understanding the University* (Cambridge: Cambridge University Press, 2008); Karin Fischer, "The Barriers to Mobility: Why Higher Ed's Promise Remains Unfulfilled," *Chronicle of Higher Education*, December 30, 2019, https://www.chronicle.com/article/why-higher-ed-rsquo-s-promise-remains-unfulfilled.
6. Robert H. Frank and Philip J. Cook, *The Winner-Take-All Society* (New York: Free Press, 1995), 22.
7. Manuela Ekowo and Iris Palmer, "The Promise and Peril of Predictive Analytics in Higher Education: A Landscape Analysis," New America, October 24, 2016, https://www.newamerica.org/education-policy/policy-papers/promise-and-peril-predictive-analytics-higher-education.
8. Douglas A. Webber and Ronald G. Ehrenberg, "Do Expenditures Other Than Instructional Expenditures Affect Graduation and Persistence Rates in American Higher Education?," *Economics of Education Review* 29, no. 6 (2010): 947–958, https://doi.org/10.1016/j.econedurev.2010.04.006; Tuan D. Nguyen, Jenna W. Kramer, and Brent J. Evans, "The Effects of Grant Aid on Student Persistence and Degree Attainment: A Systematic Review and Meta-Analysis of the Causal Evidence," *Review of Educational Research* 89, no. 6 (2019): 831–874, https://doi.org/10.3102/0034654319877156.

9. Ozan Jaquette, Bradley R. Curs, and Julie R. Posselt, "Tuition Rich, Mission Poor: Nonresident Enrollment Growth and the Socioeconomic and Racial Composition of Public Research Universities," *Journal of Higher Education* 87, no. 5 (2016): 635–673; Karina G. Salazar, Ozan Jaquette, and Crystal Han, "Coming Soon to a Neighborhood Near You? Off-Campus Recruiting by Public Research Universities," *American Educational Research Journal* 58, no. 6 (December 2021): 1270–1314, https://doi.org/10.3102/00028312211001810; Pooja Patel and Melissa Clinedinst, "State-by-State Student-to-Counselor Ratio Maps by School District," National Association for College Admission Counseling, 2021.
10. Karin Fischer, "Americans' Confidence in Higher Ed Drops Sharply," *Chronicle of Higher Education*, July 26, 2022, https://www.chronicle.com/article/americans-confidence-in-higher-ed-drops-sharply.
11. Jay Menees, "The Justice Department Has Worsened College Admissions," *Inside Higher Ed*, June 12, 2022, https://www.insidehighered.com/admissions/views/2022/06/13/justice-department-has-made-mess-admissions-opinion.
12. Jerome A. Lucido, "Lessons from the NFL for Managing College Enrollment," Center for American Progress, January 30, 2013, https://www.americanprogress.org/article/lessons-from-the-nfl-for-managing-college-enrollment.
13. Lucido, "Lessons from the NFL."
14. Julie A. Reuben, "Hypercompetition Is Harming Higher Ed," *Chronicle of Higher Education*, July 8, 2022, https://www.chronicle.com/article/hypercompetition-is-harming-higher-ed.
15. Jeffrey F. Milem, Mitchell J. Chang, and Anthony Lising Antonio, "Making Diversity Work on Campus: A Research-Based Perspective," Association of American Colleges and Universities, 2005; Jeffrey F. Milem, "The Educational Benefits of Diversity: Evidence from Multiple Sectors," in *Compelling Interest Examining the Evidence on Racial Dynamics in Higher Education*, ed. Mitchell J. Chang, Daria Witt, James Jones, and Kenji Hakuta (Stanford, CA: Stanford University Press, 2003), 126–169.
16. Jerome A. Lucido et al., "COVID-19: Understanding Changes to Postsecondary Student Enrollment Patterns," University of Southern California's Center for Enrollment Research, Policy and Practice, 2022, https://cerpp.usc.edu/wp-content/uploads/2023/04/Full-Gates-Report.pdf.
17. Phillip B. Levine, *A Problem of Fit: How the Complexity of College Pricing Hurts Students—and Universities* (Chicago: University of Chicago Press, 2022).
18. Scott Andrew Schulz and Jerome A. Lucido, "Enrollment Management Inc.: External Influences on Our Practice," University of Southern California's Center for Enrollment Research, Policy, and Practice, January 2011, https://files.eric.ed.gov/fulltext/ED537409.pdf.
19. Sandy Baum and Michael McPherson, *Can College Level the Playing Field? Higher Education in an Unequal Society* (Princeton, NJ: Princeton University Press, 2022).
20. Marta Tienda, "Economic Implications of Demographic Change: Diversity Dividend or Deficit?," *Business Economics* 51, no. 1 (2016): 11–17.

CONCLUSION

1. Paul Tough, *The Years That Matter Most: How College Makes or Breaks Us* (New York: Houghton Mifflin Harcourt, 2019), 33–38, 43–50, 63–70.

2. This is as cited in Benjamin Wermund, "In Trump Country, a University Confronts Its Skeptics," *Politico*, November 9, 2017, https://www.politico.com/story/2017/11/09/university-of-michigan-admissions-low-income-244420.
3. Milton Greenberg, "How the GI Bill Changed Higher Education," *Chronicle of Higher Education*, June 18, 2004, https://www.chronicle.com/article/how-the-gi-bill-changed-higher-education.
4. Doug Lederman, "Enrollment Managers Struggle with Image," *Inside Higher Ed*, March 27, 2008, https://www.insidehighered.com/news/2008/03/27/enrollment-managers-struggle-image.
5. Eric Hoover, "The Enrollment Manager as Bogeyman," *Chronicle of Higher Education*, July 28, 2016, https://www.chronicle.com/article/the-enrollment-manager-as-bogeyman.

ACKNOWLEDGMENTS

I began working on my book proposal for this volume in the first week of March 2020. Little did I know that the world was about to shut down as a result of the COVID-19 pandemic and I wouldn't be back in my office for more than two years. Working on this book during the pandemic was a challenge, as there were many dark days, especially before the vaccines arrived, when it felt uncertain about what the future held. But the project proved to be a blessing, as it gave me structure during such an unsettling time. I was extremely lucky to have a clear purpose each and every day, while following my passion: exposing a little-known industry that has transformed college admissions and financial aid in ways that have been largely detrimental to low- and lower-middle-income students and many students of color.

I was also blessed during these uncertain times to be working with an editor as supportive, enthusiastic, and patient as Jayne Fargnoli at Harvard Education Press (HEP). In encouraging me to pursue this project, Jayne took a huge leap of faith both in my editing skills and my vision for the book. Jayne could be tough when she needed to be to keep me on track, but she also knew when to cheer me on and build my confidence. I also want to thank her colleagues Molly Grab and Emma Struebing for guiding the manuscript to publication, and Michael Higgins and Rose Ann Miller for promoting the book. The whole team at HEP believed in the book, and for that I am eternally grateful.

When I first pitched the book to Jayne, she encouraged me to pursue it as an edited volume. I was excited but unsure of how to proceed because I didn't have any funding to offer potential chapter authors. It was my great fortune that a year earlier I had met Sameer Gadkaree, who was a senior program officer at the Joyce Foundation at the time, after he reached out to me to express excitement about work I was doing related to enrollment management and the so-called merit-aid arms race. At our first meeting, Sameer blew me away not only with his intellect but also his passion for addressing racial and socioeconomic disparities in higher education. I had found a kindred spirit, and he came to the book's rescue at a time when I was unsure whether I would be able to pull it off. I am so thankful to Sameer, who is now the president of the Institute for College Access and Success, for getting behind this project, and to the Joyce Foundation for providing the support needed to make this book possible.

I also want to thank the Gates and Lumina Foundations for all the support they have provided for my work and New America's higher education team in general.

Before selecting the book's writers, I thought that it would be important to include enrollment management experts who had concerns about the direction in which the industry has been moving. I not only wanted these experts to write chapters for the book, but also to advise me throughout the process to make sure that we didn't get anything wrong. That is why I reached out to Don Hossler and Jerry Lucido of the University of Southern California's Center for Enrollment Research, Policy and Practice (CERPP), both of whom have devoted a large part of their careers to researching and writing about enrollment management and served as enrollment managers themselves. I have gotten to know Don and Jerry over the last decade and have found them sincere in their desire to reform enrollment management so that it serves a far greater public purpose than it does today.

I am hugely indebted to Don and Jerry for all the time they put into this project for little compensation. They offered detailed feedback on each chapter, helping make the book's arguments more nuanced as a result. We did not agree on everything but had many spirited discussions that ultimately gave me much more clarity about how I wanted to frame the book. And their chapters are invaluable in showing that even supporters of the field of enrollment management have serious reservations about the outsized influence of private consulting firms that have little interest in the public mission of higher education.

In choosing chapter authors, I knew from the start that I wanted journalists involved so that we could tell the story, in an engaging way, of how the enrollment management industry came to be and how the strategies and products that these firms market to colleges affect actual students. Neil Swidey of the *Boston Globe Magazine* and Jon Marcus of the *Hechinger Report* are two of the smartest and best writers covering higher education, and I was overjoyed when they agreed to contribute chapters that expertly guide readers through the history of enrollment management and the consulting companies that have grown extraordinarily rich pushing colleges to focus almost exclusively on increasing their revenue and rankings.

I worked closely with Peter Schmidt for many years at the *Chronicle of Higher Education* and was always impressed with his encyclopedic knowledge of the case law surrounding the use of racial preferences in college admissions. As a fan of his 2007 book *Color and Money: How Rich White Kids Are Winning the War over College Affirmative Action*, I knew that Peter was the perfect person to write about the troubled relationship between enrollment management and student diversity. Peter does not pull any punches, and I appreciate the hard work and tenacity he brought to this project.

Beth Zasloff is the coauthor of one of the best books I've ever read about college admissions. The 2015 book *Hold Fast to Dreams: A College Guidance Counselor, His Students, and the Vision of a Life Beyond Poverty*, which Beth wrote with her husband Joshua Steckel, follows the stories of ten low-income and first-generation students from an inner-city high school in New York as they navigate the complexities of the college admissions and financial aid processes and their first years at selective colleges that were not designed for students like them. One of the biggest obstacles that these students ran into was the extent to which colleges "gap" students, providing them with far less financial aid than the government says they need to attend college. I felt it was important to show in the book how this often-cynical policy affects real students' lives and Beth, who writes so humanely about these issues, was my first and only choice to write the chapter. She did a fantastic job.

I have long admired Catharine (Cappy) Bond Hill and Ozan Jaquette and knew I wanted them to be part of this book from the start. Cappy spent a good part of her early career as an economist whose work focused on college access and affordability for low- and middle-income students. I got to know her when she was the president of Vassar and put her research into practice, transforming the institution into one of the most socioeconomically diverse elite private colleges in the country. Ozan Jaquette and his research team at the University of California at Los Angeles have done cutting-edge work on the recruiting priorities of public flagship and research universities. I was extremely impressed with the reports that he and his colleagues Karina Salazar and Patricia Martín wrote for the Institute for College Access and Success (TICAS) on the student list business and jumped at the chance to adapt those reports for the book.

This book likely exists only because I had the great good fortune of getting to know Jon Oberg towards the end of my tenure at the *Chronicle*. We talked for more than two hours at our first meeting, over coffee, nearly two decades ago, and he has been a mentor to me ever since. As is often the case with Jon, he recognized the hazards of enrollment management long before most took notice. Jon is truly a public servant in the best definition of that term, and it has been an honor to know him and work with him.

Asking Kevin Carey to write a chapter for the book was a no-brainer. Not only is he my boss, but he is one of the sharpest thinkers about higher education and best writers I know. Working with and for Kevin has been one of the greatest privileges of my life. In the winter of 2011, I left New America to join Kevin at the Education Sector think tank, which he had helped found. There, I met my wonderful colleagues Amy Laitinen and Rachel Fishman. Within months, I found myself back at New America with my new colleagues in tow. In a scene straight out of *Mad Men*, Kevin, Amy, Rachel, and I left Ed Sector en masse after Republican ideologues on Ed Sector's board staged a coup, hoping to create a higher education policy shop for the fledgling Mitt Romney presidential campaign. Those board members ended up destroying a great think tank. Meanwhile, Kevin has built the best education policy team in DC.

In addition to Kevin, Amy, and Rachel, I want to thank the rest of the higher education team. My colleagues make it an absolute pleasure to come into the office. They are Tia Caldwell, Da'Shon Carr, Olivia Cheche, Edward Conroy, Sophie Nguyen, Ewaoluwa Obatuase, Iris Palmer, and Sarah Satelmeyer. I also want to thank Katherine Portney and Mandy Dean of our communication staff for helping publicize the book, and, of course, New America's leaders Anne-Marie Slaughter, Paul Butler, and Barry Howard for giving me a place to come to work at least twice a week these days.

I also want to thank my family for all the love and encouragement they have provided throughout this project. From an early age, my older bother Russell made sure I loved the Beatles and thought critically about the power structures in this country, and to see clearly who gets left behind. My mother Alice believed in me from the start and has been a constant source of support. During the darkest days of COVID, when I felt the most overwhelmed by the gigantic task ahead, my mom rallied me, giving me the advice to take everything step by step and day by day. That simple advice proved crucial and carried me through.

My daughters Hannah and Leah kept me grounded throughout this process. They make me proud each and every day, not because of their academic performance, but because of who they are. No GPA or test score could ever possibly measure their worth. Their generation's passion for inclusion, rather than exclusivity, gives me hope for a better future.

My father Robert Burd, who passed away in 2019, revered the promise of higher education in this country. His life was transformed by it. Coming from a lower-middle-class Jewish family in the Bronx, he was the first in his immediate family to go to college when he entered Columbia University in fall 1956 and became a successful and much beloved doctor, who brought warmth, compassion, empathy, and generosity to his patients. My work has focused on ensuring that higher education remains a gateway of opportunity to people who don't come from wealth, just as it was for my dad.

ABOUT THE EDITOR AND CONTRIBUTORS

Stephen J. Burd (editor) is a senior writer and editor with the Education Policy program at New America, a public policy institute in Washington, DC, where he has helped shape the organization's work on higher-education policy and student aid issues. Burd has received multiple national reporting awards for his coverage of federal higher-education policy and his investigative work on the student loan and for-profit college industries. Before coming to New America in 2007, Burd worked for fifteen years as a journalist at the *Chronicle of Higher Education*.

Kevin Carey is the vice president for education policy and knowledge management at New America, and he directs its Education Policy program. He is also the author of *The End of College: Creating the Future of Learning and the University of Everywhere* (New York: Riverhead, 2015).

Catharine Bond Hill is Ithaka S+R's managing director, leading the nonprofit organization's research and consulting initiatives to broaden access to higher education, reduce costs, and improve student outcomes. Before joining Ithaka S+R, Hill served as the president of Vassar College from 2006 to 2016.

Don Hossler is a senior scholar at the Center for Enrollment Research, Policy, and Practice (CERPP) in the Rossier School of Education at the University of Southern California. He previously served as the vice chancellor for student enrollment services at Indiana University Bloomington.

Ozan Jaquette is an associate professor of higher education in the School of Education and Information Studies at the University of California at Los Angeles. His research focuses on organizational behavior, enrollment management, higher-education finance, and higher-education policy.

Jerome A. Lucido is a professor of clinical education at the Rossier School of Education at the University of Southern California (USC) and a scholar-in-residence at USC's Center for Enrollment Research, Policy, and Practice (CERPP). He previously served as the executive director of CERPP.

Jon Marcus is the higher-education editor for the *Hechinger Report*, a non-profit news organization that provides in-depth education reporting. He is also a correspondent for the *Times (U.K.) Higher Education* magazine and teaches journalism at Boston College and Northeastern University.

Patricia Martín is a PhD candidate at the University of California at Los Angeles in the School of Education and Information Studies. Her research examines the digital marketing strategies of postsecondary institutions and their effects on college access for underserved students.

Jon H. Oberg has worked at federal, state, and local levels of government, including positions as chief state fiscal officer, legislative director in the US Senate, and congressional liaison for higher education at the US Department of Education. He is also known for representing the US government in a false claims legal action against nine student-loan lenders, which resulted in the return of millions of dollars to the US Treasury.

Karina Salazar is an assistant professor in the Center for the Study of Higher Education at the University of Arizona. Her research program analyzes how the enrollment management practices of public universities shape college access for underserved student populations.

Peter Schmidt is a veteran education writer, a senior fellow at the Georgetown Center on Education and the Workforce, and a coauthor of *The Merit Myth: How Our Colleges Favor the Rich and Divide America* (New York: New Press, 2020).

Neil Swidey is a best-selling author and the director of the journalism program at Brandeis University. He is also an editor-at-large at the *Boston Globe Magazine.*

Beth Zasloff is a writer and editor and a coauthor of the award-winning book *Hold Fast to Dreams: A College Guidance Counselor, His Students, and the Vision of a Life Beyond Poverty* (New York: New Press, 2015).

INDEX